Mike Cloud at H + 1 hour, from photo plane at range of 40 miles. U.S. Government Photo

IVY-Mike

the first
HYDROGEN BOMB

W.G. Van Dorn

Copyright © 2008 by W.G. Van Dorn.

Library of Congress Control Number: 2007906231
ISBN: Hardcover   978-1-4257-7539-1
           Softcover   978-1-4257-7501-8

All rights reserved. No part of this book may be reproduced or transmitted in any form or by any means, electronic or mechanical, including photocopying, recording, or by any information storage and retrieval system, without permission in writing from the copyright owner.

This book was printed in the United States of America.

To order additional copies of this book, contact:
Xlibris Corporation
1-888-795-4274
www.Xlibris.com
Orders@Xlibris.com

42484

To my family:

Jane
Richard
Carol
Lisa

With thanks to Harold Agnew for his helpful comments and suggestions.

CONTENTS

Preface 9

Part I   The Briefing 11

Part II   The Protagonists 63

Part III Plans And Preparations 124

Part IV Deployment 210

Part V   The Test 303

Part VI The Aftermath 361

PREFACE

On Saturday, 1 November 1952, at 0715 hours local time, and three days before General Dwight D. Eisenhower was elected President, the United States detonated the world's first "Super Bomb" at Eniwetok Atoll, Marshall Islands. This is an accurate historical account of the Scripps Institution of Oceanography's participation in that test, an unpublicized event that changed for all time the lives of every person on earth.

The first half of the book treats the conception and design of the Super at the Los Alamos Scientific Laboratory, during which Scripps's assistance is sought when a late development indicates that the Mike's energy release might substantially exceed design expectations, thus mandating a drastic expansion of the Test Operation. The latter half describes the frantic efforts of 12,000 military and scientific personnel, living on a small Pacific atoll, to prepare for and conduct a test of Mike, the first thermonuclear device, to measure its effects, and to escape radioactive fallout from a mushroom cloud three times as large as the Atoll.

The account is narrated by a fictitious participant who was in a position to know everything. But from this and future events, I came to know all of the players in this drama and the details of their experiences. I have preserved the names and titles of principal Task Force officers and scientists, and employed fictitious names for other participants. The entrapment of Jack Clark in the firing bunker actually occurred two years later during the BRAVO shot of Operation CASTLE.

W. G. Van Dorn
La Jolla, California

PART I

THE BRIEFING

Friday 21 May 1952

I was halfway up the stairs of my basement laboratory when the phone rang. I hesitated, debating whether to answer it. Outside, my car was packed for a long-awaited camping trip to the High Sierra. Behind, lay years of research and experiment for my dissertation, months of study for my final orals. In hand, ready for posting, I carried the signed letters from my doctoral committee recommending the Degree of Doctor of Philosophy in Physical Oceanography be conferred on Robert A. Ward, for his work on the Causes and Effects of Tsunami Waves. But the telephone is a malevolent instrument; a few more seconds and I would have been gone for the summer; instead, I turned back to shut the thing up . . . and my life was changed forever.

The call was from our director, Roger Revelle: Could I come over for a few minutes . . . it was really quite important. I wondered what could have come up so suddenly. I had last seen Roger Wednesday evening at my exam party, pleasantly crocked, and singing an old Norwegian drinking song he had learned from his predecessor, the famous Arctic explorer, Harald Sverdrup. At that time, the Scripps Institution of Oceanography was a very small place. PhD parties were infrequent, and everybody came.

I again climbed up from the library basement, crossed the narrow roadway separating it from the old Scripps Building, and ran up the stairs to the second floor, which housed our only classroom, the director's office, and those of two other senior professors. Roger's secretary, Barbara, occupied a desk at the head of the stairs, in a sort of cubicle formed by chart files and cabinets. Through the open doorway, I could see him talking to my old friend and mentor, Jeff Knight. Roger's head swiveled and, seeing me, he hoisted all six-and-a-half feet of himself erect and shambled forward, huge hand outstretched, looking for all the world like a Great Dane, with his sad eyes, heavy jowls, and warm, engaging smile.

"Hi, Bob," he said, putting an arm around my shoulders and somehow managing to close the door without knocking the two-inch ash off his cigar. "Jeff tells me that you were about to run off into the mountains. I'm sure glad I caught you before you got away." I smiled, bleakly, and sat down beside Jeff on the settee as Roger managed to get his ash into the glass tray on his desk. Then he turned to us, his face suddenly quite grave and showing unmistakable signs of fatigue. "Yesterday morning, when I was still recovering from the effects of your party, Bob," he began, with just a trace of a smile, "I received a phone call from my old friend Al Graves, who is currently a division leader at the Los Alamos Scientific Laboratory in New Mexico. They seem to have a rather urgent problem, quite similar to one where we at Scripps were previously of some assistance, and they would like us to send somebody back there this weekend to attend a briefing on Monday. They need to generate some kind of response to Washington by the end of next week.

"Because of the sensitive nature of this problem, Al couldn't say much over the phone. But, from our past experience, I can guess pretty well what they're up against. So I called Henry Engels, and we spent most of the day mulling it over. We agreed that you two are the obvious candidates: you both have secret clearances by virtue of working on Navy contracts, and, between you, have the necessary technical competence. So, before I proceed, is there any reason that either of you can't make it?"

Jeff was shaking his head, and I could see my pack trip vanishing into the limbo. "Well," I said, with some reluctance, "I guess you have just saved me from dying of snake bite or falling off a precipice. What's the bad news?"

"I really think you'll find going to Los Alamos an interesting experience." Roger went on, as if to soften the blow. "It's quite a lovely place. Oppenheimer selected the site. It's way up in the pine forest on the slope of the

Jemez Mountains." He paused to relight his cigar, and then got up and paced back and forth, fingers of one hand grasping his temples. "I'm not exactly sure of the security classification of anything I might be telling you," he said at length, "so you should keep it all under your hats, just to be on the safe side."

"As you probably know, Los Alamos is the place where the atom bomb was developed, it is still the only place in this country authorized to continue atomic development. Of course, newly developed devices require testing before they can be turned over to the Department of Defense for use by the military. So, right after the war, quite a search was made for suitable places to do the test work.

"At the present time, small devices are tested in central Nevada, but big ones, or those requiring special facilities, are sent out to the Pacific Proving Grounds, in the northern Marshall Islands." He got up and went over to a big wall map of the Pacific Ocean, and stubbed his finger at a point just north of the Equator and about two-thirds of the way from California to China. "The Marshalls are part of the U.S. Trust Territories of the Pacific, so they can do pretty much anything they want out there without raising international questions."

I glanced at Jeff, who was pulling at his ear lobe, but he said nothing. Roger came back and sank into his swivel chair. "Well, Scripps first got involved in this testing business back in 1946," he continued. "The Defense Department wanted to shoot off an atomic bomb under water inside Bikini Lagoon in order to examine its effect on a variety of warships. We were called in to advise them where to anchor the ships, so that they could be exposed to maximum blast and radiation without all being sunk by the waves. We also made circulation studies of Bikini to determine its flushing rate, so people would know when it was safe to re-enter the area.

"Anyway," he went on, looking directly at me, "this particular test had the code name 'CROSSROADS'. Henry, Jeff, and I were all out there. We had arranged for photographic towers to be built at three locations along the shoreline, from which automatic cameras took movies of the waves passing striped poles, so that we could determine the wave height as a function of distance from the explosion."

"Did you actually see the explosion?" I asked.

"No. We were all sitting on ships fifty miles away, outside the atoll. There were low clouds. All we saw was a bright flash on the horizon. But the photo planes got some very nice pictures. Considering our rudimentary knowledge of wave generation, our wave estimates were really very good; a few ships were sunk, and we got enough wave data from the towers to explain why. It's all described in this report." Roger picked up a thin, red-covered document from his desk. It had the words "SECRET-RESTRICTED DATA" stamped all over it.

"Jeffo, you've been holding out on me," I said, taking the document and flipping the pages. "You never told me you were down in the South Seas cavorting among the palm trees with dusky girls."

"Defense secrets are like B.O.," chuckled Jeff, tugging at the chin whiskers he had acquired on a recent cruise. "Not even your best friend will tell you."

"Jeff was working at Los Alamos during CROSSROADS," interjected Roger. "In fact, that's how we first became acquainted. You were out there looking at the structural response of the atoll to the explosion." Jeff nodded in acquiescence, and Roger continued.

"Well, there were two more atomic test series at the Proving Grounds, in 1948 and 1951, but we were not invited to participate in either. And that's the way matters rested until Saturday, when Al Graves called. It seems that they have been planning another exercise for later on this fall. It's a new device, considerably bigger than anything they have tried before.

"So far, they haven't been much concerned about water waves. Now, suddenly, it appears as if their calculations might be too conservative. The device may be quite a bit more energetic than they were planning—possibly big enough to break off a piece of the atoll rim. They would like to know if they have a wave problem not in the lagoon, but in the ocean—an artificial tsunami."

Roger punched out his cigar in the ash tray and sat back in his chair, hands clasped behind his head. "So now you see why we picked you two guys to go back there; a geophysicist who has been working on atoll structure, and the world's expert on tsunamis."

"Jesus!" I said, picturing in my mind's eye rings of waves hundreds of feet high racing outward at 500 miles per hour. "Do you really think they would shoot this thing if they thought it might jeopardize lives thousands of miles away?"

"As I understand it, the probability is very low—but not zero. This test is being pushed at the highest level in the country. It has been in active planning for five months, and a whole armada of people and equipment is already starting to move out into the Pacific. My guess is that they will go ahead, short of an executive stop order. As I see it, our function is to make the best possible appraisal of the wave hazard, and to suggest a contingency plan to minimize damage in case the worst occurs. Of course, you will also want to recommend instrumentation to document what actually happens out there."

"OK," I said, feeling a little shaken at Roger's calmness. "We *do* have a warning system in Hawaii, because we lost about 270 people out there in 1946. But the Japanese have lost more than 20,000, just in this century! Are we going to tell *them* what's going on?"

Roger picked at the corner of his blotter with a finger nail. He was a gentle, peace loving man, and the thought of abetting a warlike cause obviously troubled him. After a long pause, he looked back up at me. "I hadn't realized it was quite that serious," he said, softly. "I'm not really sure about the international implications. But you should certainly point all this out to them. Ultimately, somebody will just have to make a decision."

"What about travel arrangements?" asked Jeff, pragmatically. "We're pretty short of time."

Roger smiled. "I've already taken the liberty of forwarding your clearances," he said, "and Barbara has booked you out on Sunday on TWA to Albuquerque. From there, you catch a connecting flight to the Los Alamos on a little jitney shuttle called CARCO. It's a contract carrier and no ticket is required—the manifest is prepared by the Laboratory, and they are expecting you. When you arrive, they will meet your plane and take you to the Lodge." We walked to the door, and I felt his hand again on my shoulder. "I'm sorry about your pack trip," he said, warmly. "But this test seems to have a high national priority. For what it's worth, I've recommended you for appointment as Assistant Research Oceanographer. This will give you some official academic status at LASL, and quite a jump in salary. Good luck, and I'll see you both in a week or so." We shook hands, and I went out, feeling a little like Dorothy Gale, who was plucked out of the Kansas prairie by a cyclone, and set down in the Land of Oz.

* * *

We took off from San Diego International about noon. It was a beautiful spring day, and I watched the pine-clad mountains ascend slowly beneath us, and then drop away precipitously to the barren desert to the east. Today's jets cruise above the weather, and the land below is just a distant blur. But the propeller planes of 1952 flew at ten or twelve thousand feet, from which altitude I could see everything in marvelous clarity . . . a farmhouse, with its tiny tractor plowing a postage-stamp field . . . a train of impatient cars behind a big truck, winding down the long grade into the desert. We seemed far removed from the frantic pace of the past two days.

Jeff and I had spent most of Saturday in Roger's office, going over the CROSSROADS report and discussing it from every angle. We couldn't carry a secret document on the plane, so we had dutifully memorized all the information we thought might be important at the briefing. The largest shot of the series, code name BAKER, had had a yield of twenty kilotons, or about a third larger than the device dropped on Hiroshima during the war.

The report had included a spectacular photograph of the mushroom cloud, standing on its opaque stem in the center of the placid lagoon, and surrounded by dozens of tiny target ships. The two largest ships, the old carrier, *Saratoga*, and the cruiser, *Chicago*, were both anchored within a few hundred yards of the column, whose diameter seemed larger than the length of either ship—perhaps as large as 800 feet! Because the crater from which this column issued must have been equally large, and probably extended clear to the lagoon floor, we estimated that the explosion had hurled enough water to fill four Yankee Stadiums a *mile into the sky*.

The maximum wave height was impossible to estimate from our pictures of ship motions, but had diminished to only about six feet at a range of four miles. However, these waves had become amplified in shallow water, and had overrun the lagoon shoreline in several places, inundating a number of buildings. There was a good deal more, but somehow, here in the plane, my mind refused to deal with it. It was locked away in a private drawer, to be withdrawn when needed.

I looked across at Jeff, who was sitting on the aisle, seatback reclined, eyes shut, and thumbs thrust through his seatbelt. His spectacles were tucked, bows-down, into the pocket ahead. I saw not the tall, lanky, soft-spoken scientist of thirty-five, with deep-set brown eyes, generous mouth, and cigarette-stained fingers, but the skinny kid I had grown up with in La Jolla, wearing tin-can armor, and whacking at each other with lath swords along the mud bluffs adjacent to Windansea Beach. Although two years my senior, we had remained close friends until he left for Cal Tech on a scholarship. He had received his PhD in geophysics in 1942—the same year I graduated from Stanford—and straightaway was swallowed up by Los Alamos, where he spent the remainder of the war years working on "earthquake" problems.

After the war, Jeff had accepted an appointment as Research Geophysicist at Scripps's Marine Physical Lab on Point Loma. In early 1946, and quite by accident, we had run into each other again on the street in La Jolla. As wartime flight-test engineer, I was somewhat at loose ends because of the postwar slump. Jeff had suggested that I consider going back to school as a graduate student in oceanography. "We need an engineer at Scripps," he said, "and I've always thought you had the makings of a scientist."

In 1946, Scripps had a pier, and three small buildings sitting on a bluff overlooking the ocean. It also had a faculty of nine and about ten graduate students. La Jolla was still a lovely seacoast village, fringed with pocket beaches separated by rocky promontories. One could surf alone at Windansea beach, or dive into the Cove with flippers and faceplate and come up with a fine lobster or a couple of abalone. Only the afternoon logjam of Mercedes and Bentleys in the A&P parking lot disturbed the tranquil scene. It was a place where the elderly-rich came to retire, and brought their parents. We few members of the younger set assembled evenings at Morrie's Grill, or at El Sombrero, to drink Carta Blanca and listen to Tony Vargas play his guitar and sing Spanish ballads. It was a time of peace and excitement about the future.

In those halcyon years, I was a wiry, athletic, sandy-haired egghead; a romantic introvert, shy with girls, who wrote sonnets on the beach. I woke with the dawn, worked hard, played hard, and stayed up late, reading or talking with friends, with that boundless energy known only to the young. I had a few casual girlfriends, but no fixed attachments. Ours was not a sexually promiscuous generation; we had missed four years in the war and were interested in catching up with the business of living.

After wartime industry, graduate study was a welcome change. The first two years were spent in course work, leaning about the ocean and its many moods and mysteries, and that big fish eat lesser fish . . . and so ad infinitum. Finally, I got down to picking my thesis topic. My faculty advisor, Professor Henry Engels, was interested in waves. There were four of us students in physical oceanography. So he divided the wave spectrum into four parts and gave one to each of us. Somebody got tides, somebody capillary ripples, somebody wind waves . . . and I got tsunamis.

But I found them a fascinating and practically virgin field of study. Very little was known, except that they were produced by large undersea earthquakes, and that their effects were ocean wide and rivaled hurricanes in destructive intensity.

The largest tsunami of the century had occurred on 1 April 1946—only six months before I enrolled at Scripps. It originated in the Aleutian trench, fifty miles south of Unimak Island, Alaska. Almost immediately, a huge wave struck Unimak itself, and swept the seventy-foot concrete tower of Scotch Cap lighthouse from its perch, forty feet above sea level. Four hours later, and without any warning, the sea receded all around Hawaii, and then rushed back, leaving watermarks as high as thirty or forty feet on the rugged coasts of Kauai and Oahu. Wave activity went on for two or three hours. The breakwaters at Hilo, Kahalui, and Nawiliwili were destroyed or heavily damaged, and more than 270 people lost their lives. Many of these had gone out on the reefs during the first withdrawal, and were caught when the water rushed back.

Japan had escaped much damage from the Aleutian tsunami, but a series of local earthquakes during the twenties and thirties had generated waves that killed thousands of people and devastated many small villages along the coastlines of Honshu and Hokkaido.

But the Granddaddy of all events of historical record was the explosive eruption of Krakatau Island, east of Java, in 1883. It hurled four cubic miles of rock into the sky, and huge waves inundated the coasts of many nearby islands, shredding whole villages into matchwood, and drowning more than 30,000 hapless natives. Waves from the event were recorded as far away as San Francisco, Cape Town, and London.

My own contribution to fill this scientific vacuum was a series of model experiments concerned with tsunami generation. I found a quiet corner of Mission Bay, a shallow estuary separating La Jolla from San Diego, and there, for two years, I created tiny tsunamis by disturbing the water in various ways, and attempted to describe the resulting wave systems mathematically. It was fascinating to sit there, a Gulliver surveying a Lilliputian ocean, manipulating the forces of Nature at will, and observing the results. But the greatest reward was discovery; the feeling of learning something new that might some day be put to practical use.

I spent two more years writing my dissertation, meanwhile trying to remember enough French and learn enough German to pass required language exams. I also cast about for a job. In 1952 the world wasn't exactly screaming for oceanographic engineers. The offshore oil industry didn't exist; the Navy already knew all there was to know about the sea; and the Corps of Engineers had been building breakwaters for a hundred years. As I approached my final oral exams, the future seemed a bit hazy. I decided that I needed a little respite—a time for quiet reflection—before plunging back into the stream of life. Hence my plans for a High Sierra pack trip . . . and the fateful phone call. And now, Jeff Knight and I were united on another caper. Despite our long association, because his office was at Point Loma in the Navy's Underwater Sound Laboratory, I had not seen much of him of late. He was looking forward to this trip, he told me . . . to see the changes since the war, and to look up some old friends.

We were a half-hour late getting into Albuquerque because of head winds, plainly evident from the veil of dust obscuring the sunset, as the Lockheed Constellation let down toward the two-mile twin runways that Jeff identified as Kirtland Air Force Base. Albuquerque International Airport was a tiny cluster of buildings at the west end. The pilot kept the two starboard engines running, as four or five of us descended the portable staircase that two ramp jockeys had wheeled into position at the exit doorway, faces swathed with kerchiefs against the swirling dust. Then, the instant our baggage had been hurled down from its belly scuttle, the port engines were restarted, the plane wheeled, darted back to the north runway, and bellowed its way skyward.

Following the others, Jeff and I snatched up our bags and, half-holding our breath against the choking airborne grit, sprinted towards the grubby little terminal building fifty feet away. Inside, we found ourselves alone, the others having vanished through an opposite exit marked TAXIS. The terminal was a single large room, Mexican Adobe style, showing much wear and little care. At one end, the TWA clerk was closing up. At the other, a girl was talking over a radio-telephone within a small enclosure. A sign on the wall gave the daily CARCO schedule. There were three arrivals and departures, arranged to mesh with TWA going east and west, and with Frontier going north to Denver.

The girl stopped talking and glanced over at us. She was young, but rather plain and tired looking, and her face was streaked with the red dust that permeated the building. "Ward and Knight?" she asked. We nodded, and she continued: "Your flight's late getting back here. With this wind, our schedule's blown to Hell." She glanced at the clock above the sign. "It's five-thirty now, and I expect him in about six. If I were you, I'd grab a sandwich at the snack bar before it closes. You probably won't get up to the lodge in time to make dinner, and there's nothing else open up there on Sunday night."

We thanked her and got around the corner just in time to catch the snack lackey dropping the shutter. With a little grumbling, he opened up and sold us each a packaged sandwich and a pint of juice. We bought another for the pilot, just in case. Then we sat there in the gathering gloom, chewing our soggy sandwiches, and listening to the wind howling outside. Finally, I said: "'Seems like a rather funky access to a big government laboratory—only one flight a day in each direction."

"It is," replied Jeff, quietly. "During the war, it was very busy. They had two or three flights a day with good connections—especially going east. But, after the war, things deteriorated. You had to get up at four or five to catch the morning flight west. And, if you missed the afternoon flight east, you were stuck here for 24 hours. It happened to me several time. There isn't a decent place to eat or sleep in Albuquerque."

At the sound of a plane's engines, we went to the window, and saw a Twin-Comanche braking to a stop. Its door burst open, and the pilot jumped down from the wing and bounded into the terminal, clutching a clipboard. Seeing us, he cried: "Hi, fellas. Knight and Ward, right? I'm Buz." Then, without waiting for acknowledgment, he turned to the girl in the CARCO cubicle and said, "Lilly, I'm going to stay up on the hill tonight and bring 401 down in the morning. You got the manifest?"

"Only three coming down," she said, handing him a sheet, which he tucked into his clipboard.

"Fine, you can shut down as soon as you hear me contact LASL tower. Bye, now." He tucked the board under one arm, grabbed our bags, and headed for the door. "C'mon, fellas," he yelled over his shoulder, "I want to get up there while there's still a little light. I've got to make a downwind landing, and there's no glide-slope beacon at LASL."

By the time we got into the plane, he had already stuffed our bags into the nose compartment. "Okey Dokey," he yelled, climbing up on the wing. "One in back and one in front. Who's going to help me drive?" He opened the plane door and Jeff volunteered for the rear seat. I climbed in front after Buz, who was already starting the engines. He reached across me to check the door lock and my seat belt. Then he shoved the throttle levers forward, and commenced chatting with Ground Control on the radio. We rolled out, and hardly made two hundred yards down the runway into the stiff wind, before he pulled the wheel back and we were airborne.

We climbed steeply in a wide left turn, and Buz throttled back to a steady climb. I had just time to notice that we were headed almost due north and climbing at five hundred feet per minute, when we burst out of the dust layer and were blinded by the rays of the setting sun striking the huge bulk of Sandia Mountain to the east. Far below in the gloom, Jeff pointed out the silver thread of the Rio Grande, whose course we paralleled. After a minute or two, Buz finished talking to Albuquerque and turned to me. "Ever been up here before?" he asked. I shook my head, and then commented that I had a private-pilot license, and that I always enjoyed watching a professional handle a small plane. He grinned in appreciation, "I used to be a navy throttle jockey. But . . . I like this much better . . . Much better. Short flights . . . good maintenance . . . and I'm home in a warm bed every night."

"You married?"

"No Sir . . . bachelor all the way. Got a "friend" up at the lab. That's where I'll bunk tonight. Got a couple more in Albuquerque. But, every two or three weeks, I fly a bunch of Lab people up to the Nevada Test site and catch a coupla nights in Vegas . . . Lotsa action there."

We reached cruising altitude at 10,000 feet, and Buz throttled the engines back, so we didn't have to shout to hear each other. "We're already halfway," he said, relaxing in his seat. "Those lights off to the right are Santa Fe. They say it's the oldest town in the country."

"I believe you're correct," commented Jeff, from the back seat. "As I recall, Santa Fe was founded in 1610 by Don Diego de Peralta, who at that time was third governor of the Kingdom of New Mexico."

"Whaddya know," chirped Buz, a little disgruntled at being upstaged. "Learn somethin' new every trip. You a history teacher?"

"No," said Jeff, slowly, "but I worked at the Lab for a while, and became interested in the local history. Santa Fe is sort of a cultural oasis in a literal desert. We used to run down there weekends," he continued, half to me. "They had pretty fair theater, and a first rate symphony."

Jeff sat back, and we all lapsed into silence. I looked out into the gathering darkness, with the first stars beginning to appear and the last ruddy glow fading from the peaks beyond the town. 'Sangre de Christos', Jeff had said . . . 'Blood of Christ' . . . The Spaniards had left their bloody marks everywhere in this part of the world. They weren't interested in dispensing culture, but only in plunder. For all the gold they carried back to Spain, precious little of it remains today.

The plane droned on for another ten minutes or so. I could see the Santa Fe aircraft beacon winking green and white, and had a feeling of being suspended in a warm cocoon, high above the sleeping earth. Suddenly, I remembered the extra sandwich, and asked Jeff to pass it up. Buz laughed. "Thanks, Fellas," he said. I'll be having dinner with my girl friend tonight. But I'll leave it here in the plane for early breakfast." He tucked the bag down beside his seat. Then he got on the air to Los Alamos tower, and began a descending left turn. In the last glimmer of dusk, I could see a cluster of buildings huddled on the mesa at the foot of lofty mountains. The mesa was fringed by razorback ridges that fell away into black darkness. Then I saw the airstrip, which seemed to occupy the entire top of one of the ridges. We dropped swiftly. Buz planted the plane on the very end of the strip, raised the flaps, and reversed the propeller pitch in a blur of activity, and we were down.

We taxied over to a small building, where a grey sedan was parked in the glare of floodlights. The engines stopped. We climbed down stiffly, and waited for Buz to retrieve our bags. Then we walked through a gate in the fence surrounding the airstrip, and signed a register offered by the armed guard sitting behind a small window. The driver was waiting. I turned to thank Buz, but he was already at work tying his plane down for the night. The wind was still blowing up there, but soft and cool, making a keening sound in the tall pine trees.

We got into the car and drove through empty streets for about five minutes, finally turning into a circular drive and stopping before a large building with a stone portico. All the windows were dark. We thanked the driver, who refused a tip, and carried our bags into the lobby. It and the adjoining lounge were empty. There was no sound except our footsteps. We found a note on the desk, addressed to us, and two room keys. The note read: 'Welcome to the Lodge. The dining room opens for breakfast at six-thirty. Major Davis will call for you at eight. Please don't open the windows in your room.' Jeff laughed. "VIP treatment, Laddie, he said, "We're probably lucky they left a light on for us." As we walked toward the stairs, I looked at my watch. It was only eight o'clock, Pacific Coast Time.

Up in my room, I took a long shower, but found myself too wound up to sleep. In my mind's eye, I could picture giant waves spreading over the ocean and crashing against some unsuspecting coastline. Finally, I got out a pocket book and managed to get sufficiently involved that it was midnight before I found a good place to stop. Then I woke up at four-thirty, and read until it was time to get dressed for breakfast.

Major Frank Davis joined us for coffee at quarter to eight. We had just finished a leisurely breakfast, and we sitting there in the Lodge dining room enjoying the sparkling morning, with the sunshine coming through the tall pines and lighting up the green lawn and flagstone terrace outside. Jeff had explained that this rustic building of huge peeled logs was the last remnant of the old Los Alamos Ranch School for Boys, which had succumbed to physicist Robert Oppenheimer's wartime search for a laboratory site. The Lodge had served as a dining facility for senior staff during the war years, and now was reserved to accommodate official visitors.

Major Davis was a slender man of medium height. Despite his relaxed manner and plain blue business suit, his short hair and erect bearing betrayed his military background. The small, gold-winged lapel pin further identified him as Air Force. He had a pleasant and self-confident air about him that made him seem older than his years, which I judged to be about thirty-two—my own age. He was well up the ladder of success that I had just begun to climb.

"Well," he began, after introductions were established, "Is this your first visit to Los Alamos?"

"It is for me," I responded. "But Jeff spent a couple of years here during the war."

"Then I expect you'll notice quite a few changes. They've torn down all of the old Tech area, and replaced it with a shopping center. The new Lab buildings are over on South Mesa."

"How long have you been up here?" I asked.

"Oh, only since January. I'm on a two-year assignment as Liaison Officer between the Laboratory and the Pentagon." Frank finished his coffee and glanced at his watch, a Rolex Flight Master, abristle with special knobs and dials. "Guess we'd better get rolling. The Pass Office is open by now, and we've got a big day ahead. We'll go in my car. Don't bring any written material, unless you plan to leave it inside. This is still a pretty tight security area."

Like the taxi the night before, Frank's car was a gray, 1946, Chevy sedan, with the letters ZIA printed as a logo on the front door panels. We drove through the shopping area again, now casually sprinkled with people, past a high water tower, and down through a swale that seemed to separate the business district from the residential section of the mesa. We passed through an area of nondescript housing; first, rows of Quonset huts with laundry hanging on lines between them, and then several blocks of one- and two-story, plywood, barracks-like structures, somehow divided by partitions to give a pretense of apartment privacy. Finally, we came to a wooded sector with separate, clapboard houses distributed among the trees, but all having nearly identical asphalt-shingle roofs. The whole set-up was reminiscent of a navy base, where the type of quarters depends upon rank, but none of which is architecturally distinguished. And all of this hodge podge of construction was almost obscenely planted in a spectacular mountain forest setting.

Seeing my perplexity, Frank spoke up. "You have to realize that most of this is emergency wartime housing, thrown up while the Lab was frantically trying to get a special job done. After the war, Los Alamos was all but closed down for two or three years. Now, things are picking up again, and they are building some better-quality residences over on that ridge to the north. But all these houses are government property, and are built and maintained by the ZIA Corporation, a civilian contractor that supplies most essential services to the community. There is no private land anywhere on the mesa.

"Jeff," I asked, "Where did you live while you were up here?"

"We just passed it," he replied. "I shared one of those cracker-boxes with two Post-docs from Berkeley. We felt damned glad to get it."

Suddenly, we came to a high perimeter fence, topped by three strands of barbed wire, and surrounding several large buildings. We pulled up in front of a small structure, almost hidden in a cluster of trees just outside the fence. A sign said: SECURITY.

"Pass Office," said Frank, "this won't take long."

Inside were two rooms, separated by a long counter. The front room was empty, except for a camera on a tripod, aimed at a white background screen. An armed guard sat beside it in a wooden chair. He was reading a newspaper. The back room was filled with files and other paraphernalia for badge preparation. A short, moon-faced man, with a little bristly mustache and a huge belly beneath a soiled canvas apron, was busy heat-sealing rectangular badges in plastic, and carefully trimming the edges. He looked up as we came in and, recognizing Frank, stepped forward to the counter. "'Mornin', Major," he smiled, "Couple of live ones, eh?"

"Right," replied Frank. "These are the two I called you about last night. They should be on your rush board."

"Everything is "Rush" nowadays," commented Moonface, pulling two red sheets from a pegboard on the wall. "Will you two gentlemen please step up and identify yourselves . . . a driver's license or bank card?" After he had compared our names with his requests, we were duly photographed and fingerprinted by the guard. When we had signed the print forms, Moonface embossed and initialed them, put them in separate envelopes, and popped them into his files.

"That's it, for now," he said. "I'll make these up as soon as I receive your final clearance status."

"We're going to need guided temporaries through Friday," said Frank. Moonface took two red plastic badges from a drawer. They had a pocket spring clip on the back, and a green stripe running diagonally across the front. He wrote down the badge numbers and the date on a tally sheet, which we signed. "You can go anywhere with these," he said, as he handed them to us, "but you must be accompanied at all times by someone authorized for the area you want to enter. Don't wear this badge outside the compound, and, for Christ's sake, don't lose it. Here's some reading matter," he continued, handing us each a little pamphlet. "We'll give you a security briefing when you come back to pick up your permanent badges."

During our processing, several other people had come into the office, and vaguely assembled in a line before the counter. Moonface had ignored them, and I thought I recognized in his manner the studied indifference borne of tedium and attention to trivial detail. He was King in his little card palace. Davis was a Knave, and we were a pair of ten spots. The others rated five or lower.

As we drove away, Frank remarked: "They take security very seriously around here these days. The Lab took quite a pasting from the Defense Department when Klaus Fuchs gave our little secrets to the Russians. And the fact that he was a British subject didn't help matters."

At the gate into the compound, the guard carefully examined each of our badges before letting us proceed to the parking area in front of the Engineering Building, a sprawling, five-story glass-and-concrete structure. Inside the front door, there was another guard, who looked at our passes again, and asked us to sign the visitor's log. "OK," said Frank, as we stepped into the elevator, "now we're home free."

We went up to the top floor, and walked along a hall towards the rear of the building. There were no names on the door tags, but only the letter J, followed by several numbers. We came to an open door, and Frank ushered us into a large, double office. A pretty blonde-haired girl in a long-sleeved garnet shirt sat typing in the outer room. A small card on the back of her appointments calendar read: Mona Carter.

As we entered, two men emerged from the inner office. The first was slender and of medium height, with dark hair and a ski-jump nose. He was dressed rather nattily in a black business suit, white shirt, and flowered silk tie. The second was taller and heavy set, with sandy hair, turning to white. He wore rimless glasses on a round, pleasant face, and was dressed informally in a short-sleeved shirt, open at the neck.

Recognizing Davis, the leader glanced at us. "Is this the Scripps contingent, Frank?" he queried, and, getting an affirmative nod, he thrust out his hand. "Hi, I'm Norris Bradbury. I run this shop. This gentleman behind me is Al Graves. He will be in charge of your operation." We shook hands, introduced ourselves, and exchanged pleasantries for a minute. Then Graves turned to Jeff.

"Haven't we met before?" he asked.

"Yes, Sir," replied Jeff. "I spent a couple of years up here during the war, working in X-Division. I was fresh out of Cal Tech."

"Now I remember. You were in Jack Clark's group, playing with detonators or something?"

"That's correct, you have a good memory."

"Well, welcome back. It's good to see you again." Then he turned to Davis. "Frank, you can save us a good deal of time this morning if you can bring these guys up to date on our problems. Why don't you use my office until lunch?"

"Good idea." said Bradbury. "We'll see you all in the auditorium at 1300." They were out the door, before we had time to mutter goodbyes. As we followed Frank into Graves' office, I thought I caught a flash of communication between Jeff and Mona, who I remembered had been staring at him, wide-eyed, when we first came in. While Frank's back was turned, I winked at Jeff, who smiled sheepishly. Then Frank sat down in Graves' chair, and we got down to business.

"Dr. Bradbury doesn't waste any time, does he?" I remarked, as Jeff and I took the two chairs opposite him.

"He is a very effective administrator," said Davis. "He was hand-picked by Oppenheimer when he left in 1946—about the time that picture was taken." He pointed to a large photograph of the laboratory tech area hanging on the wall to his left. It looked for all the world like a Prisoner of War camp, with rows of two-story wooden barracks, surrounded by high fencing. There were armed soldiers patrolling a muddy roadway outside the fence, and something resembling a watchtower in the background. "As you may recall, Jeff", he continued, "The Lab lacked a few amenities in those days."

"Yes, although things had improved considerably by the time I left. They had gotten rid of the soldiers, and you didn't have to get a pass to go down to Santa Fe."

Davis had picked up a pencil, and was rolling it between his palms, meanwhile gazing at us reflectively. I had the feeling he was weighing just what he could tell us. "You may remember," he began, "that about four months ago the President announced that the country was proceeding with the development of a new type of thermonuclear device—the hydrogen bomb. What isn't generally known—and this is classified information—is that the Laboratory has been actively working on what it calls the 'fusion concept' ever since it was first established. For present purposes, hydrogen fusion is the process the sun uses to produce energy. The hydrogen bomb works by the same process, only billions of times faster."

"It may sound stupid," I said, "but why do we need two kinds of bombs?"

"There is a practical limit to the size of atomic bombs, and the bigger they are the more radioactive debris they scatter around. The H-bomb uses an atomic bomb as a trigger to ignite the hydrogen, but theoretically it can be built to any conceivable size without increasing the residual radioactivity. So, it's a much cleaner device."

There was a knock on the door, and Mona poked her head in to tell us that Security had phoned to confirm interim Secret clearance status for Jeff and me.

"Good," said Frank, "that will simplify the rest of our discussion. At any rate, since January we've been gearing up for the first full-scale H-bomb test: Operation Ivy. The device is code-named Mike, and it is programmed for 1-October, out at Eniwetok . . . that is, unless the schedule is blown by Dr. Teller's new yield estimate."

"Teller?" I asked.

"Edward Teller, a physicist. He's been a primary promoter for the fusion concept since the beginning, and was instrumental in the design of the Mike device. He left the Lab last fall, when the design was frozen, but he comes down from Berkeley now and then as a consultant. But, to get back to the point I was making, when we got the go-ahead for preliminary planning last January, we were working with a design yield of two megatons. We'd have been happy with one, and were given five as an upper limit. So, the entire Ivy operation was geared to a five megaton maximum yield; everything—ships, shoes, and sealing wax. Then, just last week, Teller walked in on a supposedly-final planning session and announced that he had found some kind of error in his previous computations. He now thinks the Mike yield might go as high as a hundred megatons!"

"*One-hundred-million tons!*" echoed Jeff, with a whistle. He pulled a slide-rule from his breast pocket and began making calculations in a small notebook.

"Just how is yield measured" I asked.

"'Equivalent radiochemical yield' is the technical term," replied Davis. "It's roughly equal to the same weight of TNT."

"I see. So a kiloton yield is equivalent to one thousand tons of TNT, right? I'm just trying to get some idea of the scale of things."

"Yes. The mental image I've been using until last week is that five megatons is equivalent to a freight train loaded with TNT extending from Los Angeles to New York. So now we're looking at twenty freight trains, side by side—or one freight train extending twice around the world!"

We all sat there for a moment, stunned by the sheer immensity of the thought. Then there was another knock at the door, and Mona beckoned Frank from the room. Jeff, who was still fussing with his slide-rule, closed it up with a snap.

"Very interesting," he remarked. "Crater dimensions should vary, roughly, as the cube-root of yield. So I've scaled-up our CROSSROADS estimate to Mike size. I get a crater diameter of 13,700 feet—over two miles!"

"Not only that, Laddy," Jeff continued, ominously, "with due allowance for my unfamiliarity with these bastard English units, Mike will release about the same energy as a magnitude 7.5 earthquake."

"My God." I cried, "That's just about the size of the quake that produced the big tsunami of April 1, 1946 . . . It clobbered Hawaii . . . killed over 250 people. We really *might* have a tsunami problem."

The door burst open, and Davis grabbed his cap and uniform jacket. "My boss, General Clarkson, is at the airport," he said. "I'm going to pick him up. Mona will escort you two to lunch, and take you over to pick up your badges. I'll see you at the briefing." Then he was gone, leaving me staring at Jeff, who was staring at Mona, who was gazing back at him with that look of innocent beguilement some women affect just before setting the hook.

Part of their story came out in modest understatement during lunch, and the rest I pieced together in driblets as I got to know them better. It was pure soap . . . Mona, the beautiful young wife . . . her older, schizoid husband, a physical chemist, out of his depth in the supercharged atmosphere of wartime Los Alamos. His retreat to drinking . . . falsely accusing Jeff, his brilliant young assistant, of tampering with his wife's affections . . . Jeff leaving the Lab at war's end, crushed in spirit . . . Her resignation, and final resort to divorce. I hate sad novels, and am always happier when the guy gets the girl in the end. This one seemed to have dragged along for six years. But it couldn't have happened to two nicer people.

We got to the briefing a little late. We'd had to wait at the Pass Office while Moonface laminated our bright red badges. We got our choice of pocket clip or neck chain.

The briefing was held in an auditorium on the second floor of the Engineering building. The room seated about one-hundred, and was filled to overflowing. Although we were already in a secure area, there was a guard seated at a desk in the hall who checked our names against his list and had us sign a register. Davis was waiting for us at the door, and led us down, past rows of military uniforms from all three services, and seated us, front-and-center, in a knot of civilians. He handed us each a thick, red-bordered manual, labeled: 'Preliminary Planning Guide, Operation Ivy', and stamped SECRET-RESTRICTED DATA in red ink at the top and bottom of each page. Then he left us to join the group of people seated on the speaker's platform.

After a few moments, Norris Bradbury got up and approached the lectern. He ticked the microphone in front of him with a finger nail, and got a corroborative wince from a young man wearing earphones who was seated in the corner behind a recording machine.

"Good afternoon, Gentlemen," he began, "and welcome to Los Alamos. I am Norris Bradbury, Director of this Laboratory. I apologize for calling this meeting on such short notice. But I am sure you all understand our dilemma, and the urgency attached to resolving it. For the benefit of anyone here who may not already know, I can summarize the situation by saying that recent recalculation of the maximum probable yield for the Mike shot gives a small-but finite-probability that it might go as high as one-hundred megatons."

There was a concerted gasp from the audience, and a murmur of discussion, which Bradbury allowed to die down before continuing.

"These circumstances have been conveyed to the Atomic Energy Commission, which has discussed them with the President. We have been advised through channels that, small as this probability may be, we must revise our operation plan to allow for it. We have been asked to submit a revised time schedule, budget, and an estimate of public hazard and proposed mitigation measures, at the earliest possible time. As you are aware, there will be a presidential election this November. The present administration is exceedingly anxious that the operation be wrapped up beforehand.

"To meet this crisis, we have mobilized the Lab's resources, and have made accommodation arrangements for all attendees for the remainder of this week. We hope that by Friday we will have enough new information to put together an appropriate response to the Commission's request."

The murmur rose to an uproar as the audience strove to cope with this unexpected change and its overwhelming implications. Bradbury raised his hand and waited until the uproar subsided. "Now I'm going to turn the meeting over to Al Graves, Deputy Chief Scientist for Ivy, who will give you our *modus operandi*."

Bradbury sat down, and Al Graves came forward, holding a copy of the Ivy planning guide. "Hi," he began. "For those of you who are new here, I'm Al Graves, the guy who is responsible for the scientific part of this operation. I report to the Commander, Joint Task Force 132, General

Clarkson, who is sitting up here today, together with the rest of his staff." Graves went through the list, and each officer raised his hand as he introduced. Then he turned back to the lectern, holding up the planning guide for all to see.

"I trust you all have a copy of this document," he continued. "It's the same as that sent out to you last February, except that it has been marked up a bit. But, before we get down to tearing it apart, I want to bring you up to date on some ballpark guidelines that we are probably going to have to live with in the revised version. We've been asked to upgrade maximum credible yield for Mike from 5 to 100 megatons, a factor of twenty. The immediate effects of this change are the following." He grasped his right index finger with his left hand.

"First, owing to the expected increase of ground-level radiation from the fireball and subsequent fallout, we cannot simply withdraw all civilian and army personnel to the main camp during the shot, as previously planned. Instead, we must evacuate everybody to sea, possibly for several days. Conceivably, if Eniwetok gets too hot to return there, we might have to take everybody to Kwajalein." He paused, while another murmur of surprise and astonishment rippled through the audience, and then continued. "This mass exodus, of course, means that we will need more ships, more fuel, more small support craft, et cetera.

"Second," Graves grasped another finger, "we can no longer safely fire this device from the bunker on

Parry Island. It will have to be detonated from the *Estes*, while at sea. This will, no doubt, give EGG additional headaches."

"Who's EGG" I whispered to Jeff.

"A specialized electronics firm in Boston; EGG stands for Edgerton, Germeshausen and Grier. They have a practical monopoly on civilian communications and hardwire control of firing systems."

Up on the platform, Graves grasped his ring finger. "The third major change will be in the area of hazard evaluation. In all previous tests, our concern has been more or less limited to radiation and air-blast effects in the immediate neighborhood. Thermal effects were confined to the lower atmosphere, and we minimized fallout by shooting when the wind was blowing in the right direction. Each Task Group command was given a prediction manual, and took over its own monitoring and policing. There was coordination, of course, but only at staff level."

"Now, we have a whole new ball game. Our physicists tell me that a 100-megaton explosion might blow a hole right up through the tropopause and into the stratosphere. The thermal updraft will carry with it several million tons of ionized coral and water, much of it highly radioactive. We know very little about stratospheric winds, except that they sometimes blow at very high velocities—hundreds of miles per hour—and in strange directions. So we have to face the possibility that radioactive fallout may occur hundreds—or even thousands of miles away from its source.

"There is serious concern that an explosion of this magnitude may set the atmosphere itself on fire. We are presently re-examining these calculations.

"We now have also to consider whether such an explosion might break off a large piece of the island—large enough to generate a dangerous tsunami, like the one that devastated Hawaii six years ago."

Graves stopped for a moment, pulled a handkerchief from his pocket and wiped his glasses. He looked quite drawn and anxious from the stress of the past few days. Then he addressed us again. "I am sure that we can cover the mechanics of protecting the task force within the framework of this operation plan, at some increase in time, effort, and expense. But the questions of long-range fallout and wave damage are beyond our expertise. Moreover, they have international implications that are of serious concern all the way up the ladder. "So, we have decided to bring in some outside help, and to reorganize our task group structure a bit.

"Task Unit 7, Radiation Safety, will be renamed: Hazard Evaluation. Radsafe will become TU 7.1, with the same responsibilities as before. Then, we have created two new sub-task units. TU 7.2 will be Fallout Prediction, for which we have brought in Doug Calder, from the Weather Bureau's Long-Range Forecasting Section, and George Ellingwood, a radio chemist from Columbia University. Will you gentlemen please stand and be seen?

"We have also created TU 7.3, Water Wave Prediction, for which we have invited Jeff Knight, a physicist, and

Bob Ward, an oceanographer, both from the Scripps Institution in La Jolla. We rose and turned to the sea of curious faces.

"The Hazards group will be headed up by Bill Ogle, whom many of you already know, and who is sitting up here with us on the platform. Bill has been Assistant Test Director at Nevada for the past four years, and took time off to lead the firing party last spring during Operation GREENHOUSE, out at Eniwetok."

Ogle's hand rose and fell. My first impression of our new boss was the unvoiced independence expressed by his informal attire in that array of uniforms and business suits. As always, when we knew him better, he had a pipe in his mouth, although it appeared unlighted at the moment. Graves, still at the lectern, picked up his copy of the operation plan, and waited for the buzz of conversation to die down.

"I will now give you the op-plan for revision of this Op-Plan," he began, waving the document in the air. "The copies passed out to you when you came in are your personal property for the duration of this workshop, and should be identified by writing your name and task unit on the cover. They will be collected each evening and redistributed in the morning. You will notice that every alternate page is blank, but numbered. This space is for your own notes and comments.

"Over the past weekend, we task group commanders have gone over our copies jointly, marking those sections requiring revision. We will spend the remainder of this afternoon going through the plan, section by section, so that you can mark yours similarly. There will be time for questions and limited discussion to clarify issues. Tomorrow, we will divide up into task units for group discussion and recommendations. The last page of your manual is an office assignment chart for the rest of the week. We have arranged for any necessary secretarial and telephone service. Now, I suggest we have a coffee break, before we begin demolition."

And so, we sat there, throughout the long afternoon, drinking numberless cups of coffee to combat lack of sleep, until our hands shook and our stomachs burned. More than anything, I was amazed at the magnitude of the effort required to transport and maintain 12,000-odd men, and thousands of tons of equipment, 6,000 miles across the Pacific. The green light for Ivy had been received in January to construct and test a device conceived of only a few months previously, and allowing only nine months to execute. We were almost halfway to D-Day and nearly all hardware had been procured and shipped to the Forward Area. Now, suddenly, the scope of effort was increased by perhaps one-third, and at a time when the task force had also to compete for planes and ships needed for the new, undeclared war in Korea.

Radiation effects were clearly uppermost in everyone's mind. Every personnel-carrying ship had to be provided with a team of radiation monitors, and equipped with a wash-down system and decontamination facilities. At the test site, many modifications would be required to immunize important buildings and equipment from searing heat and shock waves. Then there remained the problems of re-entry and decontamination after the shot, in order to retrieve data records and to render facilities habitable for future use.

All through this discussion, Jeff's mind was clearly elsewhere. He had his slide-rule and pencil working on tomorrow's problems, one hand running repeatedly through his long hair, until it stood out like a rag mop. It was almost six, and things had gotten down to the question of rollup of the exercise, when Davis came over and indicated that there was no need for us to remain longer. We turned in our copies of the op-plan, and went up to Mona's office to phone for a cab. When we got to the Lodge, it was ten of seven; happy hour was over. So we each ordered a double martini, wolfed down a dinner I cannot even remember, and fell into bed.

In the morning, Jeff and I were joined for breakfast by Ellingwood and Calder. Ellingwood was a small, slender professor-type, in a neat gray suit that matched his gray hair, gray eyes, and little gray mustache. His brisk air belied his apparent age, which I judged to be late fifties. Calder was tall, gaunt, and deliberate, and spoke so haltingly that I wanted to fill in the words he seemed to be searching for. He had been twenty years with the Weather Bureau, which put him in his mid forties. He wore a rumpled black suit, and a white shirt, with the collar tips curled outward, and seemed the perfect example of a career civil servant.

Ellingwood told us that the briefing had lasted until eight-thirty, a Happy-hour, promised yesterday, had been postponed until tonight. Ogle had phoned him at seven, asking him to round us up for a meeting in his office at 0930. We had a second cup of coffee and exchanged pleasantries until it was time to leave. I was surprised how difficult it was to be conversational when the subject dominating all others in our minds could not be discussed in public.

Ogle's office was on the fifth floor, just across from Graves'. As usual, there was no name by the door, but someone had taped a card on the wall labeled, 'TU-7', in red pencil. He must have heard us fumbling around in the corridor, for the door opened and he motioned us in. It was a small office, but somehow he managed to squeeze four extra chairs into the space between his desk and the opposite wall. Two large metal filing cabinets stood in one corner. One of the file drawers was partly open, and a red warning tag had been slipped into its handle. There was a chart of Eniwetok Atoll clipped to the blackboard, and another of the Pacific Ocean lying on the desk. A single window looked out over the pine-clad mesa.

We shook hands and sat down, while Ogle searched in his jacket pocket and produced a zippered pouch holding two pipes and some tobacco in separate compartments. He proceeded to fill one of the pipes, packing the charge in with a blunt finger. He was of average height, but solid—with an air of quiet dynamism, of great strength, perfectly controlled. With his swarthy complexion, intense brown eyes, and jet black hair, combed straight from a high forehead, he looked for all the world like the portrait of an Apache chief that used to hang in my uncle's study.

When his pipe was going, Ogle swiveled his chair toward the window and sat back, eyes lidded, blowing clouds of purple smoke at the ceiling. He seemed lost in thought, almost as if he had forgotten our existence. Finally, he turned back to us, speaking in a soft, direct voice.

"Perhaps there are a few things about this operation I should mention that didn't receive much emphasis in yesterday's briefing. First of all, Ivy is not an "effects" test. There are no targets waiting to be scorched or blasted. The whole object of this experiment is to confirm whether we can produce the expected fusion reaction, and to measure its efficiency. Now, suddenly, just as things have gotten up to full momentum, it turns out that the energy release might be twenty times larger than originally calculated. Large enough so that side effects may persuade the people on top to cancel the operation. That decision is more far-reaching than you may think. This is the first all-out fusion test, but planning for the next operation was commenced coincidentally with Ivy, and there is a whole battery of new devices awaiting the outcome of this test."

He paused, as if to let the impact of his words sink in. "Our part of this scramble is to estimate the worst-credible combination of these side effects, taking into account all the mitigating measures we care to recommend. It will then be up to the White House to decide whether or not we go ahead.

"Well, that is the end of my prepared speech. We don't expect any miracles—only the best advice we can get. We have quite a decent library on explosion phenomena here at the Lab, and I can fill you in on any technical specifics, except how this device works. If you have any questions, shoot. If not, I propose to put you fallout and wave types in adjacent offices, and simply remain available. I'm still Chief Radsafe Officer for the task force, and we have a lot of overhauling to do in that department."

Ellingwood was the first to come out of shock. "I presume that what you want from me is an estimate of the radioactivity that might be produced in the atmosphere by neutron activation of coral dust."

"And sea water."

"Then I'll need some help with the dynamics—you know . . . how much material will be suspended . . . and, of course, the neutron flux."

"I can give you some help with your first question," replied Ogle, rising to show us out. "But neutron activation, of course, is all over in a millionth of a second—before anything starts to move. All I can do is to give you our previous flux model and hope you can scale it up to fit this first go-around. We'll have time later to re-run the program properly."

As we started out the door, Ogle opened the red-tagged drawer and withdrew two packets of documents, each neatly tied with string. He handed one to Calder and one to Jeff. "This is some material I put together from our files this morning that might help you get started," he said. "I've signed it out, so please return it to me before leaving the building." He led us next door into a pair of connected rooms. There was a table and two chairs in each, and nothing else—not even a wastebasket. An assortment of pads and pencils, and a desk calculator, lay on the table in the first room.

"Well, here you are, "said Ogle. "Nice new offices, just been repainted. If you want anything else, including me, just ask Mona. She's right across the hall. The material I gave you includes your copies of the op-plan, and also a questionnaire that should be filled out as soon as you can. It's for logistics planning revision. You know, numbers of bodies you will bring out to the forward area, accommodations and office space, special equipment you want the task force to furnish . . . it's all self-explanatory. The sooner this information gets into the hopper, the better chance we have of meeting our target date. Right now, it's 1 October, but I expect it will slip two or three weeks. That is secret information. Any questions?"

"Can we borrow those charts in your office?" I asked.

"Help yourselves, I got them out for you anyway." Then he was gone, leaving us to our own devices. We affected salutes to Ellingwood and Calder, who returned them, gathered up a few pads of paper, and retired to their inner sanctum.

"Well, Jeffo," I said, leaning back in my chair and stretching, "how do you size up our options?" We had been sitting there for two hours, pouring over the stuff that Ogle had provided, and making independent notes. In addition to the CROSSROADS report, there were quite a few papers on cratering in assorted media, although nothing on coral. There was a British report on waves produced by very small TNT explosions in water. It was classified SECRET, for no apparent reason. Not really very much to base an extrapolation to 100-megatons.

"I think my job is the easier," he responded, getting up to empty the overflowing ashtray and breaking out his second pack of Pall Malls. "Several years ago, the Geological Survey drilled a test hole on Bikini Atoll to see how far down the coral extended. As I recall, they were down to about 4,000 feet before they hit the old volcano underneath. I don't suppose that Eniwetok is much different, but we can find out much quicker by seismic refraction. Our ship, the *Horizon*, is already scheduled for a geophysical cruise in the western Pacific this fall. I will try to borrow her for a couple of weeks to run seismic profiles across the atoll rim near the shot site. I suggest we also ask the task force to drill a row of shallow holes across the rim, just to get an idea of its permeability and water content. Then we can scale up the data we have to estimate the Mike crater size."

"But, what do we tell Ogle this week?"

"Well, we know already that most atolls are riddled with cavities and pretty much water saturated. So, I would expect that the Mike shot will blow a crater in the atoll rim roughly the same size as it would make in water, except that it won't collapse back like water. Rather like blowing a crater in crackerjack. The coral is probably too crumbly for the shot to break off a big piece of the atoll. Even if it did, its density is so near that of water that it would sink slowly, without making a big wave disturbance. The worst scenario will arise if the crater is large enough to break clear through the atoll rim into deep water outside."

"So that the waves will be produced by direct blast, and not by some sort of coral landslide?"

"Exactly," said Jeff, removing his glasses and rubbing his eyes. "So, I see my job as making the best estimate of crater dimensions, later, perhaps, to be modified on the basis of the on-site surveys. This should give us the fraction of total blast energy available to produce waves—if the crater breaks through the rim."

"I see. Then we use that energy to scale up the CROSSROADS data, and anything else we can dig up, to estimate the size of the waves Mike will generate."

"There you go. Then all that remains is for you to figure out how dangerous these waves might be in places like Hawaii and Japan!"

"That's the hooker," I said. "We really don't have a good theoretical basis for calculating waves, let alone their run-up on irregular shorelines. We can only give average figures, based upon previous experience—such as the 1946 tsunami."

"What happened in '46?"

I described the details as well as I could remember them, pointing out that we knew practically nothing about the seafloor motion that produced the waves, nor about their open-sea characteristics.

"Do we have any other relevant examples?"

"None in such detail, but several earlier tsunamis were more destructive. There was a big one off northern Japan in 1933. It killed 12,000 Japanese, but didn't affect Hawaii at all. The worst historical event was the eruption of Krakatau in the East Indies. The whole volcanic island blew its top, and the tsunami drowned 30,000 people on nearby islands."

"Yes, I remember reading about that one. A couple of guys from Columbia studied it. They concluded that the waves were produced mainly by the air blast. As I recall, their energy estimate works out to about 500-megatons." Jeff got up, shoving his hands into his pockets, and paced back and forth. "Isn't it amazing," he went on, slowly, "compared with other animals, men are such a weak, defenseless creatures. But now, suddenly, we seem close to rivaling the more-destructive forces of Nature." He sat down again, elbows on the table, and chin resting in his laced fingers. "But you mentioned something about a new tsunami warning system."

"Yes," I replied. It was set up by the Coast and Geodetic Survey after the '46 tsunami. It's essentially a seismic and tide-gauge network tied together by good communications. The headquarters are in Hawaii. An earthquake of magnitude seven or larger rings a bell in headquarters. They locate the epicenter by triangulation with seismic labs in Berkeley and Caltech, and send an alert message to key tide stations. Then the local tide observers are supposed to go down to watch their gauges and report any unusual wave activity. If the reports sound bad, Headquarters sends out a general warning to a whole list of people . . . civil, military . . . all around the Pacific."

"Has it ever been activated?"

"Oh, sure. There have been a couple of false alarms. They also have fire drills now and then, just to check it out."

"Would you propose to use this system if Mike goes to maximum yield?"

"Just the communications, perhaps. That decision will go up to the task force. But I think we should put our own observers on key islands. We could equip them with special tsunami detectors, and a communications link with the Command Center at Eniwetok. Then I can make a recommendation to Ogle, and the task force can take it from there."

"And what about Japan?"

"That will be up to the White House, I imagine."

"Sounds to me like a whale of a responsibility for a young oceanographer."

"Can you suggest anything better?"

Jeff thought for a moment. "No," he said, "although I think Ogle would like the earliest possible information. Is there any way to anchor wave gauges in deep water a few miles away from the shot site?"

"Maybe," I replied, looking at the chart of Eniwetok. "There are two or three sea mounts up north, here, that come within a few hundred fathoms of the surface. We might put some gauges on top of these things, and have surface skiffs moored to them, with a radio link to the command ship. Would you like to ponder that problem?"

"OK. I can use the *Horizon* to plant the moorings. She won't be busy after we finish the seismic profiling." Jeff leaned back and yawned, stretching his arms above his head, just as Ogle burst in, nearly catching a knuckle in one eye.

"I'm going next door to learn something about fallout," he explained. "How's the wave business progressing?"

"Fine," replied Jeff. "We've solved all the big problems, and thought we'd grab some coffee before tackling the details."

"OK, the coffee machine is in Mona's office, unless you want to go down to the canteen in the basement. They've got rolls and sandwiches. If you both go out, just drop the literature into my file. Security gets a little uptight if they see anything classified lying around in an empty room." He entered the annex, and then leaned back through the doorway. "If you like, we can go down to lunch together."

"Sounds good," I said "whenever you're free."

But about 1130 Ogle reappeared, looking grim, and went out without speaking to us. He returned shortly with two laboratory types, judging by their informal attire, and holed up again. Later, Mona went in with a tray of sandwiches and coffee. So we gave up and went to lunch without him.

It was almost three when the annex door opened, and five of them emerged, expressing, if nothing else, exhaustion and relief. Ogle, who was carrying their documents, sat down with us, and began filling his pipe. The others waved in mute salutation, and went out, closing the door behind them.

"Well," Ogle said, firing up, "I hope the wave predictions are in better shape than the fallout."

"That bad?" asked Jeff.

"I am forced to admit," he said carefully, "that I vastly overestimated present understanding of upper circulation. The meteorologists know there are high-velocity jet streams up there in the stratosphere, but they seem to have only the foggiest notion of their day-to-day variability. The kindest thing I can say is that we have essentially no synoptic prediction capability."

"So where does that put us?" I asked.

"It means that we have to ask the Air Force to set up additional observation stations on outlying islands, and to extend all their daily sounding balloon ascents up into the stratosphere. And we've got to do this long enough before the test to establish some sort of pattern, so that we can make sure the stuff we may inject into the stratosphere is going to go in the least-harmful direction."

"Which is?"

"Due east. Then it can go 6,000 miles without encountering populated areas. Ellingwood seems to believe that most of the dangerous stuff will have decayed to low level or will have fallen into the ocean by that time.

"But, what about the stuff that never gets up into the stratosphere?" mused Jeff.

"We have a better handle on that," said Ogle. "It consists of heavier particles. Most of it will go nearly west, with the trade winds, and will fall out within two or three hundred miles. So, if we evacuate the fleet to the southeast of Eniwetok, we should be well clear of almost everything. However, just to be on the safe side, all of the ships will have radiation monitors aboard, and be equipped for decontamination. This means a wash-down system, hot suits, and automatic showers . . . the works. If one person gets needlessly overexposed, we'll never hear the end of it."

He relighted his pipe and said, "OK, what about the *good* news?"

"Not all that great in here, either," commented Jeff. "As near as I can make out, Mike could go as high as 15 or 20 megatons before it breaks through the atoll rim. Even if it goes to 100, we don't think it would cause a landslide that could generate a big tsunami. But about half the blast energy would be available to make waves. We can't scale CROSSROADS-BAKER directly, because it was underwater, and Mike will be at the surface. So our best guess is that it might create a dangerous wave situation—but not exactly like a tsunami."

"Can you explain that to a landlubber?" asked Ogle.

"Well," I interjected, "We believe that tsunami waves are something like a hundred miles long in deep water. The Mike waves might be ten miles long, and the biggest storm waves are less than one mile. The end result is that we don't have any reliable way of predicting what might happen in places like Hawaii."

"And, if it goes less than fifteen, we don't have a problem?"

"Less of a problem—but not zero. There are too many imponderables."

"OK," sighed Ogle. "What do you recommend we do to protect people?"

"It could be worked out through the warning system, I suppose," thinking off the top of my head. "You know . . . we'd have to make a value judgment about the local waves. If they seem dangerous, we could have the Warning Service issue alert of a large, fictitious earthquake. Then, we upgrade the report by wave observations at more distant observations stations. After all, that's all the information local authorities have about a real tsunami . . . And, there's no breach of security."

"That reads OK to me," said Ogle. "Tell me more."

We sat there another hour, explaining the warning system, and our instrumentation plans. Ogle was remarkably prescient in his comments. He suggested that we should arrange for observers in Hawaii to document any unusual wave effects, and also that we measure waves within Eniwetok Lagoon as guidance for future testing. Finally, he glanced at his watch and stood up. "I've still got a few things to attend to today," he said. "But I think you two have gotten pretty much on top of things. I especially like the fact that your proposal puts very little extra burden on the task force. I don't see any reason why you can't finish up your preliminary proposal tomorrow, so that you can go home and start things rolling. Mona can help with your reservations."

We followed him as he carried all the documents to his office and put them back in the file. He removed the red tag, slipped a steel bar through the drawer handles, and secured it with a padlock. Then he turned to shake our hands. "I'll see you both at Happy-Hour," he said. "It should be a good chance for you to meet the people you'll be interacting with in the next few months." He looked at his watch again. "If you hurry, you might make the bus back to the lodge. There's quite a traffic crunch when the bell rings."

PART II

THE PROTAGONISTS

There are happy hours and happy hours. Mostly, they are a feature of your neighborhood bar—such as the Snug Harbor, on Lido Island in Newport Beach, where I used to hang out in the war years. It's a place where locals drop in to meet friends and touch antennae before heading on for dinner. Everybody knows everybody else, and a relaxed and convivial atmosphere prevails.

Happy hour at the Lodge was quite different. Most of the people were strangers. The officers had changed into civvies, and I couldn't recognize a single face. Jeff had gone off to pick up Mona, so I came down stairs alone, eased my way into the sea of bodies, and aimed for the bar. There is a knack for manipulating massed humanity. Steady pressure works best. Standing drinkers, rapt in conversation, behave rather like loose pack ice in a winter harbor. They strongly resist frontal assault, but yield slowly to persistent insinuation of shoulder and elbow. I ordered a double scotch, and had just turned to worm my way to some quiet eddy, when I felt a hand on my arm. Frank Davis pulled me over and presented me to General Clarkson, and to Admiral Wilkins, Commander, Task Group 3.0, the naval arm of JTF-132.

Clarkson in mufti was less impressive than in uniform. But his booming voice more than compensated for modest stature, just as the little smile crinkles at the corners of his intense blue eyes belied the square set of his jaw. He shook my hand as though he meant it, and made me feel at ease. Wilkins was taller, thinner, and balder than his superior, and I could hardly hear his quiet voice above the conversational background.

"Well, Young Man," rumbled the General, "Ogle tells me you are the world's expert on tsunamis."

"I guess so, if there is any such thing," I replied. His jaw tightened imperceptibly. I realized he wasn't being facetious, so I continued, hastily, "You see, Sir, it's a very new field. About all we've learned so far is what the shoreline effects are like when there's a big disturbance. But we know very little about the disturbance itself."

"I understand that not much is known, but Ogle tells me you've cooked up some sort of game plan. As long as we're all out here together, I'm hoping that you can find time this week to make us a little presentation—just me and my staff . . . very informal. Most of us have never heard the word tsunami before yesterday."

"Of course," I said, "How about tomorrow afternoon?"

"Fine. I'll ask Major Davis to work it out with Ogle." Then he turned to greet a new arrival, and I realized our conversation had ended.

Someone had opened the tall doors leading out of the dining room onto the terrace, and I allowed myself to be drawn outside with the general exodus into the cool evening air. Then I spied Jeff and Mona coming around the corner of the building and across the wide lawn beyond the terrace. Mona had changed into a light lemon chiffon dress, and had let her hair down. She wore a beatific smile, and appeared to be floating about four inches above the grass, like a balloon on a tether, only restrained from soaring off above the treetops by her grasp on Jeff's arm. He caught sight of me and began to grin.

On sudden inspiration, I rushed toward them crying, "Congratulations! I just heard the wonderful news."

"News!" shrieked Mona. "How could you know? We haven't told anyone."

"All I had to do was open my eyes. You both look as if you'd swallowed canaries." Then we all burst out laughing.

"Honestly, Robert," Mona sighed, taking my arm as well, as we walked back to terrace, "you have no idea how stupidly intelligent adults can act in good faith. Each of us thought he was being so noble and self-sacrificing . . . . and all we've done is to waste several precious years. So, we've decided that, as soon as this 'business' is over, we'll get married, and try to make up for lost time."

"Well," I said, "this certainly calls for a celebration." I left them standing at the edge of the terrace, and plowed my way back to the bar. There was no champagne, so I settled for a bottle of Lancers and three glasses from the kitchen. When I got back, they had been joined by Ogle and another mutual friend, Jack Clark, whom Jeff had worked with during the war. This required another trip for more glasses, but eventually the appropriate toasts were drunk. Ogle, Clark, and I all agreed that Jeff was a traitor to bachelordom, but that the circumstances were sufficiently extenuating to approve his resignation from the ranks.

The wine gone, the happy couple wandered blissfully away, and Jack glanced at his watch. "My God," he exclaimed, "I've got a bunch of people coming over for pot-luck in an hour. I better go polish the door knobs." He turned to go, and then looked back. "Say, why don't you guys come on over? There's always plenty of food."

"Fine with me," I said, and looked at Ogle, who hesitated, and then shrugged his shoulders. "I was going back to the office to finish some homework . . . but, what the Hell . . . I'm really not in the mood."

"Great," said Jack, "Just straggle over whenever you feel like it. You know how to get there, Bill."

He trotted off across the lawn, and Ogle took me in tow. For the next hour we meandered around the terrace, pausing to introduce me and chat briefly with a dozen or so people whom he considered might be useful for me to meet. I have a lousy memory for names and always carry a little notebook, in which I busily scribbled Ogle's comments as we moved about.

Around seven, they turned off the spigot at the bar, and began setting tables in the dining room. "I guess it's not too early to wander over to Jack's," commented Ogle, "Perhaps we can talk a little before the guests arrive. He's quite an interesting guy."

As we walked around the Lodge, Ogle explained that Jack had replaced him as Test Director at the Nevada Test Site three years previously, but would probably head-up the firing party for the Mike event. "That's why there's such a high percentage of single men in this racket," he confided. "The Laboratory is our home, but we're away three-quarters of the time. A couple of years ago, Norris Bradbury tried his best to persuade the government to let us get out of the testing business altogether. The long separations are too hard on the staff . . . too many problems with wives left at home. He couldn't sell it, though. Nobody wanted the military running the tests."

"Were you ever married?" I asked.

"Yes . . . for a good many years." He got out his pouch and proceeded to fill his pipe. "She died last spring . . . while I was out on GREENHOUSE. It was cancer . . . not altogether unexpected. I couldn't get back, but my sister was with her at the end . . ." His voice trailed off, and I suddenly felt a flood of warmth for this lonely man I scarcely knew, a man who lived a secret life, except for a little circle of confidents. Somehow I felt flattered that he seemed to accept me as one of them.

* * *

It turned out that the party was right next door to the Lodge, in one of the staff cottages left over from the Ranch School. Jack Clark shared the place with another physicist, Nick Metropolis, who was away. The front half of the cottage contained a big L-shaped living-dining area, with the kitchen in the corner. Behind, there were two small bedrooms with a bath between. Like the Lodge, the structure was built of peeled logs, and comfortably furnished in a rustic fashion.

When we walked in, Jack was bustling about in a red apron, pulling trays of hors d'oeuvres from the refrigerator and putting them on the bar that separated the kitchen from the dining area. A small table in the living room held an assortment of glasses upside down on a towel. There were also bottles of scotch, bourbon, and mix, and a large earthen crock, frosted all over, and labeled Nitroglycerin. It held about a gallon of martinis.

Jack came out to greet us, taking off his apron. He was short and slightly built, with horn rims, a crew cut, and an engaging smile. We helped ourselves to martinis with a silver dipper; they were so cold that they frosted the glass and numbed the lips. Jack explained that hereabouts martinis were customarily pre-mixed and stored in the freezer. By decanting off the ice slurry as it formed, the proof of the remaining mixture could be raised to about 120, which indeed gave them about the same impact as nitro.

Very shortly we heard voices, and other guests came crowding through the door. From their laughter and general air of familiarity, it was apparent that these were not people from the briefing, but Laboratory regulars who were all close friends. There were several women, carrying boxes and casseroles, all of which were set out on the dining room table.

Over the next ten years I was to become well acquainted with most of these individuals, but on that occasion I had scarcely heard of any of them. My post facto recap for that party, compiled the following morning with Ogle's assistance, includes quite a list of scientific luminaries:

Fermi, Enrico, Physicist, Univ. Chicago (kind, thoughtful, gracious). Demonstrated the first atomic chain reaction in a 'pile' of carbon blocks, interspersed with enriched uranium pellets.

Von Neumann, John (Wife, Klara), Mathematician. Inst. for Advanced Study, Princeton. (impulsive, talkative, very bright). A one-man think tank. Invented game theory, and designed the first large electronic digital computer.

Teller, Edward (Wife, Mici), Physical Chemist. Univ. of Chicago (very opinionated, argumentative, intense). A pivotal figure in the development of atomic bomb, and the present Mike device.

Bethe, Hans, Physicist, Cornell Univ. (gracious, thoughtful, wide interests). One of the first to work out the reactions whereby the stars burn hydrogen to produce energy.

Ulam, Stan, (Wife, Francoise), Mathematician, LASL (chess fiend, skier, climber, amusing intellectual). Number theory specialist, who conceived 'trick' that made Mike possible.

Feynman, Richard, Physicist, Cal Tech (very bright, amusing, musical, versatile). Specialist on nuclear structure.

Mark, Carson, graying Canadian mathematician, and director of the Mike design team.

John Marshall (Wife, Leona) both Physicists, LASL (shy, reserved, wife talkative, gossipy). Experimental physicist and Fermi protégée, respectively.

There were several others, including a couple of freelance ladies from the J-Division secretarial pool. So far as I could make out, there was no particular reason for this occasion, except that so-and-so were in town. I was told that the Laboratory staff was divided among a number of close-knit social groups, within which such parties were frequent, and usually impromptu. But there was more to it than that. As I later learned, this small group of charming, gracious people comprised, in fact, the hard core of brain power that had developed the atomic bomb. All during the war, they had lived here together, in meager circumstances and enforced social isolation, and had somehow remained friends. Through mutual travail, failure, and success, they had formed common bonds much stronger than normal in the fiercely competitive world of science. But you would never have guessed all this from their conversation. As distinct from a social gathering among artists, wherein little but art is ever discussed, these people talked about everything but science. Just standing alone for a moment in the center of the room, I caught fragments of Roman history, economics, music, skiing—and how to prepare Hungarian goulash.

Because I was the only stranger present, Ogle went to some pains to make sure I met everyone, always introducing me as the world's tsunami expert. Reactions to this pronouncement were diverse, but generally interested. Teller proceeded immediately to explain his own hypothesis of wave interaction with obstacles, whereas Bethe asked many questions, and seemed astonished that even such everyday phenomena as wave-breaking on a beach had no satisfactory mathematical explanation.

Dinner was buffet, Mexican style. There were bowls of frijoles and beans, casseroles of enchiladas and tamales, and trays of tacos and quesadillas. Under the table, there was also a large tub filled with crushed ice and bottles of dark Dos Equis beer. People helped themselves when hungry, and most of us ended up sitting cross-legged on Navajo rugs in front of the stone fireplace, listening to Feynman pounding expertly on a pair of bongo drums, while Leona Marshall played the guitar and sang plaintively.

After dinner we had coffee in large, earthenware mugs, and talk reverted to storytelling. Somebody told of a German physicist, named Houtermans, who fled into Russia to escape the Nazis at the beginning of the war. He was captured and thrown into a Siberian prison, where he remained until the war ended. He spent the time evolving a brilliant mathematical theory, all of which he scribbled on his cell wall with charcoal, having no paper or pencil. Finally freed, he promptly wrote up his results and mailed them in for publication—only to find that he had been scooped two weeks previously by another scientist with the same idea.

Then, there was George Gamov, a huge bear of a Russian, who defected to America after the 1934 Solvay Conference in Brussels. Gamov had a great sense of humor and loved practical jokes. He and a former student, Ralph Alpher, once wrote a paper together. Without telling Bethe about it, they sent it in with the title: 'The ABC,s of Atomic Abundance', by Alpher, Bethe, and Gamov. This work became internationally famous as the Greek Alphabet Paper, although, when the theory went out of fashion, it was reputed that Bethe had threatened to change his name to Zacharias.

Sitting there, leaning against the raised stone hearth, with the warm glow of brandy suffusing my system, I suddenly realized that I felt perfectly at home. In any other society, I might have felt a need to establish my identity and to defend it, through some social contrivance. Here, I was accepted, solely on Ogle's recommendation—and that sufficed.

At this point, Clark appeared in our midst, carrying a portable tape recorder. which he set down on the coffee table. Then he plugged in a microphone on a long cord and held up his hand for silence. "I hope you'll excuse me for interrupting things," he began, "but it suddenly occurred to me that this may be the last time that the old LASL Super Snoopers are all together in one place. It's also an auspicious occasion . . . you know . . . dawn of the nuclear era, et cetera. What I'd like to do is have all you theoretikers say a few words about what you think the nuclear age will be like within the next, say, twenty years. OK? Then I'll put the tape into a bank vault, and we'll get it out in 1972 and see who's the best guesser."

There was a murmur of accordance and interest as Jack turned the machine on and spoke a few introductory words. Then he handed the microphone to Teller, saying, "OK, Edward, you're sort of Father of the Super program, we'll start off with you."

Teller took the Mike and quipped, "How long does this tape run, Jack, I don't want to use it all up myself?" Then he sat there a moment, reflectively, holding the microphone before him like a scepter. With his deep-set eyes, bushy, black brows, and his mop of black hair, he resembled some sort of messiah about to pronounce judgment. Then he began to speak, rapidly and impulsively. He likened the discovery and control of nuclear fusion to that of fire among primitives. For 1972, he predicted a military stalemate among nuclear powers, with none willing to risk the awesome consequences of a nuclear war. He foresaw the first convincing experiments in the control of fusion reaction energy for power production, leading to practical utilization by 1990. Meanwhile, peaceful uses of uncontrolled (explosive) devices would include the digging of harbors and canals, the creation of deep underground reservoirs and waste disposal cavities, and the enhanced exploitation of oil and gas deposits.

These views, I suppose, coming hardly as a surprise to the assembly, were greeted with mild applause. The Mike was then passed on to John von Neumann, who was more succinct. In his opinion, international power politics was like a game. In game theory, among opponents of equal aptitude, the odds favor him with the greatest number of powerful pieces. A stalemate could only exist as long as the balance of power remained static. In his opinion, the only way to ensure this was to maintain an aggressive nuclear development program. He wasn't sure how things would look in 1972, except that such new developments as computers and rockets would play a significant role.

Bethe was next, and stated that he had only returned to Los Alamos after the war hoping to prove that the Super concept would not work. "Unfortunately," he concluded, "it now looks as if it might." His view of 1972 was cloudy but guardedly optimistic: "I really do not see any prospect of producing useful energy from controlled fusion in the near future . . . but, as I have just noted, I am usually wrong in such practical matters."

Fermi remarked simply that he was enthusiastic about learning more—quantitative details of nuclear reactions, but felt that the military aspects of thermonuclear experiments were better left to professional statesmen. Although it isn't on the tape, Ulam later told me that, at the time of his death by cancer two years later, Fermi had become very apprehensive about the arms race and its impact on society, and regretted not having become more involved in public affairs.

At about this time I ran out of notebook paper and, in my slightly inebriated state, gave up trying to chronicle what seemed to be a portentous insight into the future. After all, I thought, I can always borrow Jack's tape. But, as I recall, nothing much else was said of great moment.

The taping session introduced a note of sobriety among the celebrants, most of whom began to gather up their effects and slip away. The two secretaries hung around long enough to empty ashtrays and rinse glasses. One of them was rather cute. I had chatted earlier with her long enough to learn that her name was Suzy, and that she had only worked at the Lab for a couple of months. She came over to hug Jack goodbye and, catching my eye over his shoulder, nodded toward the door. But it was after eleven, and a little late for hanky panky, so I made a sign that I would telephone her tomorrow. She smiled and skipped out after her companion, leaving me and Ogle alone again with our host.

"How about a little nightcap?" asked Jack, filling a coffee cup and adding a jolt of Irish.

"Thanks," I replied, "but I think I'd better stick to coffee."

Ogle smiled. "The Los Alamos pace getting to you?"

"Either that or the altitude. But I did get a bit of a head start at happy hour. Anyway, it was a lovely party; I got a big kick out of Teller. He comes on like a charging lion. Isn't he sort of responsible for this whole thermonuclear business?"

"Well, Edward was certainly its principal proponent, but there is some feeling that things might not have turned out much differently if he hadn't been in the picture at all. I'm sure they would have run more smoothly." He leaned forward and tapped his pipe ashes into the fireplace. Then he fished out his little pouch and zipped it away for the night.

"You mean, someone else would have thought of it?" I asked, as he got to his feet and shook hands with Jack.

"Probably," he replied, reflectively. "Edward was by no means the only person in this country worrying about fusion reactions. He just worried about them more energetically."

I said goodbye to Jack, and we walked out the door and down the path to the curving driveway where Ogle had left his car. He fumbled for his keys. "And besides," he continued as he opened the door and got in, "the whole fusion program has been up-and-down like a yo-yo ever since the beginning. It has several times been saved from extinction by sheer coincidence . . . and it wouldn't surprise me in the least to find out tomorrow that the Mike test has been cancelled by presidential order."

"You make it sound like a dime-store thriller."

"It is," he replied. "Perhaps some day I can tell you all about it." Then he drove off.

* * *

Ogle ultimately told me the story—but thirty years later!

I hadn't heard from him since we were both up in Alaska for the last Pacific test series at Amchitka Island in 1971, when he suddenly phoned me at Scripps and invited me to lunch. He picked me up a few minutes later and we went up to the Sky Room in the La Valencia Hotel. It's a creaky old place that cascades seven stories down the bluff in the center of La Jolla, but the view from the top is spectacular. It was a beautiful spring day. Yesterday's showers had swept the horizon free of smog, and we could see all the way from the Coronado Islands to the south clear up to Santa Catalina, ninety miles to the north. We got a window table, ordered drinks, and sat there enjoying the view, while Ogle fished out his little pouch and fired up his perennial pipe. To my mind, a pipe is much more than an instrument for oral gratification, as psychiatrists would have us believe. It is an extension of personality. The indecisive man plays with his pipe, constantly popping it in and out of his mouth, using it to point or gesticulate, or simply sucks on it upside down when empty. Ogle was a smoker's smoker. Once his pipe was filled and lighted, always clenched in the same mid-section of his left jaw, he never touched it again, except when speaking, or until it was time to switch to the second pipe he always carried in the same pouch.

"Is that the same pipe you had in Alaska?" I asked, idly.

"Hell, no. They burn up or I bite the stems off in six months. I order these custom-made, a dozen at a time, from Joe Roth's in New York. I always get the same Bulldog Stubby . . . it fits my pouch, and doesn't wear my jaw out holding it up all day."

I laughed. "When they dig up your skull a thousand years hence, they'll be able to identify you by the custom Roth stem clenched between its teeth."

The waiter brought our drinks and two menus, and stood by while we examined them. Ogle ordered a crab salad; I chose cold salmon with Sauce Verde, and asked for a bottle of good Vouvray. Then I raised my glass and said, "Here's to whatever brought you out this way. What are you doing with yourself these days? I heard you left the laboratory."

"That's right. I became a square wheel when Pacific testing stopped. So, I retired to Colorado and set myself up as an energy consultant. Got a new wife, too; you remember Holly Jurgens, from Anchorage?"

"The Senator's wife?"

"Yes, I traded him two good saddle horses and a cabin in Taos for her hand. But, she couldn't hack New Mexico and I couldn't hack Anchorage, so we bought a little ranch near Boulder. She's got horses and a garden, and it's close to fishing and hunting. Good airline connections out of Denver.

"As usual, I'm traveling about half the time. Suits Holly just fine. She says she couldn't put up with me longer than a week at a stretch." He was as close as he ever came to smiling, and his brown eyes twinkled.

"You're looking fine," I said. "Married life obviously agrees with you."

"You're looking pretty fit yourself," he remarked, tactfully ignoring the obvious thickening of my midriff. "How're all the family?"

"Just fine . . . the children are long gone, except for Laura . . . she's in her last year at Mills. Say, can't you stay over for dinner? Susan will shoot me if you leave without saying hello."

He thought a moment, and then shook his head. "No, I'm afraid not. Just on principle, I never accept invitations when traveling, because I can never repay them. I've been here two days talking to Harold Agnew at General Atomics. I'm sure you remember him from the Ivy days. He was head of the arming party, and later replaced Bradbury as LASL director. He mentioned you were still connected here with Scripps, so I thought I'd give you a call and see what you're up to."

"Well, I'm not worrying about nukes any more. I recently discovered that asteroid impacts may have produced tsunamis on the moon—but nobody really believes me. We all believe that asteroids falling into the ocean could make prodigious tsunamis. Waves 20,000 feet high. There was an asteroid impact into the Yucatan about 65 million years ago that kicked up such a dust cloud that it cooled the earth for 100 years and killed off all the dinosaurs."

"'Way out of my class," he remarked, We're just worrying about the MX missile. You know, the ultimate ICBM."

Our lunch arrived and there was momentary pause as the wine was poured; it was a Roger Salmont '79, and quite acceptable. Then I said, "What about the MX, Bill? I've never heard a convincing argument for building it in the first place."

"Then you obviously haven't been following Freeman Dyson's excellent series in the *New Yorker*. He regards it as a great technical folly—second only to the greater technical folly of the philosophy of nuclear deterrence as a permanent guarantee of survival."

"That's quite a mouthful. For starters, what does he mean by technical folly?"

"The MX was intended as a replacement for the thousands of twenty-year-old Minuteman missiles we've got sitting in silos all over this country, which are now considered vulnerable to the increased accuracy of Soviet missiles. The folly is that MX was designed without any clear concept of where to hide it. Hence all this flimflam about minisubs, truck mazes, and so forth."

The waiter being busy, I refilled our wine glasses. Then I sat back and looked at Ogle. He was a little gray at the temples, but his rugged, 'Apache' face seemed otherwise immune from the ravages of time.

"Where will it all end?" I reflected, half to myself. We were all so damn naive and excited back in 1952, floating around out there in the ocean off Eniwetok, waiting for Mike to go off. I wonder how different things might have turned out if it had been a dud . . . No . . . That wouldn't have changed things much. What I meant was . . . if the whole thermonuclear program somehow had never got started."

"In the United States?" asked Ogle, reaching for his pipe pouch. "Don't forget, the Soviets detonated their first device only nine months after Mike. There is fairly good evidence that they had been working on it for over three years. And they really didn't need our input. Once you have succeeded in making an atomic device—which they did in 1949—then the thermonuclear step is technically a trivial undertaking by comparison.

"So, if you're going to play the 'if' game, you probably have to go back to the discovery of atomic fission, which, as you may recall, occurred in 1938—in Germany! If Hitler had clamped the lid on that discovery, and fully exploited it to his own ends, the political history of the world might have come out quite differently."

I pondered Ogle's remarks, while he signaled the waiter for more coffee. "Something bothering you?" he asked.

"Just a little *déjà vu*. It seems to me that, if your analysis is correct, the United States really owes Edward Teller something of an apology. Back in the testing days he was a hero . . . you know, 'Father of the H-Bomb' . . . 'Savior of the Country'. Wasn't he awarded the Fermi Prize in 1962? But, in the last decade or so, he has become a public whipping boy, particularly among the liberals. I've even heard scientists refer to him as the 'Villain of the Century', and 'Father of the Nuclear Holocaust'. Where do you place him, Bill?"

Ogle sucked on his pipe for a moment, looking not at me but at the distant horizon, where white flecks of sails bent on the afternoon breeze. "You've asked a moralistic question," he said at length, "which I don't think I'll attempt to answer. But what I *was* attempting to convey is that, historically, new discoveries in science are inevitable when the time is right, and that, with modern communications, they are apt to occur almost simultaneously in different places. If you accept that hypothesis, then, in my opinion, it's better to be at the front of the line than at the end—particularly when the other guys have a longstanding avowed intention of destroying your system of government."

"You think that was Edward's motivation: fear of the Russians?"

"Oh, certainly. He stated it publicly. But I think there was also his ego. In science, the name of the game is discovery. Edward was one of a flock of bright young

European scientists who came over here in the mid thirties to get away from Hitler. Before he came to Los Alamos to work on the fission program he didn't have much of a track record. Shortly thereafter, he conceived of a possible way to make fusion work using atomic energy. From then on, it became his obsession; he refused to work on anything else. When he couldn't get adequate support for his "Super" project, he went to Washington, where he had some friends among congressmen and military types, and lobbied very persuasively. I believe he saw the successful demonstration of a fusion reaction as his big chance for lasting recognition.

"I also feel," he continued, "that Edward's role in the Super drama has probably been overplayed by the media. He was always a principal character, but the history of the fusion program in this country was not all that black and white. It almost died several times."

Ogle paused to tap his pipe ashes into the planter by his chair. Then he pulled out his little pouch, switched pipes, and refilled the other. It struck me that he often used such devices to marshal his thinking. Finally, he said, "It seems to me that I promised to tell you that story some day . . . or is that what you've been leading up to?"

"Not really. But I'd like to hear it. Everything was so secret in those days I never knew what the Hell was going on."

"All right. To the best of my knowledge, most of the mumbo jumbo has come into public gaze in the last few years. Is there a quieter place we can sit?"

I paid the bill, and I took him down to a garden terrace overlooking the grassy expanse of Scripps Park, with the surf breaking off the point beyond. There were several tables with patio umbrellas, but we had the place to ourselves.

"Well," he began, after we had seated ourselves and he had got his pipe going, "you asked me about Edward, and I had mentioned that he was not the only person in those days who was thinking about fusion. It may not be common knowledge, but Los Alamos had a fusion program going since it was first founded by Oppenheimer—and, to the best of my knowledge, it still does. The prospect of limitless cheap energy from controlled fusion remains a viable objective. During the war years, Edward was in charge of the Laboratory's program. But, when the war ended, the Manhattan Project was terminated, and most of the scientific staff trickled back to the safety and comfort of their ivory towers. Edward accepted an offer from Chicago; Oppenheimer went to Cal Tech, and Norris Bradbury replaced him as Director. There was some question whether the Lab would survive at all. In the summer of 1946, we were down to about eight theoretical people, and fusion was on the back burner.

"However, in the fall, Congress passed the Atomic Energy Act, which provided, among other things, that atomic development should remain permanently in civilian hands. After that, things picked up again; by 1949, we were back up to twenty-two physicists. In summer, a good many of the old guard came back. They could double their university salaries by two months consulting. However, about all that the fusion group had been able to accomplish since the war was to convince itself that Teller's classical fusion theory wouldn't work. As far as most people were concerned, it was a dead issue.

"Then, all of a sudden, several things happened that got the Super project back on target. In August, 1949, the Soviets shot off their first atomic device. This caused a flurry of introspection at top level in the administration. President Truman asked the AEC whether the Super should be accelerated. Their General Advisory Committee, headed by Oppenheimer, recommended against it, principally, as I recall, because it was not a military weapon, but an 'instrument of genocide' . . . . and that, even if the Russians were to develop a super bomb, our atomic stockpile should prevail against it."

"Pretty wishful thinking, wouldn't you say?" I asked.

"Perhaps," replied Ogle, "but, in retrospect, it seems clear that on essentially emotional grounds the GAC was doing just about everything it could to torpedo the Super program. At least, they persuaded a majority of the AEC Commissioners, who also voted 3:2 against it.

"Meanwhile, Teller and John Von Neumann had both returned to work full time at the Laboratory, and between them had stirred up a lot of pro-Super feeling among key congressmen and defense officials. So, both the establishment and the few scientists who knew anything about these matters, were polarized—and Truman was on the fence.

He decided to get another opinion from a special subcommittee of the National Security Council, composed of the Secretaries of State and Defense, and the AEC Chairman. He gave them a February 1, 1950 deadline for responding." Ogle sat back, rubbing his palms together, his eyes twinkling. "So, you see, with Defense (Louis Johnson) strongly pro-Super, the AEC (David Lilienthal) strongly opposed, and State (Dean Acheson) undecided, the fate of the U.S. fusion program was again equivocal." He fluttered one hand palm down, to emphasize the point.

"Then, on January 27, the British advised us that Klaus Fuchs had confessed to spying for the Russians ever since 1942. Fuchs was a German expatriate to England, and he had also been a member of the British team at Los Alamos. He knew almost everything about the Super."

"Good Lord!" I exclaimed. "What a potboiler. How many people knew about all this at that time?"

"Not very many," said Ogle, relighting his pipe with a wooden match. "Maybe a hundred altogether. But the Fuchs business seemed to have tipped the balance. The Special Committee voted to go ahead, and about three weeks later the President issued a public statement to the effect that (because of the Russian test) the United States would now proceed with production of all types of nuclear weapons, including the H-Bomb."

"Do you mean to say that if they had voted against it our whole thermonuclear program would have ended?" I cried.

"Very probably, at least until the Soviets shot off their first H-bomb in 1953. You have to realize that, until the Fuchs business was announced, most scientists privy to these matters were quite opposed to the Super concept.

"Anyway, Truman's announcement opened the floodgates; money came pouring in, and Los Alamos went out recruiting talent again. They brought in a lot of bright new faces, and many of the old wartime staff came back, including Hans Bethe, who had done all the work on solar fusion reactions. And they all went to work on Teller's scheme for producing a little supernova right here on earth. One of the first things they discovered was that Edward had made a lot of mistakes in his calculations. But, after these were patched up, the thing still wouldn't work on paper. Teller had apparently sold the whole Super program without actually knowing how to build it."

I could see a twinkle in Ogle's eyes as he leaned back in his chair and tapped his bulldog's into a nearby flower pot. "Well, the most of 1950 went by without any breakthrough; the greatest array of scientific talent in the country tried every trick they could think of—and the Super still wouldn't work. Teller walked around talking to himself and smacking his fist into his palm. The only guy who was not miserable was Bethe; he had come back to work on the Super hoping to prove that it was impossible—and it looked as if he were right. Christmas was a dismal time. Nobody sang or laughed. We were all worn out and exhausted."

He stopped to reload his pipe, taking an infernally long time at it. I found myself leaning forward, gripping the arms of my chair. "Well, God dammit," I said, "What happened?"

"What happened? Why, another miracle, of course." Ogle was now thoroughly enjoying the moment. "You remember Enrico Fermi—he was at the party the night Jack Clark got us all to talk into his tape recorder?"

"Sure, he built the first atomic pile under the basketball stands in Chicago."

"Well, you may recall that almost all atomic devices are comprised of a small sphere of plutonium surrounded by a larger sphere of chemical explosives, and are detonated from the outside. The chemical explosion compresses the plutonium sphere until it goes critical and produces a fission reaction.

"The problem that the Super group had been wrestling with all year was how to wrap an atomic device around a tank of liquid hydrogen (deuterium), so as to compress it to fusion conditions, such as those that exist in the center of the sun. The calculations always showed that the device would blow itself apart before the reaction could take place."

"And Fermi thought of a way to do it?"

"Yes—he made a suggestion to Teller, when they were out hiking. Teller talked it over with Stan Ulam—the mathematician who was also at the party. Ulam spent the night doing calculations, and found an idea that looked plausible.

"Fermi had suggested putting the primary (atomic device) at the end of the secondary (deuterium tank), which looked like an oversize water heater, and enclosing the whole assembly in a thick steel casing, leaving a foot or so of space all around. The casing is lined inside with an inch or two of light plastic.

"Now, the new twist. Instead of depending on a burst of neutrons from the primary to initiate the fusion reaction in the secondary, you block them with a thick steel plate. Then, when the primary goes off, the internal void is flooded with an enormous burst of radiation, which vaporizes the plastic into a hot, high pressure gas, like the interior of the sun. The idea is to compress the secondary tank to half its size, before the outer casing is blown away—like a hand grenade."

"Good Lord," I said, "what a fantastic concept."

"Absolutely," said Ogle, gazing into space. "And it was also a fantastic intellectual exercise for the design group, who spent the next week confirming its feasibility. But it was not until we pushed the button at Eniwetok that we were sure what might happen; anything from a complete dud to Teller's 100 megatons.

"The principal problem they had designing the Mike device was computational insufficiency, using slide rules and Marchant calculators. Now, all these devices are designed by computer codes. Nobody worries about the physics any more."

He stopped to fill his other pipe. I was gazing blankly at Scripps park and the ocean beyond, but remembering only my vision of the giant Mike 'sausage', twenty feet high and seven feet across, standing in its cradle, all alone on it's own little islet on the rim of Eniwetok Atoll.

"Well," Ogle finally continued, "we were not completely ignorant. In 1951, While the Mike design group was calculating, we ran a preliminary fusion test out in the Pacific, using a big fission device to squeeze a little sample of deuterium. Edward went out to watch the test. He was not experimentally inclined and fretted constantly during the rather tedious preparation. Then he fretted again while things cooled down enough so that the films could be retrieved from the instrument bunker. When he finally got to see them, he cried out: 'Aha. Last summer we didn't know if the Super could be built. Last fall we still didn't know if it could be built, but we didn't know it on much better grounds. Now, we know it will work.'

"Then he came back to the Lab and helped finish up the Mike design, which he now regarded as a *fait-accompli*. In December, he left Los Alamos and Carson Mark replaced him as head of the design group. Edward took a teaching position at UC Berkeley; he had always been unhappy with the way Bradbury was running things, and this move gave him freedom to lobby for his own lab, and a power base among his Berkeley friends. When the Mike device was tested in November, 1952, Edward didn't even go out. He had already moved into his new Livermore Laboratory. So far as I know, he never witnessed another test!"

"That's quite a story," I said, after a considerable silence. "But, it leaves me a little perplexed. Teller obviously made mistakes, but he must have had something on the ball. Just how good a scientist was he?"

"Oh, don't get me wrong. Edward is very bright . . . He is probably among the top twenty physicists in the world." Ogle paused a moment, again a little twinkle in his eyes. "But, then, we also had Bethe and Fermi. They were probably among the top two!"

He glanced at his watch, and rose to his feet. "Well, I think I've got just enough time to drop you off and make the three o'clock plane to Denver." We drove back down the hill in silence. Just before we got to Scripps, Ogle said, "Say, I wonder what ever happened to Jack Clark's tape. Doesn't he live here in La Jolla now?"

"Yes, he does. He was over for dinner just a few days ago, and I asked him about it. He seems to have lost it."

"Too bad," he remarked. "It was an interesting window into the past—future." He extended his hand as I got out. "Do give us a call if you come through Boulder. I've got some reindeer steaks in the freezer."

"I sure will," I said. But of course, I never have.

* * *

Despite Ogle's assurances, we stayed at Los Alamos for two more days. We finished our preliminary task unit report Wednesday morning, although Jeff was almost a total loss to the joint effort. He had a bad case of heart trouble and, unless responding to a direct question, he would simply sit there with his eyes out of focus and a silly grin on his face. I finally told him to take a walk, and completed the job myself.

Ogle came in about eleven to see how things were going, grunted approval of my scribbling, and then disappeared into the fallout annex. So I went out to lunch alone. When I returned, he was sitting at my desk, chewing on a canteen sandwich. "You've suddenly become very popular," he said, finishing the last bite, and pitching the crumpled paper wrapper expertly over his shoulder to make a backboard shot into the wastebasket. "Everybody wants to know more about water waves. So, I've taken the liberty of postponing your departure until Friday morning, and have set you up for another briefing tomorrow morning and a seminar in the afternoon. Do you mind if I come along while you talk to General Clarkson?"

"Seminar?" I exclaimed, stricken with apprehension.

"Sure. You made such an impression at the party that the academics would like to hear it again . . . in greater detail. Don't feel alarmed, physicists are omnivorously curious, and it's SOP to have visiting scientists talk about their work. Actually, it's partly my fault," he said, slyly, "We have regular Thursday seminars. This spring, I'm in charge of picking speakers, and several people at the party did suggest that we finger you this week. It's all very informal . . . just tell them what is known and what is not . . . especially the latter."

"OK," I said, "and what about General Clarkson?"

"He'll have his most of his operational staff there. They'll be interested in how a worst-case tsunami scenario might affect their respective operations. Ellingwood and Calder will talk about fallout after you're finished. I didn't invite Jeff . . . he seems to have other matters on his mind, and I don't think the task force really cares if we blow a piece off the atoll." He stuffed tobacco into one of his pipes and fired up. "Anything else? We've still got a few minutes."

"Sure. I really haven't had time to look at the Operation Plan carefully. Can you give me a thumbnail outline of how the Task Force functions?"

"Of course," he replied. "I should have remembered you're new to this game. Well, to begin with, this is the fourth Pacific test operation. Each of them has been conducted by a joint civilian-military task force. The first was JTF-1, which ran Operation CROSSROADS back in 1946. Then we had SANDSTONE, JTF-2, and GREENHOUSE, JTF-3. By all rationale, IVY should be JTF-4 . . . but, instead, it's JTF-132. Don't ask me why.

"The task force structure is always the same: only the faces change. It's composed of four task groups. TG-1 is all civilians . . . scientists, technicians, engineers and laborers.

They design, assemble, and fire the devices, and make whatever observations and measurements are necessary to determine the 'effectiveness' of the shots.

"TG-2 is Army. Their duties are essentially housekeeping, internal communications, and security. I believe that they are actually supposed to be prepared to defend the atoll against enemy attack. So they have a firing range out there and practice shooting.

"TG-3 is Navy. They provide logistic support. In plain English, that means they haul people and things in ships and aircraft between here and the Proving Grounds. They also provide small craft for operations within the atoll. The Navy will evacuate us from Eniwetok for the Mike test, and it will have destroyers and aircraft patrolling an enormous circle of ocean to keep us safe from prying eyes.

"Then, last but not least, there is TG-4, the Air Force. For Mike, they will be based almost entirely at Kwajalein Atoll, about 400 miles southeast of Eniwetok. They will perform quite a variety of functions; such as, providing weather information to the task force, vectoring and flying deep-penetration aircraft through the explosion cloud to sample radioactive debris, and flying various kinds of photographic missions."

Ogle paused to relight his pipe, which had gone out from too much talking. "Then, of course, there is Holmes and Narver, an AEC civilian contractor. In effect, they provide the glue that keeps the whole operation together. They build roads, bridges, and buildings; they dig ditches, string wires, and run the commissary, the liquor store, and the movie theaters. Somehow, they also manage to feed ten or fifteen thousand men in two sittings three times a day. H&N are the people who want to talk to you tomorrow morning. They have quite an investment in buildings and equipment that might be subject to wave damage." He knocked the ashes from his pipe, looking up at the clock on the wall. "I guess we'd better get going," he said. "General Clarkson appreciates promptness."

As we started down the hall, I could see Mona's desk through the doorway of Graves' outer office. But, instead of Mona, Suzie was sitting there, typing away. I aimed my forefinger at her, pistol-fashion, and mouthed "Bang". Displaying remarkable reflexes, she managed to zap me back before I passed out of range, hardly missing a stroke.

Today's briefing was in a small conference room near the center of the main corridor. The room was empty, except for two tables placed end to end, and a dozen chairs. There was a blackboard on the wall opposite the windows, to which was taped a chart of Eniwetok and another of the Marshall Islands. A small cart held a Pyrex coffee pot, a stack of foam cups, and a tray of doughnuts.

General Clarkson came forward to greet us, and I recognized Admiral Wilkins, the Navy Task Group Commander. His Air Force and Army counterparts were introduced as General Glantzberg and Colonel Burritt. Glantzberg appeared to be a youngish fifty, with a handsome face and flashing teeth. He was in uniform, having just flown in from Albuquerque, and sported four rows of service ribbons. Burritt was short and studious, with curly gray hair and steel-rim glasses beneath bushy eyebrows. Among several others, there was also a tremendously tall, slender officer with hawk-like features and jet black hair, whom I later identified as General Wise, Clarkson's Deputy for Air.

General Clarkson came immediately to the point. "Doctor Ward, we appreciate that Mike is a first-of-a-kind event, and that you have not had time to make detailed calculations. But, the Task Force Command is responsible for the safe conduct of this operation, and we have been asked to upgrade our hazard plans in many sensitive areas. It would be of great help to us to have even a rough, order-of-magnitude estimate of what we're up against. So, I'd appreciate your giving us first a physical description of the wave phenomena, and then responding to a few specific questions from my staff."

Clarkson knew how to handle men. I was standing there with my knees knocking, a 32-year-old pipsqueak with a brand new PhD, coming—perhaps for the first time—to the full realization of how many lives might depend upon my advice. And yet, he put the question to me without condescension, as if I were a trusted senior advisor. My stomach relaxed and the knees firmed up.

I went to the blackboard, picked up a piece of chalk, and drew a big circle, which I labeled Eniwetok, a circular chain of low islets and reefs about fifteen miles across, enclosing a lagoon about 150 feet deep. I put an X at the top of the circle and labeled it Mike, and another at five o'clock, labeled Base Camp. I paused to let this picture register, and then continued.

"The wave system generated by an explosion is very similar to the familiar pattern you see when you toss a pebble into a still pond. Rings of waves spread out in all directions. They become lower as they travel outward, but our best guesstimate indicates that the waves inside the lagoon might still be high enough near Base Camp to surge over the atoll rim, sweeping away everything not actually buried in the ground." I could detect a sense of anxiety in the ranks, so I hastened to add, "This picture is not altogether hypothetical, Gentlemen. Typhoon waves of about this size periodically inundate atolls in much the same manner—but usually from the outside. They wash everything . . . pigs, chickens, and houses . . . right into the lagoon."

I put down my chalk, and there was urgent buzz of conversation. Admiral Wilkins was the first to pose a question. "Dr. Ward, the fallout contingency seems to require that ships evacuating Eniwetok prior to the shot will rendezvous in a sector southeast of the atoll. Would you anticipate a wave problem anywhere in that area?"

"Probably not, Sir," I replied. "Ships at sea are relatively immune from waves of this type. All you might see is long, low swells from the northeast, lasting for an hour or so."

"What about Kwajalein, Doc?" asked General Glantzberg. "It's also a low atoll. We'll have forty or fifty planes on the ground at the Naval Air Station there, and a big air operation going on—with no alternative landing facilities."

"I think Kwaj will be OK, too. The shot site is on the north side of Eniwetok, so most of the wave energy will be radiated in that sector. Kwajalein is nearly 400 miles southeast of Eniwetok, and the naval station is at the lee end of the atoll. All the actual protective factors would act to reduce local wave heights. But I really can't tell you anything more specific."

There followed a good deal of internal discussion among the several command groups. Then Wilkins spoke up again, addressing Ogle rather than me. "Bill, many of our post-shot activities depend upon using the Eniwetok airstrip. If it becomes eroded by wave action we may have problems."

"Yes, I know," replied Ogle. "However, early radsafe and photographic surveys will be flown by choppers from the command carrier, *Rendova*; they can land almost anywhere. Homes and Narver tells me that the fuel storage is underground, and we can fly in portable pumps if necessary. H&N will leave a D-6 bulldozer chained in a wave-proof bunker, so they can start clearing debris and filling potholes as soon as the field is cleared by the radsafe teams. We should have it back in operation within two days, even if we have to rig portable runway lights. We'll probably also be able to assess lagoon wave effects visually on the first chopper survey—probably within H+2 hours."

Then, shifting gears, he said, "You know, General, we really haven't got much to go on. We're playing a gigantic guessing game, expanding a 20 kiloton bust like Bikini Baker to 100 megatons. Our present Op-Plan is a guestimate for a five-megaton explosion. Most explosion dimensions scale like the cube root of energy, which says that, at 100 mt, Mike might look about three times bigger. Since it is necessary to evacuate the atoll, we will have to trigger Mike by a radio link to the present firing bunker near Base Camp. So now, quite irrespective of any fallout effects, if Mike actually goes to anything like 100 megatons, everything on the atoll gets a triple whammy.

"Do I take it you don't quite buy 100-mt?" ventured Clarkson.

"I don't have a crystal ball," replied Ogle, "but the smart money is coming in somewhere between 15 and 45 . . . not enough lower to help much . . . and we'd still have to worry about fallout." He stood there a moment, as if expecting further comment. Then he picked up a wooden pointer, and smiled somewhat mischievously as he flexed it between his hands. "Well," he continued, "this brings us to the subject of cloud dynamics, about which I expect we'll have quite a bit of discussion.

"The first thing I'd like to emphasize," he began, "is that, because of the finite thickness of the atmosphere, Mike is not just a blown-up copy of our 1946 Bikini BAKER shot. The cloud dynamics are quite different. In both cases, the fireball is a hot, low-density plasma. As it expands, it also rises, like a hot-air balloon . . . but at hundreds of miles an hour! At full expansion, the BAKER cloud was only about two miles high. But, at 100-mt, Mike might blast its way right through the troposphere, and way up into the stratosphere—perhaps as high as 30 miles!

"At H+60 minutes, when our cloud sampling operations are supposed to commence, the mushroom cloud base could be at 60,000 feet, have a diameter of 100 miles, and a stem 20 miles across!"

As he rattled off these statistics, Ogle was busily scribbling numbers on the board and drawing arrows to represent the pertinent dimensions. "With the rapid rise of the hot gas cloud," he went on, "we could have surface winds as high as 250 knots converging towards the stem, and updrafts of the same velocity within its central core." He added some more arrows to represent the winds, and then stood back to admire his handiwork.

"So, you see," he concluded, fishing for the inevitable pipe, "the problem of radioactive cloud sampling has suddenly become rather complicated. To penetrate the cloud at all, we might have to fly above 60,000 feet."

"But . . . we just don't have anything that will fly that high," interjected General Wise.

"Okay, then our next-best option is to sample the stem between the tropopause and the cloud base; that is, between 40,000 and 60,000 feet."

"What have we got in that department?" asked Wise of Glantzberg.

"At 45,000 feet, and with 250 knot updrafts, we'd have to use high-performance jets—B47's or F84G's," replied Glantzberg. Then, to Ogle: "The B47 is a twin-jet bomber with a three-man crew. It can operate at 48,000 feet and roundtrip from Kwajalein without refueling. It would be ideal for this mission, except . . ."

"Except that, during this Korean mess, I'd never on God's green earth be able to steal ten 47's for eight months from the Bomber Command," interjected Wise.

"Okay," Glantzberg resumed, jumping to his feet, "that leaves us with F84G's—and beaucoups problems. The F84 is a single-place fighter with a two-hour max cruise, or one-hour max high-altitude performance. We'd have to put up orbiting tankers and refuel twice, just to get through each leg of the mission. To follow the original Op-plan—two sniffers followed by three pairs of sampler aircraft at hourly intervals—would require three KB29 tankers plus fourteen operational F84's.

"Then, to replace the three-man crews, we'd need pilots with three heads and six arms. They not only have to fly a hot ship blind in a turbulent, radioactive cloud, but also to navigate, refuel twice, and record and report instrument readings." Glantzberg pulled out a handkerchief and mopped his perspiring face, his initial joviality now transformed almost to outrage.

"Well, Walt," rumbled Clarkson to Wise, "what do you think?"

"I don't know," replied Wise, thoughtfully. "It strikes me as a complicated operation. We've still got the three C54 photo planes up there, and a B36 command ship to vector the fighters and tankers. With all that air traffic, we'll probably need a destroyer with ground-control radar just to keep track of things. Obviously, we're going to have to do our homework all over again."

These comments provoked a flood of discussion, with Clarkson acting as moderator. It seemed that Kwajalein's initial function had been as a navy transport and personnel staging base in support of task force operations. Its single 10,000-foot concrete runway could handle much larger and heavier aircraft than the 5,600-foot macadam airstrip at Eniwetok. The normal complement of the Naval Station was sixteen aircraft and 300 personnel. Since January, the operational requirements of JTF-132 had steadily ramified to about thirty-two aircraft and 1,200 residents. To meet this anticipated expansion, the navy had refurbished a bunch of wartime Quonset huts, and utilized the taxiway for aircraft parking.

Now, suddenly, with the new operational demands and the unavailability of the Eniwetok strip during the test, it looked as if Kwajalein might have to double its support facilities. As Captain Pahl, Clarkson's Navy Deputy, put it: "Christ, we'll be parking planes on the baseball diamond and sleeping under the wings!"

Amid the hubbub, I could hear Ogle and Admiral Wilkins discussing what should be done if Eniwetok were closed out for early re-entry by fallout and the whole fleet had to seek alternate refuge. The only options were Kwajalein—already hopelessly overcrowded—and Guam, 1,000 miles to the west, and directly in the path of the low-altitude fallout.

Suddenly, we were recalled to attention by Clarkson, rapping on the table with the wooden pointer. "Gentlemen," he boomed, "We're obviously not going to resolve all these questions today. So, I propose another coffee break, after which we'll hear the fallout story."

The break was short because we were all getting saddle sores. Ogle started things off again, holding a cup of coffee in one hand and a doughnut in the other. "OK, Because Mike is a surface burst, we anticipate that the main contribution to fallout radioactivity will be due to neutron activation of water-saturated coral beneath the detonation site, a great deal of which will be blown out of the explosion crater and sucked up into the rising cloud by violent circulation in the mushroom stem." Ogle took another sip of coffee, and then remarked, matter-of-factly, "This morning at breakfast I figured out that the total mass of material removed from the crater might be as much as five million tons; about equal to that of the great Egyptian pyramid at Giza. And it takes less than one per cent of the Mike energy to throw it ten miles up into the sky." He stopped for a moment, and I fantasized the Giza pyramid, somehow intact, turning over and over in the stratosphere . . .

"Anyway," Ogle continued, "all of this material is vaporized, sucked up, and dispersed throughout the mushroom cloud, where it condenses into dust or water again as the cloud cools, and falls out according to particle size as the circulation slows down. Just what kinds of things we can expect, and when and where they will come down will now be tackled by Dr. Ellingwood and Mr. Calder, respectively."

Ogle helped himself to more coffee and sat down as Ellingwood proceeded to the blackboard. He stood there facing us for a moment, in his neat gray suit, with his little gray mustache quivering slightly, like a rabbit pausing between nibbles. I sensed that like many academics he felt deferential to military authority, but was unsure how to present technical matters understandably to a non-technical audience.

"Dr. Ogle has asked me to talk about the fallout hazard as it affects task force operations," he began, tentatively. "The hazard, of course, we take to be the risk of biological damage resulting from cumulative exposure to ionizing radiation . . . that is, radiation that causes irreversible cell damage, and which arises from the disintegration of radioactive atoms among the fallout into two or more fragments, at the same time releasing gamma radiation."

Ellingwood was now warming to his task, rising to his toes and making graceful gestures, as if evoking music from an unseen orchestra. "Some of these reactions also produce alpha particles (helium nuclei) and beta particles (electrons), but these have low energies and can scarcely penetrate clothing. They are not dangerous unless fallout particles are allowed to remain in contact with the skin or are breathed or ingested—and then only if they are incorporated into body tissue. Therefore, the short-term fallout hazard reduces to gamma radiation, which is easily measured, and whose duration can be accurately predicted once the fallout has ended. As Dr. Ogle mentioned, gamma rays are hard X-rays that can produce cell damage in any part of the body.

"The measure of radiation intensity is the Roentgen, usually indicated by the symbol R, or by mr, for milliroentgen. Similarly, the units of total radiation exposure, or dosage, are the rem (one Roentgen hour) and the millirem. By way of reference, the average daily background radiation from purely natural sources is about one rem per year, which corresponds to a continuous background intensity of 1/8 mr.

"At the other end of the hazard scale, the largest short-term dose that can be sustained by the human body without clinical evidence of radiation damage is about 100 rem; dosages between 100 and 1,000 rem represent increasing severity of radiation damage; and doses over 1,000 rem are usually fatal."

"If I read you right," rumbled General Clarkson, "a medical laboratory couldn't detect physical damage if I received a single radiation dose 8,000 times bigger than the natural daily background, and it would take a dose 1,000 times bigger than that to kill me."

"That's right," replied Ellingwood. "The body has a remarkable redundancy, and is constantly replacing cells destroyed by many agents other than natural radiation. We could probably withstand radiation levels hundreds of times higher than exist at present without ever knowing the difference." He pulled a flash card from his pocket and squinted at it through his bifocals. "Now, where was I? . . . ah, yes, here we are . . . Until we know the average density and porosity of the coral, there is no practical way to estimate the total amount of radioactive fallout that will be produced by the Mike event, but it will be only a tiny fraction of the 5-million tons of material carried up in the cloud—perhaps one billionth, which would represent about 10 pounds of radioactive nuclides. This would be quite close to the total weight of fission products produced by the primary device . . . but then, it could easily be a hundred times as much.

"What kinds of things are we talking about, and how fast will they decay?" He consulted his card again. "Altogether, I estimate that there will be more than fifty different isotopes produced by neutron activation in such materials as the structure surrounding the bomb . . . er . . . device, its concrete foundation, and the coral-water basement. These will be mixed with some two hundred other radioactive fission products from the trigger device.

Each of these species decays at a different rate. Some have half-lives of less than a millionth of a second, and a few are longer than a million years."

"Would you refresh my memory on the concept of radioactive half-life?" asked Admiral Wilkins.

"Oh, certainly. Left to itself, each atomic species decays at a statistically constant rate; that is, half of the individual atoms present in a sample decay by fission into two or more daughter products in a fixed time interval that is characteristic of that particular species. Decay is usually accompanied by emission of radiation in the form of alpha, beta, or gamma rays. In most cases, the daughter products are also radioactive, and decay further, but with different half lives."

"So, you're telling us that right after Mike we'll be looking at 250 different radioactive species, each having a different half-life, and emitting different radiation?"

"No, no, nothing like that," said Ellingwood, defensively. "By the end of the first hour, when the fallout on the island will largely end as the cloud moves downwind, all of the short-lived stuff will have disappeared. We'll be down to, perhaps, twenty or thirty species. Within 24 hours we should be down to a dozen; and within two weeks there will only be four or five isotopes left: carbon-14, cesium-137, strontium-90, and iodine-131 . . . ."

"Dr. Ellingwood," interrupted Ogle, "I don't think these people are interested in a species abundance list . . . just an estimate of the rate of gamma decay with time . . . you know . . . the general power-law?"

"Oh, yes," squeaked Ellingwood, now quite flustered. "For an assembly of mixed species, the average gamma intensity decays by a factor of ten for seven equal time increments. For example, suppose that at H+1 hours your survey helicopter gets a gamma reading of 1,000R over some spot on the atoll rim. They then can expect that at H+7 hours the reading will have decayed to 100R, and at H+14 hours it will be down to 10R, et cetera."

"But, we won't know the initial values in advance, right?" said Wilkins.

"No, we won't; the local fallout is extremely variable. The initial activity will have to be surveyed as early as possible, and then monitored to make sure it is decaying in a predictable fashion."

Sensing his opportunity, Ogle sprang to his feet and thanked Ellingwood for coming. "Most of the variability you mentioned is due to weather factors," he said, "which is why I've invited a meteorologist to wind up this briefing. He took the pointer from Ellingwood's unresisting hand, and extended it to Calder, who was shuffling forward, still clad in the same rumpled black suit and turned-out shirt collar he had worn since Monday.

In his slow, halting manner, Calder explained that the climate of the northern Marshall Islands in summer and early fall was stable, and governed by the wet-monsoon circulation over Indo-China. One could expect brisk westerly trade winds day-in and day-out, up to the thermal inversion at about 3,000 feet. Below this level, bands of cumulus marched across the sky with occasional rainsqualls. Above the inversion, the sky was generally clear, with the winds swinging south and then east with increasing altitude. At the top of the tropopause, or weather layer, there was supposed to be a tropical jet stream meandering about, with easterly winds up to 150 miles an hour. Above 50,000 feet, the clear, dry stratospheric air was thought to drift eastward at about 150 miles per day.

All during the course of this explanation, Calder had been drawing a vertical chart of the atmosphere and labeling the various layers and wind data. Now, he wrote: 'Summer Monsoon' at the top, and began another chart beside it labeled: 'Winter Monsoon.' "Somewhere between mid-October and mid-November, it seems, everything changes. This Intertropical Convergence, which is the zone of latitude where the southern and northern trade wind belts meet, reaches its maximum northerly position, at about ten degrees north latitude—which happens to be right over Eniwetok. At the same time, the wet southeast Asian monsoon switches over to the dry northwest monsoon. The net result in the Marshall Islands is a cessation of the westerly surface trade winds, and a disappearance of the dry inversion above them. The weather becomes humid and sultry, with cumulus thunderheads rising to 40,000 feet. There are short periods of torrential rain, interspersed with calms and fitful breezes from all directions. Eniwetok, being in the northern Marshalls, lies right at the edge of the Convergence—sometimes within it and sometimes without, until December, when the whole system moves slowly south again, and the trade winds resume."

Calder's presentation had been tedious, and when he paused as if searching for more material, Ogle jumped up again to wring his hand, and then summarized the situation quite rapidly himself. "As you can see," he said, "the fallout picture is quite complicated. We must combine the Mike explosion model with the radioactive decay model and one of these two weather scenarios in order to estimate the total fallout history. This will take some time—perhaps several months. We will be looking for a combination that will enable us to collect the diagnostic information we need to confirm the device performance, but without risk to the task force—or anyone else.

"At first look," he added, tapping Calder's Winter Monsoon chart with the pointer, "I don't think we'd shoot under these conditions, for a lot of different reasons. If we aren't ready before November, we'll just have to hope for a good day." He put the pointer back in the chalk tray and asked for questions. There was nothing but a sort of stunned silence. I had the feeling that Ogle had planned this briefing as something of a snow job. As he later confided to me, he felt it wise to keep the military slightly off balance. "If you give them the slightest opportunity," he said, "you're liable to find everything welded down and painted three coats. In this kind of operation it's absolutely vital to maintain a high degree of flexibility."

Whatever his reasons, the afternoon had had that effect on me. I was beginning to develop an overwhelming sense of omnipresence about Mike, as if he were Zeus, standing atop Mount Olympus, poised to hurl a lightning bolt that would shatter the world and obliterate all humanity.

*   *   *

About four-fifteen Jeff and I slipped out of the briefing, leaving Ogle and Ellingwood still engaged in a lively conversation with General Clarkson and several members of his staff. As we walked down the hall, I could see that his color and reflexes had decidedly improved since the morning. Evidently, today's session had sobered him and he was coming to grips with our mission. As we passed Graves' office, I stopped and held out my hand. "You're leaving in the morning, right?"

"You're not coming too?" he asked, surprised.

"No, it looks like I'll be leaving Friday instead." I told him about Holmes and Narver and my seminar.

"Maybe I should stick around as well," he said. "I want to ask the navy for an M-boat to drop charges for seismic profiles, and I should talk to H&N too, about drilling a row of wells across the reef."

"Why not," I responded, grinning at his hesitancy. "Anything you can accomplish now will save us time later on. But if you're going to stay over, we'd better see about changing your reservations right now, okay?"

We turned into the office. Suzie was still sitting there, typing busily away. "Hi, Stranger," she piped, displaying a pert nose and a lovely set of teeth. "They seem to be keeping you pretty busy." She was wearing a simple cotton-print shift that showed her brown arms, and a bit more, to good advantage.

"That's right," I responded, "and more of the same tomorrow. Jeff has decided he really ought to hang around another day also. Can you try to switch his reservations?" I managed a wink without his noticing.

"But, he's already set up for Friday," she cried, pulling a card from her file. "Dr. Ogle requested it this morning."

I glanced at Jeff, who was blushing to his hair roots. "That's Ogle," I smiled, "always thinking ahead. Well, Jeffo, looks like you're stuck for another dull evening in Paradise." Then I turned to Suzie. "Okay, Midget, I know my buddy has plans, would you care to share the fare at the Lodge?"

"Damn," exclaimed Jeff, "you beat me to the punch. Mona and I were going to invite you both to join us tonight."

"Great idea," cried Suzie, jumping to her feet. "Either way, I accept. Will 7:30 be okay? I've got a grudge tennis match with Jack Clark at five."

I laughed. "Sure, 7:30's fine. 'Seems like you've got quite a social life going. Won't Jack think you're two-timing him?"

"Oh, no," she giggled, "he's been trying to beat me at singles ever since I got here. But tennis is really the only thing we've got going between us."

IVY-MIKE

We waved goodbye and just managed to catch the shuttle bus back to the Lodge. It was another beautiful day, with a cool breeze from the north. On impulse, I bent forward and found I was too stiff to touch my toes without bending the knees. "I need some exercise," I said. "Care to take a walk?"

"No thanks," said Jeff. "Whenever I feel that way I lie down until it goes away." He shuffled off toward the Lodge, and I struck out on my own.

The area northeast of Fuller Lodge seemed to be in the process of drastic modernization. About four square blocks had been resculptured into a shopping mall, complete with movie theater, bowling alley, and numerous shops. The mall enclosed a large, grassy park, bordered on the west by trees. To the east were several blocks of new frame-stucco dwellings—no fifty alike, but certainly superior to the barracks they replaced. My northerly progress was shortly arrested by a deep canyon, evidently separating this promontory of the mesa from the next, but across which I could see acres of cleared land and clusters of new residences. The abyss was bordered by a paved road, appropriately named Canyon Drive, and separated from it by a high fence, evidently the perimeter fence for the whole establishment. Apparently I was in an unfrequented sector of a large cage where, like animals in some enormous zoo, its thousands of denizens lived in peace and harmony. The laboratories and tech buildings were all encaged within this largest cage; and within them, in my fantasy, there were less still smaller cages, wherein the deepest secrets were matured under armed guard, and locked at night in steel vaults. I walked west for a half a mile or so through a pleasant pine forest, empty of buildings, until I came to a major intersection with Diamond Drive. To my left, I could see the bridge leading to the south mesa and the lab complex. To the right, against the foothills of the Jemez mountains, there was a large development of new and fancier houses, with individual styling . . . the abodes of senior scientists and staff that Davis had mentioned.

Retracing my steps, I took the right fork off Canyon onto Central Avenue, being guided by the high, white-and-orange water tower that I remembered standing just across from the Lodge, and which loomed above everything else among the trees. On the left, again was the pine forest. There were also pines to the right, but sprinkled among them were row on row of two-story redwood, board-and-batten duplex apartments, that Jeff had described as the premium housing of wartime Los Alamos.

I arrived back at the Lodge about six, and having nothing better on my mind, decided to see how the title match was progressing. The tennis court, as I recalled, lay beyond the cottages of bathtub row, and north of the big lawn behind the Lodge terrace. As I approached the vine-covered fence surrounding the court, I could hear the plunk of balls, punctuated by male grunts and feminine squeals. When I judged the point had ended, I opened the gate and strolled inside to the bench at one end of the net.

"No kibitzing," cried Suzie. "I told you this was a grudge match. She had on very brief magenta shorts and a white bra-halter with head band to match. Despite her diminutive stature, she was all girl . . . and all muscle, a perfectly-blended lady dynamo. Jack wore floppy shorts and a soiled visor. From the streams of sweat on his chest, he was getting the worst of things.

"Score?" I asked.

"She's one up, and I've got her four-to-three in the second," he wheezed.

It was Suzie's serve and, judging from Jack's position three feet behind the baseline, she packed a wallop. She let fly a cannon ball and, when he blooped it back, she was ready at the net and volleyed it expertly into the opposite corner. I can't bear to see a man cry, so I strolled out again and went up to my room, looking forward to a long, hot shower.

Although the Lodge accommodations were somewhat primitive, they had recently been upgraded with new plumbing, including all-tile shower stalls of ample size. I had disrobed, got the shower blasting at just the right temperature, and was busy lathering my scalp, when I felt a pair of soft little arms snaking around my waist, and two pointed objects pressing against my latissimus dorsii. Still blinded by soap, I fumbled behind me and encountered a small but firm pair of shoulders, and heard a familiar giggle.

"Guess who?" said Suzie.

"Lady Godiva. What the Hell are you doing in here, Midget?"

"I thought I could save an awful lot of time if I just showered over here instead of going all the way home and back. Are you mad at me?" She came around in front and pulled my head down to be kissed, thus assuring herself that, while fully aroused, I wasn't angry.

So, we had a long, wet, soapy, blissful shower together, and then tumbled into bed. I discovered that Suzie's agility on the court was second only to that in the sack. I think I won the first set; but she broke my serve midway of the second, and the match was hers—hands down. Then we lay there exhausted, hearts pounding, bodies intertwined, in that ecstatic oblivion which briefly transcends time and space.

I must have fallen asleep, for the next thing I knew she was bending over, kissing me gently, her wet hair falling around my face. "Wake up, Sir Galahad," she laughed, "your chariot awaits, and your Ladyfair is famished." She had just come out of the shower, and was standing in a puddle of water, clutching a towel around her hips—a beautiful, pointy-breasted, little animal. She had crushed Jack Clark on the tennis court, ground me to a sexual pulp, and now she craved fuel to keep her blast furnace roaring. I wondered what kind of man could keep up with such insatiable physical demands. I sprang up manfully and hobbled into the shower, but before I emerged she was dressed and ready. No makeup, no perfume, wet hair combed straight down, she was pert and adorable . . . and she knew it. I struggled into my clothes and we went down to meet Jeff and Mona, who had been waiting half an hour over cocktails. Although nothing was said, they exchanged meaningful glances, and I knew the shoe was now on the other foot. Jeff inquired solicitously after my health, but I refused to rise to the bait. The conversation went on without me, gay and artless. But, after a couple of dry martinis, and with a prime sirloin inside me, the blood started coursing through the shrunken veins. Like the Phoenix, I sprang up from the ashes, and we all went on to a long and hilarious evening, ending up with champagne. The festivities lasted till they closed the bar at eleven-thirty. Suzy and I watched Jeff drive Mona unsteadily away. Then I kissed her goodnight and tendered a perfunctory dinner invitation for the morrow. "I can't, Lover," she whispered, "I'm going down to Santa Fe for the weekend. Anyway, I think it's better to leave on a high note. I wouldn't want you to become a habit." Struck by a sudden thought, she opened the door of her little Volkswagen Bug and fished around in the back for paper bag. "'Present," she said. "Don't open it until Christmas."

She pressed my hand, hopped in the car and drove away. I walked slowly back and went up to my room before opening the bag; it contained two brand-new, fuzzy, orange tennis balls.

* * *

Compared with the previous three days, Thursday was relatively uneventful. In the morning Jeff and I talked to Olaf Anderson, H&N's Manager of Overseas Operations, and to Paul Spain, his AEC counterpart. The two reminded me of the old cartoon characters, Mutt and Jeff. Anderson was a huge, lumbering Swede, bald as an onion, with a belly that overlapped his belt several inches; Spain was thin and wiry, with sharp features, dark hair, and an eager, helpful manner.

The meeting was short and to the point. We were told that both agencies maintained field offices in Honolulu for the purpose of arranging and expediting movement of people and materials to the 'Forward Area'. We were again enjoined to submit advance requests for any facilities and equipment needed at Eniwetok.

Then Jeff described his seismic program and inquired about drilling the test wells. This turned out to be no problem, since H&N already had a drilling rig at the shot site to drill holes for pier pilings. All we had to do was to provide the well locations before the rig was moved elsewhere . . . probably within a week. When Jeff remonstrated that he hadn't yet even seen a map of the area, Anderson pulled one from a chart file and handed it to him. "But, this chart is classified," cried Jeff. "I can't take it out of this office."

"Ja?" replied the Swede, "vy don't you sit over dere and mark de vell locations. Den ve drill dose holes next veek and cap dem off. Dey vill still be dere ven you come out.

Hah, Hah, Hah." Floored—but also mollified—by such instant logic, Jeff accepted the chart and spread it out on a desk in the corner, while I waded through my wave scenario, mostly for Anderson's benefit. He took it all in, and then remarked that he had already been briefed on air blast, radiation, and fallout. "So far as ve can see," he smiled, jovially, waving his huge hands, "dere is no vay in God's vorld ve could protect all dose buildings at Base Camp from all dose effects. No, aye t'ink ve yust move out de light stuff and go on de ships. Den ve yust pray Teller vas wrong and Mike is not so big. If de camp is vashed by vaves, ve rebuild it in six months. If ve get clobbered by fallout, ve vash it down—yust like de ships. Hah, Hah, Hah." He slapped his knee as if it were all a huge joke, and then got up to take the chart that Jeff had marked up for his inspection. "Hokay," he commented, slipping it back into the file, "Aye send you a copy tomorrow, yust in case you vish to change somet'ing." Then he bent over to half his height and shook his big forefinger under my nose in mock ferocity. "Don't vorry, young fellow. Ven all you scientists go avay to make new tricks, ve vill stay dere to clean up de mess. Hah, hah, hah."

My afternoon seminar to the LASL staff was somewhat more interesting. Jeff excused himself, having heard the story before. At lunch, he told me that he and Mona were driving down to Albuquerque for a little prenuptial honeymoon. They had decided not to have the wedding until after Ivy, when they could both get away for two or three weeks. We agreed to meet at the Albuquerque air terminal.

Ogle dropped by the office at three as I was finishing up my notes. I could tell he was in a good humor by his jaunty air and the twinkle in his brown eyes.

"Everything must be going your way," I ventured, "you didn't kick the wastebasket." I had by now become adjusted to the fact that he used me as a sounding board when he wished to vent some minor irritation or to try out a new idea or concept.

"You're quite right," he said. "Things have turned out much better than I had any reason to hope at the beginning of the week. And as soon as you and Jeff leave for La Jolla, Al Graves and I will get our secretaries back, and perhaps we can begin to get some work done around here." He had pulled out his pipe and was busily engaged in scraping the bowl with an intricate-looking tool. Then he tapped the scrapings into the waste basket, folded up his tool, and began stuffing tobacco into the pipe.

"I'm sure you know that Jeff is going to make an honest woman of Mona," I countered, a little defiantly, "but I wasn't aware that I was sabotaging the Ivy effort."

"Perhaps you weren't," he responded, lighting up and blowing a cloud of smoke at the ceiling, "but Suzy has been sitting at her desk all morning with a mountain of correspondence—and she hasn't typed a line . . . And when I inquired about her tennis match with Clark, she burst into tears."

"I'm sorry to hear that. I think she could make the right man very happy."

"What kind of man would that be?" he said, skeptically.

"As Kipling put it: 'One of infinite resource and sagacity'." That stopped him, so I suggested we go over to the seminar room where I could write some things on the blackboard ahead of time.

The room was the same as that used for Monday's briefing. I was quite surprised to see it more than half full. "Don't worry," confided Ogle, unflatteringly, as we seated ourselves in the first row, "most of these people come here every Thursday just to get off work a couple of hours early."

"Can I talk about the present problem?" I asked.

"You can talk about anything, except sex and politics."

While I was scribbling away at the blackboard, I noticed that the last to arrive were several guests from Clark's party, Hans Bethe, Leona Marshall, and Clark, himself. I finished sketching and walked over to the lectern. The room quieted, and I had a flash of apprehension, thinking of my own meager presence among all the great minds that had opined from this platform. But, as suddenly, it vanished. Ogle had invited me here, confident that no one would be disappointed . . . it was his way of expressing gratitude . . . and of showing off.

I decided to come out of my corner with the gloves flying. So I started by saying that tsunamis were among nature's most catastrophic phenomena, but that there was still no adequate theoretical treatment of most aspects of their behavior. Hence my talk would be more descriptive than analytical.

Then I gave them the facts. Tsunamis are most always associated with great submarine earthquakes. The occurrence rate has averaged ten per century for the past 1,000 years, but there have been only three since 1900. Physically, the waves are produced by vertical dislocation of the sea floor by a few feet over an area as big as the state of Florida. The wave system spreads out as a series of concentric rings, perhaps 100 miles apart, and traveling at 500 miles per hour. Although these waves may be only a foot high in mid ocean, they are greatly amplified in shallow water over the continental slopes, and rush ashore as swift surges in low-lying areas or splash up to great heights against steep cliffs. I recounted some of the fatality statistics, and gave examples of the kinds of damage produced.

And what kind of tsunami would Mike make, if it were detonated in deep water? The crater might be a hundred times deeper, but the dislocated area ten-thousand times smaller, than for a big tsunami. In the open sea, the waves might be a hundred times higher, but also a hundred times shorter, and they would decay faster as they traveled.

How would their effects compare when they reach shore? "That," I said, "is the sixty-four-dollar question I've been asked to answer. I would appreciate any suggestions."

There was quite a burst of applause, followed by a flurry of questions, most of which I don't remember. A number of people came up to thank me, and then I was left with Bethe, Ogle and Leona, who insisted we all come to her house for drinks. "We always have a few people over after seminars," she said. "It's part of the Los Alamos tradition."

We parted company at the guard gate, and I drove over with Ogle. "You did it just right," he said. "Never tell a group of scientists anything. Just give them a few facts and ask the right questions."

The rest of evening was Jack Clark's party all over again, only with a little more of everything, people, food, and booze. Only, Suzie wasn't there. Somehow, it put a damper on things. I tried drowning the feeling with margueritas—a Marshall specialty—but all I achieved was a thumping headache. I don't recall getting back to the Lodge, but suddenly it was four a.m., and Frank Davis was pounding on the door, waiting to drive me to the airport to catch the morning CARCO flight to Albuquerque.

PART III

PLANS AND PREPARATIONS

Jeff and I got back to La Jolla too late and too tired to accomplish much on Friday. But we spent all of Saturday holed-up with Roger Revelle and Henry Engels, thus establishing a weekend work precedent that was to carry through the whole operation.

We started, of course, by describing the results of our trip, including summaries of the old and revised estimates of the Mike yield, and their implications regarding fallout and wave-making. Roger, as much humanist as scientist, immediately foresaw the fallout consequences. "Good Lord," he exclaimed, shaking his huge head, "if that stuff really gets into the stratosphere, we'll be breathing and eating radioactive dust for three or four years—at least that's how long it took for fine dust from the Krakatau eruption to disappear from the atmosphere. And most of the early fallout will go directly into the ocean. There is bound to be some uptake by filtering organisms that may work its way up through the food chain, perhaps ultimately affecting commercial fisheries . . . The Japanese fish tuna in the western Pacific. We obviously should have some sort of long-term program for monitoring fallout in the ocean." He volunteered to pursue that objective himself.

Responsibility for the test foregone, Henry was vastly intrigued by the scientific aspects of Mike's wave-making potential. As Jeff and I had worked out, the important wavelengths were about half way between those for big storm waves and tsunamis. He elected to look at the theoretical aspects of the problem, and I would conduct some 'explosion-generated' wave experiments in one of San Diego's remote reservoirs, where the noise wouldn't create public alarm. As Henry put it, "The only really sticky part is the presence of the atoll. It's a pity," he reflected, "that they couldn't do a small-scale nuclear test in the open sea . . . just to check our hypotheses."

Henry Engels was at that time a young associate professor, who combined a curious old-world charm with boundless energy and enthusiasm. He had come over from Austria at seventeen on a physics scholarship to Cal Tech, a short, stocky, diffident young man, speaking hardly a word of English. He had surprised everyone by completing undergraduate work in three years, while still finding time to compete in rugby and skiing. After two years of graduate work, he had suddenly switched to geophysics, and had come down to Scripps to complete his PhD. During the ensuing seventeen years, he had acquired a prodigious command of our language. He was now so thoroughly Anglicized that his tendency to swallow his r's appeared more an affectation than a hangover from a European boyhood, as was his predilection to lederhosen and shaggy sweaters, out-at-the-elbows, irrespective of the weather.

Henry and his effervescent blond wife, Margaretha, lived in one of the small campus cottages in total disarray. There were stacks of books on every horizontal surface, articles of clothing tossed randomly about, and a week's accumulation of dirty dishes in the kitchen sink. They were very social and entertained often, usually spontaneously, with students or friends, sitting around outside on the grass beneath the Cyprus trees drinking martinis from frosted silver goblets and cooking mussel stew on a brick barbecue. Both Henry and his wife were hopelessly myopic and wore coke bottle specs to compensate. A neighbor's wife once confided to me that she was often called over, mornings after, to help find their glasses, misplaced when they had tumbled into bed a little tipsy.

These eccentricities aside, Henry was an outstanding scientist. During, World War II, he had developed a surf forecasting method as a guide to planning landing craft assaults on enemy-held beaches that was credited with saving many lives. He had acted as my faculty advisor during the long struggle to get a degree, and I looked forward to working with him on this novel and exciting project.

We next considered the ship problem. In 1952, Scripps had two ocean-going vessels, the *Horizon* and the *Spencer F. Baird*. Both were converted navy auxiliary tugs, 143-feet long, 1,500 horsepower, diesel-electric drive, and single screw. The stern of these ships was open deck space, with a massive A-frame aft and a giant winch ahead of it holding five miles of steel cable for dredging on the sea floor. For more than a year, both vessels had been scheduled to embark in September on a four-month joint geophysical cruise exploring for sea mounts among the island groups of Micronesia, returning by way of Fiji and Samoa.

It now appeared that the *Baird's* departure would be delayed, owing to a steel strike that had deferred completion of a new, seven-mile tapered cable for dredging in the deep Marianas trench. Normally, the schedule for a two-ship operation was inviolable. But circumstances seemed to have arranged themselves so that the *Horizon* could leave on schedule and have two or three weeks to carry out Jeff's Eniwetok surveys while waiting for the *Baird* to join her.

Always the opportunist, Roger foresaw this delay as a chance to get more work done. "We might have time for a circulation study at Eniwetok, or to set some moorings downwind of the island for fallout collection. Both of these things should appeal to the navy . . . our funding comes through them, irrespective of who pays for it. Of course, this means the ships won't be home for Christmas," he added, grimly, "but it won't be the first time we've been at sea during the holidays." Then, an afterthought: "I suppose we'll have to get secret clearances for every man Jack of the *Horizon*'s crew."

And so, Scripps' participation in Operation Ivy became Leg-II of Capricorn Expedition. Leg-I comprised the long voyage from San Diego to Eniwetok, by way of Honolulu, during which the many routine observations common to all oceanographic expeditions would be religiously conducted.

For planning purposes, we broke our total effort down into four sub-tasks. First was the size of the Mike crater, the related problems of an associated landslide, and the type and quantity of material blown out of the crater that could contribute to the fallout. This involved a detailed study of the atoll rim structure in the vicinity of the shot site, and was clearly Jeff's bailiwick. Aside from the row of holes that we had requested Holmes & Narver drill across the rim, the seismic-refraction equipment for atoll profiling was already on the ship, and no new instrument development was required.

Water wave measurements were my responsibility, working with ocean engineers John Isaacs and Willard Bascom, newly arrived from U.C. Berkeley. Isaacs was a big, burly, contemporary of Roger's. An idea man and a competent administrator, he was put in charge of our group, to relieve Roger of technical details. A hands-off type, fortunately, he left us largely to our own devices. Bascom was original and mechanically versatile. Together, we would have to design and have the shop build special wave recording equipment to be installed inside Eniwetok lagoon, outside the lagoon on nearby seamounts, and at several remote islands still to be selected.

Henry Engels, as already noted, would attempt to develop a theoretical model for wave generation by an explosion, with fudge-factors to account for the presence of the atoll rim. I would attempt a model experiment making waves with small explosion in a nearby reservoir. I don't think either of us was too sanguine about obtaining useful results in the time remaining, but it was an interesting hydrodynamic problem, so far unstudied.

Roger would write an amendment to our proposal for a follow-on study, in which fallout into the ocean would be tracked as long as it could be detected. Perhaps without realizing it, he was initiating a program that was to continue for thirty years, in which newly-produced radioactive tracers would provide a powerful method for tracking water mass movements all around the world.

As Director of Scripps, Roger automatically became the de facto commander of TU-7.3. Isaacs was deputy commander, probably, as Jeff put it, because somebody would have to write up our contribution to the final Ivy report. We agreed to hold a weekly recap on Fridays, when our peripatetic director was most apt to be in town.

The main issues resolved, we turned to the more mundane, practical matters of office space, people, and money. Ours was a highly-classified program, and even this fact had to be kept secret from our fellow workers. We needed a place to work that could be screened from all casual visitors without appearing to be exclusive. We settled on the Library basement. Aside from my tiny lab, the basement was reserved as an archive for biological collections—thousands of glass jars containing specimens preserved in formaldehyde ... the life work of three or four of the Institution's most venerable researchers.

To this day I don't know where the stuff went; but suddenly a giant moving van appeared, and uniformed workers began carrying out packing cases of jars, while the biologists ran frantically around labeling the cases with marking pens and jotting down their contents in field notebooks. A week later, we went down, ripped out the shelves, and painted everything. We made some interesting discoveries, such as a nest of large rats that had long terrorized the librarians upstairs but defied all attempts to localize their whereabouts. We also found the odor of formalin as difficult to eliminate as that of rat urine.

Then the carpenters came in and put up partitions, giving us several offices on the west side of the building, where there were windows at ground level, and a large laboratory-shop area behind. All of this sanctum was reached by a flight of concrete steps that descended directly from the sidewalk adjacent to the rear door of library above. There was no other access. A small sign read: 'Archives: *Authorized Access Only.*'

The paint was scarcely dry when we brought in the furniture, shop tools, and a very large steel safe. The safe weighed about a ton. It arrived at night, and was offloaded by a forklift onto timbers. Six of us managed to slide it down the steps and into an inner office where, to the best of my knowledge, it remained until they tore down the building twenty years later. When everything was ready for occupancy, an AEC security type came by, poked about a bit, and gave the premises his blessing as an adequately secure area.

Two weeks to the day after returning from Los Alamos we moved into our new quarters. Meanwhile, our little task unit had been supplemented by the addition of four staff members—all "borrowed" from Jeff's Point Loma laboratory on the bases of exigency and existing security clearances. There were two lab-mechanicians—all-purpose handymen—the kind of guys who could build a house, drive a truck, operate machine tools, and fix anything. Of course, they both were skin divers and could handle small boats, which requirements are fundamental in our line of work. Jack Jensen was stout, husky, and mild mannered, while Charlie Black was tall, stringy, and taciturn. They had worked together for several years and had achieved that level of amicable association essential to teamwork, where each recognized and compensated for the other's shortcomings. More surprising for two such disparate personalities, their friendship extended even to their home lives. Jack was married and Charlie, a bachelor, lived with them, taking many of his meals there, and riding to work in Jack's battered station wagon as often as he rode his own BMW motorbike. Half-humorously, Jeff once referred to them as the Bobbsey Twins, and it stuck.

There was also a skinny little electronics wizard, Franco Carlucci, who hailed from Chicago and had learned his trade as a wartime navy ET. He combined the scrappy antagonism of a street fighter with a brooding defensive nature, and consequently was the target of much good-natured ribbing from his shopmates. They called him the Mafia Kid because of his allusions to a Sicilian connection, from which he threatened dire reprisals for any fancied insult. Carlucci couldn't swim, hated the ocean, and got violently seasick at the mere sight of a ship bobbing alongside a wharf. He seemed hopelessly miscast in the role of oceanographic technician, but Jeff averred complete confidence in his abilities. "Frank is just like (Horatio) Nelson," he argued. "He's always sick the first three days at sea. Then he recovers and is steady as a rock. The only thing we have to remember is not to let him ashore before we need him."

Lastly we enjoyed a sparkle of Divine light in the person of Lorraine Buck, whom we all called Mrs. B. She sat in the front office as receptionist—secretary and bulwark against the outer world. She was also our purchasing agent, business manager, and security officer. On the side, she taught voice, and played piano in the La Jolla civic orchestra. Most importantly, she played the role of mother confessor to our little group, offering not advice, but sympathetic understanding to all comers.

Mrs. B's first task was the typing of our proposal to the Office of Naval Research, the Institution's umbrella agency for all federal funding. The money would come from the AEC by way of the Armed Forces Special Weapons Project, under whose aegis we would operate as a task unit of JTF-132. The proposal was the briefest in Scripps' history—and also the largest. The work statement read, in effect, that we were to receive an award of $365,000 for a one-month field study of atoll structure and circulation.

To appreciate the significance of this circumstance, one must realize that in 1952 the Scripps Institution had only the loosest association with its parent agency, the University of California, to whose Regents our facilities comprised: "a museum and a pier, both in constant need of repair." Our handful of graduate students had to go to UCLA to take their foreign language exams. All purchases in excess of $25 had to be authorized by the Berkeley business office, and contract proposals had to be approved by the Board of Regents and the President of the University. This normally required 2-3 months. Then, if the contracts were awarded, an equal period elapsed while the funds were absorbed into the university system and duly allocated so that the money could actually be spent.

Our proposal somewhat upset this orderly state of affairs. Two days after it was mailed to Berkeley, Roger received an anguished phone call from George Gibson, the University's Vice President for Business and Finance. Gibson had in hand a U.S. Treasury draft in the amount of $365,000, payable to the Scripps Institution of Oceanography. He wanted to know whether this was a prank or an unsolicited gift. When Roger told him that our proposal should already be on his desk, he heard only slight choking noises. "After Gibson had recovered enough to talk," Roger told us later, "I explained that we had been asked to do some urgent, classified studies for the government, and that I had said we would need the money even more urgently. What I failed to realize was that the government might actually respond more quickly than the university." In any event, we received an advance spending authorization within the week, and were finally in a position to concentrate on the mission itself.

During renovation of the basement, Jeff was mostly down at Point Loma, prepping his graduate student for leg III of Capricorn expedition, which he himself planned to rejoin after Ivy and (presumably) a hasty Hawaiian honeymoon. Meanwhile, I took temporary refuge in the library chart room, which was upstairs and to the rear of the book stacks. From there, I could keep an eye on work progress, and still devote most of the time to looking for suitable instrument sites, and to devising schemes for measuring the Mike waves in three very different physical environments. Here, I use devise advisedly. In those days there were no oceanographic catalogues from which parts could be ordered; everything had to be designed and built from scratch. If you wanted 400 feet of waterproof electric cable, you bought a reel of ordinary industrial cable, and immersed it piece by piece in a tub of sea water, until you found one that didn't leak. It was an interesting and challenging assignment.

When the basement was finished and furnished, our small staff got together and celebrated with a bottle of wine. The workmen had done a nice job. And, since the twins had painted the place, we had had our choice of colors. The entry hallway and the shop beyond were pale green. Mrs.B's annex with its huge safe opposite, was coral, and the large room beyond it, which Jeff and I would occupy, was light blue overhead, with a darker wainscot. Our office was furnished with back-to-back grey metal filing cabinets, green metal desks, and black telephones, all arrayed against the west wall, with its shoulder-height windows. Each of us had a swivel chair, a wastebasket, and a guest chair, as well as a ceiling-height metal bookcase against the opposite wall. There was also a drafting table with a chart file beneath it, a large blackboard, and a small bulletin board, already replete with a tide calendar and cautionary notices with respect to secrecy. And all of this largess, Mrs.B advised us, was government surplus, obtained through the assiduous efforts of John Kirby, our business manager, at no cost to our grant or to the university.

Around the first of June, Jeff and I got together to review our individual efforts and to divvy up the work load. When I came in, he was standing at the drafting table leafing through a big stack of charts that Ogle had sent us. He had extracted several, which he now carried back to his desk. I shifted the towel and bathing trunks from his guest chair to mine and flopped down beside him.

"Might as well start with the big picture," he grunted, setting his ashtray on one corner of the pile and the telephone on the other to suppress curling. The top chart, the Western Pacific Ocean, showed the Marshall Islands as two parallel chains, trending northwest to southeast. I counted about twenty atolls altogether, way out there in the middle between Hawaii and the Philippines, and just north of the equator. Bikini Atoll, the site of Operation CROSSROADS, lay at the northern end of the western chain, with Eniwetok, all by itself, 200 miles to the west. Beyond Eniwetok, there was nothing but Guam, 1000 miles farther west. Five hundred miles to the north, there was only the pin prick of Wake Island between Eniwetok and the Aleutian Islands, way up near the Arctic Circle. Eniwetok's nearest neighbor seemed to be Ujelang, 120 miles south, and, somewhat east of it, Kwajalein, our main base for air operations.

"Crazy names," I said, reading randomly down the chains, "Wotje, Ailinginae, Uterik . . . Wotho."

"You ain't seen nothing yet," said Jeff, leafing through the chart pile. "The Marshalls are mainly large atolls with deep lagoons, relatively free of coral heads. They made ideal harbors for fleet operations during the war. Ah, here we are." He pulled out the chart for Eniwetok and put it on top of the pile. The atoll, nearly circular and about 20 miles in diameter, was surrounded by a continuous strip of intertidal reef, nowhere more than a mile wide and often much narrower. Scattered along the reef were dozens of tiny islets, covered with symbols for palm trees and other vegetation. The barrier reef was broken only in the southern sector by a shallow pass about five miles wide, and by a deep, narrow navigation channel on the west side. Except for a few isolated coral clumps in its western part, the lagoon appeared uniformly about 180 feet deep. Outside, the barrier reef was depicted as fissured, like the fingers of a hand, and dropped abruptly to a flat ten-fathom terrace, representing a lower, glacial stand of sea level. Beyond the terrace, the reef dropped precipitously to oceanic depths. Our pre-war chart showed a native village and a stubby pier on the largest islet, adjacent to the navigation channel.

"If you think the atoll names are crazy, get a load of these islands," said Jeff. Starting at the south pass and reading the counterclockwise, the first few were not so bad: Eniwetok and Medren, the largest islets, were separated by the navigation channel from Japtan, Jinimi, Ananji, Jinarol, and Runit. But, up towards twelve o'clock, near the shot site, there were some real tongue-twisters: Bokenlab, Kidrenen, Mijikadrek, and Enjebi. And one right out of Gulliver: "Drildrilbwij."

"Well, Jeffo," I said, "what's your action plan?"

He pointed to one of the islets on the north rim of Eniwetok. "This is Eluklab, ground zero for Mike. As I'm sure you remember from graduate geology, all of these atolls are relic volcanoes that were eroded down to sea level, and then sank slowly enough so that coral growth could keep their tops at the surface. Hence, their very steep exterior flanks. The natives sometimes believed that they actually overhung . . . like mushrooms. As I believe I mentioned at Los Alamos, there is something like 4000 feet of coral on top of the Bikini seamount . . . and probably just as much above Eniwetok. To make any reasonable estimates of crater size and fallout material, I need to determine the average density and composition of the reef in a profile section across the rim from the lagoon to the ocean. You see, the reef isn't solid. It's porous, like crackerjack, and to some extent sea water can flow slowly through it. So I'm having H&N drill a row of twelve holes, 400 feet deep, on a line across the rim. This will give us samples of material as far below the surface as I expect the crater to go. By measuring the tidal rise and fall of water in these holes, relative to that in the ocean and the lagoon, we can determine the average porosity and density of the structure.

"Then, to extend this estimate still deeper for landslide calculations, we'll shoot a series of seismic refraction profiles across the rim. We'll have a boat inside the lagoon detonating TNT charges at various distances from the reef. The *Horizon*, will be outside, along the same line, listening to the explosions with an array of hydrophones. By timing the arrival of shock waves traveling by different paths, we can deduce the rock density as far down as the old volcanic peak."

"How long will all this take?" I asked.

"Oh, a week or so, depending how things go. Sometimes we have to go back and repeat some shots, or add some more to fill in gaps. You worrying about the seamount recorders?"

"Not worrying, just trying to make sure everything falls into place. I've got the hardware sketches about ready to go into the shop, so maybe this is a good time to fill you in on how the pieces go together. Have you got a chart of the Marshall group handy?"

"Sure," he said, fumbling through the stack, "but it may be too old to show your seamounts."

"That's OK," I said, going to my desk. "I've got an up-to-date chart, and I've made up some sketches of the installation. Nothing's final. Feel free to make any comments or suggestions." I put the chart on his desk and indicated two seamounts I had circled with crayon, about 30 and 75 miles northeast of the shot site, respectively. "Both of these peaks are shallower than 500 fathoms and have flat tops, so the *Horizon* can be anchored by her dredging cable if necessary. Okay?" He nodded, and I went on. "Isaacs and Bascom are designing a special mooring which the *Horizon* can set on each seamount." I handed him the first sketch. "The mooring consists of an anchor clump connected to a spherical, steel, subsurface buoy by a thin steel wire. If the buoy is, say, 400 feet below the surface, and has an excess upward buoyancy of 500 pounds, then the wire is stretched very tight; the buoy sits there virtually motionless in the presence of the weak currents and wave forces at that depth."

"I see," said Jeff. "The buoy is sort of a stationary platform for your wave gauge. How do you get the signals up to the surface?"

"There's a thin mooring rope going up to a surface raft. The signal cable is tied to the rope every few feet."

"A raft?"

"Right." I handed him another sketch. "The raft is four truck inner tubes sandwiched between two crossed sheets of plywood, top and bottom, like a four-leaf clover. On top there are two boxes of batteries and a waist-high frame holding another box containing the spring-wound strip-chart recorder." It runs for a week. But someone has to get on the raft to see the recording.

"Couldn't we also have a light on a mast that would flash if the waves exceed a critical value? Then we might wait to see the record, until later."

"We can do that," I said. "But Henry will be on the *Horizon*. He's got to issue a warning report to me in the task force command center aboard the *Estes*, and would prefer to see the whole record—even if you have to go back to the raft and remove it. It would raise Hell if we issued a false warning."

"I guess that makes sense," mused Jeff, leaning back in his swivel chair and fishing a pipe and a paper tobacco packet out of his desk drawer. He began poking shreds of tobacco into the bowl. The pipe looked brand new. I noted that his ashtray was clean and shiny.

"I didn't know you smoked a pipe," I said.

"I used to when I was at LASL," he commented, lighting up with a paper match, "but, I gave it up when I came out here. Then, when Mona and I became engaged, she said she missed it—and so did I, actually." He removed the pipe from his mouth and examined it reflectively. "But, I'd sort of forgotten all the ritual and trauma attached to pipes . . . you know . . . it makes me dizzy, bites my tongue, et cetera—and, if I don't clean the filter religiously, I get a real shot of bitter goo in the mouth." He made a wry face. "I don't know how Ogle manages; his insides must be petrified.

"Anyway, you were talking about seamount recorders. How do you propose to distinguish the explosion waves from all the other stuff out there . . . you know, the swell and wind waves?"

"Good question. It turns out that the magnitude of the pressure fluctuations produced by surface waves—the phenomena we are actually trying to record—diminishes as you go deeper. The effect is related to wavelength. Five hundred feet down, the depth equals the wavelength of the wind waves, and the pressure signal is reduced to about five per cent of that at the surface. But the bomb waves will be thirty or forty times longer, and scarcely affected by depth. Their signal will come through full size."

"I see," said Jeff. "You're using the ocean like a natural filter; by putting the pressure sensors at just the right depth, you can filter out the wind waves without affecting the explosion waves at all . . . ARRRGH!" He leaped to his feet, coughing and spitting. Then he hurled his pipe the length of the room and ran for the washroom. He emerged shortly, grinning sheepishly. "Sorry about that. My concession to domesticity seems not to have worked out." He sat down and retrieved a pack of cigarettes from his desk drawer. "Okay," he said, lighting up with evident satisfaction, "where were we?"

"If you're satisfied with the seamount systems," I said, "we can move on to the lagoon wave recorders."

Despite General Clarkson's druthers, we had convinced Ogle that there was no real need—nor any practical way—to communicate early lagoon wave information to the task force command. Our recorders would be only documentary, with the objective of improving future wave predictions under similar circumstances.

Their design was in some ways simpler and in others more complicated than the seamount instruments. In the protected lagoon and at shorter range, the wind waves would be much smaller and bomb waves much bigger. There was no communications requirement, but the instruments would be subjected to enormous shock pressures from the air blast, transmitted through the water surface. After much discussion, Isaacs and Bascom hit upon a system that satisfied us both. It consisted of an 800-pound streamlined lead fairing, shaped like a sleeping turtle, but flat on the bottom, so that it could lie undisturbed on the lagoon floor as huge waves swept over it. The center of its 'back' was hollowed out to receive the recorder housing,

IVY-MIKE

made of two pressure-tank ends bolted together. The housing was held in place by hatch dogs, and had an eye welded to its top, from which a retrieving line ascended to a surface float. Thus, by sending a diver down to unlatch the dogs, the housing could be hauled up to a boat at the surface. The recorder itself resembled a sturdily-built phonograph turntable, except that the aluminum record disk, after being actuated by the shock wave, revolved only once, taking ten minutes, as (hopefully) the recording of surface waves from the explosion was scratched into its surface by a diamond stylus driven by a stiff bellows.

On the whole, I thought it a very clean design, and even Ogle, who saw it on one of his ad hoc, whirlwind visits, seemed suitably impressed. "You'd be surprised," he remarked at lunch, "how much effort and ingenuity sometimes goes into making a single, critical measurement." He described a quarter-million-dollar experiment designed to capture prompt gamma rays from a new type of atomic device at the Nevada Test Site. There was a mile-long, evacuated light-pipe aimed at the center of bomb case. The other end went into an 'expendable' building, where the light beam was reflected vertically downward through a razor-thin slit onto a sensitized steel disk rotating at 50,000 revolutions per second! There was some sort of explosive gate to close the slit a millionth of a second after the gammas arrived, and before the following thermal pulse incinerated the building and everything inside—except the block of steel housing the precious disk.

"The tough thing about that experiment," he said in his typical laconic manner, "was that there was no way to test it ensemble before the fact."

We had the same problem testing our 'turtles', as Jeff had named them. There was no way to simulate a billion-pound shock wave lasting a thousandth of a second, followed by 100-foot-high water waves for half an hour. We settled for simulating the shock with a small TNT charge a few feet away in a deep reservoir, and the water waves by raising and lowering the recorder package 100 feet with the hydrographic winch on the *Horizon*, anchored in the lee of San Clemente Island.

Ogle also brought us presents, and the news that Mike had slipped a month. The new test date was 1 November, just three days before the forthcoming presidential election. "We've all been forewarned to double-check security about this change," he said. "If there's a news leak, somebody's liable to try to make political mileage out of it. With even a two-day weather hold, we'd be forced to postpone the test until spring."

But to us, there was nothing but relief. It was already mid-June. The *Horizon* would have had to sail by 1 August to reach Eniwetok a month before the test—and all our instruments had to be on board. Now, we had an extra month!

Jeff's gift, when unwrapped, proved to be a heavy, nubby sweater, of the type suitable for mountain climbing or skiing. "Just the thing for the tropics," he commented dryly, holding it up for all to see. It was white, with blue-and-red zigzag stripes around the upper arms and across the chest.

"You'd better be wearing that the next time she sees you," grunted Ogle solemnly, chewing on his empty pipe. "She's been at it every spare minute since you left."

My present was a sealed envelope containing a postcard of a scene from Monument Valley. The central feature was a smooth rock obelisk about 200 feet high, with an enormous boulder balanced on top. The caption read: "Thinking of you always—S." I felt a sharp pang of remorse—or was it guilt? In the six weeks since Los Alamos, my social life had plunged to zero; my image of Suzie had dwindled to a micro dot, buried in some secret recess of my brain. Coveted, perhaps, but scarcely acknowledged. I made a mental promise to reciprocate as soon as I had a free moment.

The last item on our work schedule was instrumentation for the distant island stations, which were to serve the dual purposes of documenting the explosion waves far from their source, and of providing early warnings in Hawaii and Japan if Mike achieved its maximum yield.

Island selection was easy—there weren't many choices. They had to have airstrips, good communications, and, preferably, a military facility to handle classified radio messages. We picked Guam and Wake, already mentioned; Midway island—an atoll 1200 miles northwest of Hawaii and midway to nowhere; and Johnston Island, a tiny sandbar with an airstrip, 750 miles southwest of Honolulu. Johnston was just an Air Force stepping stone between Hawaii and Kwajalein.

Instrumentation was tougher. We needed a gadget that could be strapped to a seawall or pier piling, that required no external power, and which could faithfully resolve the relatively small bomb waves from much larger tides and wind waves. What we came up with was, in effect, a hydraulic radio, tuned to the bomb-wave frequency band, and designed to discriminate against all other unwanted signals. The only moving part was a copper bellows, whose motion was transmitted via a piece of fish leader to a pulley that moved a pen across a clock-driven chart drum. The chart had to be changed and the pen re-inked once a day.

To operate such an instrument for a vital one-shot event, perhaps weeks hence, you don't put a technician out there alone on a little island with limited diversionary resources. Instead, you would like to send a scientist who knows the purpose of the experiment, the cause of any possible malfunction, and how to fix it. You need a guy who will sit up all night beside his beloved machine waiting for the precious signal, correctly interpret it, and make sure the word gets back to Headquarters.

We didn't have any spare scientists. Instead, we went over our list of graduate students and selected six doctoral candidates (four operators and two alternates). Henry and Roger then persuaded them that it was vital to the progress of science that they participate in a field experiment, somewhat in the nature of a solar eclipse. They were advised that they would get a free air trip to a beautiful south sea island, with diving, snorkeling, and minimal demands upon their activities. They were given no details about Ivy, except that there was to be an explosive test whose waves we were anxious to document. With relatively little complication, they could be certified as naval technicians, giving them temporary travel and billeting privileges at military installations.

The only snag in these arrangements was Wake Island, which was operated by civilians under jurisdiction of the Federal Aeronautics Authority. There was no military communications center to handle classified traffic, whereas it was necessary that all our operators know approximately when to expect wave signals, and to be able to respond with coded messages giving the wave characteristics. Ogle put this problem to the task force. After some delay they advised us that the Wake operator and his alternate would be given a one-week code-encrypting course in Honolulu, and be entrusted with the special equipment necessary to code and decode secret messages. A DOD SECRET clearance was required. Fortunately, two of our candidates had seen military service, and their clearances could be reactivated without too much difficulty. Just to be on the safe side, I decided to take the course myself.

The translation of all these thoughts, discussions, and sketches into hardware was accomplished right at Scripps.

The pieces were fabricated in our research support shop, specifically equipped to create specialized doohickeys to order. To meet our busy ship schedules, often made erratic by accident or misadventure, shop personnel were accustomed to working long hours and weekends. In return, they enjoyed a flexibility unknown in journeyman shops. Each man was assigned a project for which he alone was responsible, and made to feel that his efforts were as valued as those of the scientist who submitted the request. He rarely worked on the same job twice.

The shop foreman, Frank Hetzel, was a master craftsman in all materials. He used to say: "If it will freeze, we can machine it; if it will melt, we can weld it." He had piercing blue eyes, a firm jaw, and big hands, capable of incredible delicacy. It was alleged that in his youth he had been a steeplejack, had raced motorcycles and stock cars, and now devoted his spare time to building super Baja-Buggies for exploring the rugged terrain of Baja California.

Hetzel was a favorite among grad students because of his interest in their projects, and he was not above making sly design changes to insure that something sketched up by a neophyte would function as intended. Because I was an engineer, we had a good deal in common, and struck up a friendship that was to last for many years.

In this curious but warm fraternity of workers in ocean science, our shop people often went to sea to make jury repairs or adjustments to new equipment, and each ship had a small shop aboard. Thus, as our own instruments neared completion, I was pleased to find that Hetzel was interested in the project and would have time to join us for Leg II of Capricorn. His special talents could tip the balance between failure and success.

Somewhere in July, and with all instrumentation under construction in the shop, we got around to the model-explosion experiments. Henry Engels reported that the problem of waves from an explosion in deep water had never been solved. All we had to go on were some experiments done in a river by the British, using one or two pounds of dynamite. Isaacs suggested that we do the experiment using a hydrogen and oxygen mixture. This combination would release the greatest thermal energy of any chemical reaction, and there would be no reaction products except steam.

I found the ideal site for the experiment at a private reservoir hidden in the midst of a eucalyptus forest on the old Scripps Ranch east of San Diego. Because cattle were no longer run on the ranch, the reservoir had fallen into disuse, and was surrounded by a jungle of cattails and marsh grass. It consisted of two acre-size ponds separated by a low earth dam. With a little shovel work, it would be possible to steepen the slope on one side of the dam, thus creating a good simulation of the reef profile separating Eniwetok lagoon from the ocean.

Our 'firing team' went out there on one of those still summer mornings when La Jolla is characteristically chilly under a low overcast, but the back country ten miles inland is blistering hot. We had a one-ton stake truck, with Jeff, Henry and me in front, and the Bobbsey Twins in back, together with all of our test gear. There was a welding cart, with the acetylene cylinder replaced by one containing hydrogen, a big coil of plastic tubing, a motion-picture camera and tripod, a dozen survey staffs marked at tenth-foot intervals, and an inflatable rubber dinghy. We also had a telephoto lens for the camera, a box of large rubber balloons, a sextant (for measuring angles), and the ignitor assembly, which Hetzel had cobbled up according to my verbal instructions. That was the great thing about Hetzel—you only needed to get the idea across and he would take it from there.

As we drove I explained the mechanics of our operation to Henry Engels, who had previously been exposed only to the philosophical concept of detonating a given mass of combustible gases. The ignitor was a small piece of brass rod, designed to screw onto a steel bar driven into the ground. The idea was to slip the neck of a balloon over the top of the ignitor and tie it in place with waxed twine. The balloon could then be inflated by separately admitting oxygen and then hydrogen through plastic tubes running from the supply cylinders, located a safe distance away. There was also a spark plug for igniting the gas mixture. Water waves produced by the explosion would be photographed as they traveled past the survey staffs stuck into the bottom at known distances from the explosion.

We drove down the dirt perimeter road that gave access to the reservoir and parked under a big eucalyptus near one end of the earth dam. I put the twins to work on the dam chopping reeds with machetes. They stripped to the waist and went at it like a couple of samurai warriors, grunting and whistling through their teeth at each stroke. Jeff and I went out in the boat with the survey staffs and began planting them a few yards apart in the soft muddy bottom along a line perpendicular to the center of the dam. Henry Engels remained in the truck, making calculations.

An hour passed. The sun had climbed above the protection afforded by the trees. It was very hot, and I noticed that the chopping had ceased. Jensen had walked back to the truck and was poking around in the back. Henry had gotten out of the truck and was sitting on the ground with his back against a tree trunk—apparently asleep. Suddenly I remembered what it was we had forgotten . . . the ice chest, with our lunches and everything to drink!

We called a smoking break while Jack drove back to Scripps for the chest. By the time he returned, Charley and I had chopped our way to center of the dam and established the shot point by driving the steel bar into the ground. Jeff and Henry were out in the boat measuring the distances of the survey staffs from the shot point with a steel tape.

The last job was to screw the ignitor onto the steel bar, and to run the tubing and electric wires to the 'firing bunker', a drainage ditch about fifty yards away and six feet below the top of the earth dam. We also set up the camera back among the trees behind the upper pond, where it had a narrow-angle view of the survey stakes between the tree trunks. The camera had a 300-millimeter lens, so that the stakes looked as if they were all side-by-side and fifteen feet away. Then we sat down to lunch.

I don't know whether it was the heat or the physical exertion, but everyone was strangely quiet as we sat there eating. We were miles from any highway, and there was no noise except the rustle of the dragonflies swooping across the pond or the occasional rasping of eucalyptus leaves in response to a breath of air. I fell to musing about the disparate personalities in our little group and the vagaries of scientific research that had brought us all together in the midst of nowhere. Give or take a few years, we were all about the same age, and would be thrown together often in the months to come. As Chief Honcho, I would have to earn the respect of all of them if we were to bring home the bacon. Ours was a vital and awesome responsibility. For the first time, I felt a tiny twinge of anxiety, and wondered if I could really cut the mustard.

Charley Black, with his hypnotic blue eyes, blue-black hair and curly beard, quick manner and wide-ranging interests, was clearly too intelligent for the job of Marine Technician; yet he seemed too independent and impulsive to persevere in a more responsible occupation. Charley had been married and divorced within a few months. He had a small daughter on whom he doted—but rarely saw. With his hyper-acute vision, he would have made a good foretopmast hand and lookout on a square-rigger. But he would never make Mate.

Jack Jensen was Charley's counterpoise. Solid as oak and dependable as dawn, he never volunteered, but went about any assignment carefully and methodically. Married twelve years, he had three children, a bald head and a paunch—an old young man. After fifteen more years, he and Charley would still be doing the same thing—but Jack would have enjoyed it, while Charley rankled.

And Jeff, my oldest friend, technically brilliant, ultra sensitive, and socially awkward. No, that wasn't quite right . . . he was just so introverted that he scarcely noticed the real world around him.

Henry, my mentor, was easiest to understand and deal with. He was Nobel Prize material, on his way to the moon. Henry would never pick up a machete and chop reeds, a task beneath his European class sense. He would be quite content to concern himself solely with the theoretical aspects of our operation and leave the worrisome details to us. But he would be there with his charming smile when they handed out the ribbons.

It was Henry who interrupted my soliloquy. "Bob, what is the scale of this experiment?"

"Well, taking account the water depth and the dam width, the optimum oxy-hydrogen explosion is about equivalent to a pound of TNT."

"Aha," said Henry, scribbling on his note pad. "That's ten billion times smaller than Mike . . . or ten nannoMikes."

"Ten what?" asked Charley.

"NannoMikes," I ventured. "The prefix, nanno, means one billionth in scientific gibberish. Dr. Engels is saying that our puny little test will only amount to ten billlionths of the most probable energy of the Mike test . . . and that's classified information. Don't even whisper it to your mistress."

"I don't have a mistress right now," said Charley, "but I'm working on a couple of hot prospects."

"I was only trying to think of a good name for our experiment," complained Henry. "It's too small to be a picoMike and too big for a nannoMike."

"It doesn't have to be exact," commented Jeff, "just euphonious. How about micro-micro-Mike . . . or, root-twelve-Mike?"

Jennings was shaking his head in disbelief. He crumpled up his lunch bag and got to his feet. "When you guys decide what we're going to call this test, give me a yell." He trudged off and began to pick up the gear we had left lying around.

So, we cleared the decks for action, moving the truck back up the road out of harm's way. Jeff and Charley were on the camera, Jack at the gas valves, and Henry was official observer and recorder. After Jack had bled a little gas to purge the tubes, I strolled out and tied a balloon over the ignitor. "Shot—1 will be a tenth of a pound of TNT," I said, picking up the sextant. Setting the angle I had precalculated, I focused it on the balloon. "Okay," I said to Jack, "turn on the oxygen first." I could hear the gas hissing in the regulator as the balloon expanded, and I watched its split image come together in the telescope. "Stop!" I said, and readjusted the sextant angle. "Now the hydrogen . . . slow . . . stop. Better give it an RPH more . . . Fine." The balloon was now almost two feet in diameter.

"What's an RPH?" asked Henry.

"It's an international standard unit of measurement among machinists. It's the thickness of a red pubic hair."

"Aha," said Henry, both amused and embarrassed. "Is a red hair thicker than a black one?"

"No. Red is the thinnest of all possible hairs—about 50 microns." I set the sextant down and picked up the little box that contained the firing switch. "Camera ready?" I asked. There was an affirmative wave, and I slid the safety off. "Okay, countdown of ten, start camera on three.

I began the countdown. At three, I heard the camera whir. At zero, I pressed the button. There was a bright flash of light and a resounding BLAM, about like a 20-mm cannon at the same range. There was a brief shower of sand and small pebbles, and then the camera stopped. We all cheered and ran out on the dam. As I had hoped, there was a two-foot crater, about an inch deep, with the blackened ignitor still standing on its rod in the middle.

The lip of the crater was only a few inches from the rim of the earth dam, which bulged slightly into the water.

"Good shot," I said to Henry. "You see, the crater is just about the same size as the balloon, just as I calculated from the scaling laws."

"Yes", he agreed, "but I didn't see any waves. According to my hypothesis, most of the energy should go into air shock, which should interact with the water surface beyond the crater."

"Long, low waves might be hard to see. They'll probably show up better on film," I said, consolingly. "Anyway, we didn't expect much to happen unless the crater broke through into deep water, did we? What's say we go all out next time?"

Henry nodded in agreement, still looking a little crestfallen. I put the twins to work filling in the crater and tamping the earth down. They retrieved the tubing ends, which had been blasted into the water, and reconnected them to the ignitor. Then we retired again to the dugout.

This time, we pumped the balloon up to four feet diameter, corresponding to Henry's estimate for a 100-megaton burst. As I began the countdown, I was conscious of a curious transmigration in time and space; we were standing, not in a glade of trees, looking at a bright red balloon tangent to the surface of a muddy pond, but on the deck of a warship, fifty miles from the Mike fireball. I heard the camera start, pressed the firing button, and all Hell broke loose!

I was blinded by the flash and deafened by the blast. There was a ripping sound and a flutter of leaves as debris blown from the crater tore through the trees. Then I saw the waves; a beautiful series of circular swells radiating outwards. "Henry," I cried, "look at the waves!"

But Henry was lying on the ground, hands clamped to his ears, eyes scrunched shut. His forehead was bleeding slightly where a pebble had struck it. His glasses were lying ten feet away among the leaves. I helped him up and we walked out on the dam, as Jeff and Charley came running around the pond. "We got it," gasped Jeff. "Waves a foot high, Charley says." Then we all trooped out to survey the damage.

The first thing we noticed was that the reeds on the earth dam beyond the shot site had been neatly sheared off at ground level for four or five yards, and laid flat away from the blast for another ten. The new crater was about five feet across, and had ruptured into both ponds. A substantial chunk of the bank had collapsed on the 'ocean' side of the dam, and water was draining through the crater from the 'lagoon' side, which evidently was an inch or two higher. There was no sign of the ignitor or its support bar, although Charley alleged to having seen something resembling it turning over and over high in the sky just after the blast. Some of the nearest reeds were smoking slightly, so I asked Jack to throw water on them. Then I turned to Henry, who was poking a stick around in the crater, trying to estimate its depth.

"What do you think," I said, "was this test a reasonable model for Mike?"

"I can't be sure until we've analyzed the films," he said. "It seems to fit most of the scaling criteria. But I wish we had tried an open-water shot first. Do you suppose we might find the ignitor?"

"I sort of doubt it, Dr. Engels," said Charley. "What I saw was way up above the trees, and it didn't fall in the pond. I'm not even sure it was the ignitor."

Just then a pickup truck drove up and two men jumped out. One wore a badge and carried a shotgun. "Howdy, folks," he said, taking in at one glance the welding cart, the smoking reeds, and the gaping hole in the dam. "You fellas hear any shooting up thisaway? We've had some problem with duck hunters poaching 'round this pond."

I told him we were from Scripps, and were testing a new kind of underwater explosive device that had gotten a little out of hand. I said we had permission from the Scripps family to use the reservoir.

"Need a permit for explosives in the County," he commented. "How much more work you figure on?"

"We're all finished," I said, which appeared to mollify them. With a last look around, they climbed back into the truck and drove off, and we began picking up our gear.

We got the film into the photo lab that afternoon and spent the next morning plotting wave heights on graph paper. By noon we had been able reasonably to reconcile hypothesis with fact. At 100-megatons, the Mike crater seemed certain to break through into both the lagoon and the ocean, so there was nothing to be gained by displacing the shot site. In the ocean, the waves could be 360 feet high five miles from ground zero, and still about 25 feet high at our seamount recorders 75 miles away. Conceivably they might pose a significant hazard to coastal facilities around the north Pacific. At ten megatons, corresponding to our smaller test, the crater would probably remain contained within the atoll rim. The waves produced by air impulse would be longer, but much lower. Our monitoring network should provide adequate advance warning of potential hazard to shore installations in all directions. The critical yield for crater rupture into the ocean seemed to be about 20 megatons.

The implications of these results, of course, went up the pipeline, with the result that Roger and Henry bustled off to Washington to say it in person. I was invited, but declined. We were having some instrumental problems, and there seemed nothing more that I might contribute. Roger, I knew, would be beating the drum for his long-term surveillance surveys. They returned two days later, quite exhausted. The program was still on track, but waves had been upgraded in priority among task force activities. Nothing ranked higher, except deployment, servicing of the Mike device itself, and the observations connected with yield determination.

* * *

Late in July, Jeff and I were summoned to Los Alamos for another briefing. "Purpose: Final Review of Revised Plan for Operation Ivy," the cryptic message read. In keeping with our seventy-hour work week, the briefing was scheduled for Saturday; confirmed air reservations for Friday and prepaid tickets awaited us at the airport. Someone back there was always thinking of us.

"What a break for you, Jeffry, old buddy," I commented, as TWA Flight-11 to Albuquerque reached cruise altitude and we could lower our seat backs. "Did you notice that our return reservations are for Monday? You may have time to spend a whole day with your betrothed, before we head out into the wilds of Oceania."

"Yes, I noticed. Just like Ogle to give us an enforced holiday. You can bet *she* won't be taking Sunday off."

"I guess you're right," I said. "How did W.C. Fields put it? 'Anybody who hates children and dogs can't be all bad'. Tell me. Why did you and Mona decide to wait? It'll be nearly Christmas before we get back."

Jeff winced in reproof at my mentioning hard dates in public, one of the most stringent no-no's emphasized by the security troops. Then he replied, casually: "Several reasons. As you probably know, she's not just a secretary. She runs the whole damned division. Everything would fly to pieces if she dropped the reins before the merry-go-round slows down. Then, as must also be obvious, my own efficiency seems—er—to diminish when she's around." He gave me a shy smile. "After three years, three months isn't long to wait."

"Perhaps you're right," I said, "but, when we were back there in May, I had the feeling Mona was prepping Suzie as her replacement."

"Could be. But I think she decided Suzie was out after bigger game. In fact, Mona thought she was stalking you."

"Stalking? I was ambushed!" We both laughed, and then I said: "Right now, I could do with a little more stalking, if that's the right word. But I'm afraid she's given up on me. She actually turned me down the last night I was there."

Jeff settled back and opened his latest John D. MacDonald paperback. I toyed with the *Newsweek* I had plucked from a rack on the bulkhead, but my mind kept slipping back to that small brown body, half wrapped in a bath towel, hair dripping water all over my face. I'd have to give stalking another try.

Albuquerque was Hot with a capital H. I could sense it before landing by the way the plane dropped the last few feet onto the runway, and by the shimmer of heat waves over the taxiway. It hit like a hammer when I stepped through the plane door, and I could feel it through my shoe soles before I got inside the little terminal. Fortunately, the CARCO pilot was waiting, together with two other passengers. As soon as our bags were brought in, we grabbed them and followed him out to the little twin Comanche. Three minutes later we were struggling up out of the haze layer that seems always to lie over the desert in summer.

Our new pilot was tall, thin and angular, with deep-set eyes hidden behind amber sunglasses. Despite the heat, he wore a tie and a faded air force flight cap, peaked at the bow and pulled down at the stern, like the "twenty-mission crusher" affected by wartime bomber crews. I tried a couple of conversation gambits, but he didn't respond. His attention was focused on the huge bank of white cumulus clouds filling the Rio Grande valley to the north, and rising higher than the mountain peaks on either side.

As we got closer, still climbing, he swung far to the east in an attempt to flank them. As we approached Santa Fe, it became obvious that we couldn't go over or around, so he turned west and began to thread his way through the narrowing defiles between the clouds. "Seat belts . . . tight," he yelled, as our wing tip brushed the gauzelike filaments to one side and shuddered violently. He fought the controls as we swooped and swerved, until at last we ran out of clear space, and plunged, full-bore into the heart of a maelstrom.

Instantly, bright sunlight gave way to darkness; all visual reference was lost. We were flung violently in all directions, hammered by hail, and blinded by stabbing flashes of lightning interspersed with bursts of rain. The plane seemed to be pursuing its own course, wholly independent of the pilot's efforts, and I could almost believe that some vital interconnection had been disabled. Then, suddenly, through a patch of murky gray below, I glimpsed the tops of pine trees, frighteningly close. The pilot saw them too, and with masterful effort, stood the plane on its ear and dove through the hole in the cloud. We came out directly above the end of the airstrip with just enough altitude for him to wrench the plane level and plant it, before the downpour again enveloped us.

We taxied to the hardstand, and he cut the engines and removed his earphones. "You earned your pay today," I ventured.

"Typical summer afternoon up here," he said, laconically. "Sort of fun tryin' to outwit those thunderheads. I make it more often than not, but sometimes there's nothin' left but to brute force it." He reached across me to unlock the door. "'Be pretty dull drivin' this taxi back and forth all the time in calm weather. Bye, now."

Ogle greeted us at the gate and handed us our badges. "Glad to see you made it," he grunted, puffing out clouds of smoke. "The two earlier pilots elected to abort, but Gus'll tackle nearly anything. I don't envy those other guys having to rent cars and drive up in this. They've had some washouts down by White Rock." He drove us up to the Lodge and came in for a drink, but refused to join us for dinner. "I just came in from Washington myself," he confessed, "and I've got a pile of paperwork to catch up on before the meeting tomorrow. Why don't you guys come over to my office about 0830, and I'll have an hour to prep you before the briefing. Okay?"

He had hardly disappeared when Mona slipped in, as if on cue, and I realized that Ogle must have been playing a discretionary role; now, I was odd man out.

Mona, sizing things up, gave Jeff a quick embrace before turning to me. "Bob, how wonderful to see you. Let's all go in and eat before they run out of food."

"Look," I said, "I feel like a square wheel. Why don't I call Suzie and see if she can join us?"

Mona hesitated. "I . . . I'm afraid you may not be able to reach her. This afternoon she muttered something about going to the library . . ." Her voice trailed off.

"She didn't know we were coming up?"

"Oh, yes, she knew all right. But, in all honesty, when you didn't call earlier, I think she realized she may have been reading too much into your relationship, and decided to make herself unavailable. After all, three months without a word?"

I stood there feeling foolish, thinking of Ogle's little asides, the unanswered postcards, all brushed away in the frantic pace of our preparations. "Good Lord, I said, half in self defense, "I had no idea I represented more than a friendly passing interlude in her life. I mean . . . we only spent *one evening* together."

"Suzie's not a complainer," said Mona, softly, "and I am not her confidant. But, I reviewed her personnel file when she was hired. There are some things about her history that might help you understand her behavior." Jeff had gone off to get her a drink, so we sat down and she eyed me levelly.

Suzie Small, it seemed, was the only child of Jonathan Small, a gentleman California rancher and outdoorsman, her mother having died in childbirth. Jonathan had raised Suzie in the image of the son he had always wanted, imparting to her his love of sports, and the competitive edge necessary to overcome the disadvantage of small stature. She was no mental slouch, either, having earned a BA in political science from UC Berkeley. She had applied for an advertised position in Public Relations at LASL because it offered: "intellectually challenging work in a country atmosphere." The subsequent transfer to J-Division had resulted from her acquaintance with Mona, and her general efficiency at getting things done.

"As I recall," Mona continued, "she had only been in our division two months when you blew into town. She'd whomped the field in tennis, but I don't think she'd had a single date—lots of parties, but no solo events. Los Alamos isn't the greatest hunting ground for unattached women. We were both in the boat—but for different reasons." She paused as Jeff arrived with her martini. She took a sip and then sat there a moment, reflectively twisting her glass round and round by the stem. Finally, her eyes returned to me. "I don't know what happened between you two last May, and it's really none of my business. But ever since, Suzie has been in a funk. Somehow, the Prince didn't come back to find who owned the glass slipper." She gave a little sigh and pressed Jeff's hand beside hers on the table. "Anyway, Prince Robert, if you really want to see if the slipper fits, I'll tell you where to find her—I'll even loan you my car. But, if you don't, I suggest we go eat. There isn't any point in reopening a dead issue."

Suddenly my mind was reeling. I felt like a white rat I had once seen in a high school psychology experiment; it couldn't find its way out of an impossible maze, and just crouched in the corner with its eyes screwed shut, trembling all over. It seemed that the last thing in the world I needed right now was a lovesick girl on my hands, much less a full-blown love affair. And Suzie, for all her undeniable attractions, was just not my cup of tea.

Since boyhood, I had tendered the secret mental image of my ideal mate. She was a tall, slender ash-blonde, with hollow cheeks and gray eyes. She had a gracious carriage, a queenly presence, and was always the center of attention. I had fantasized the winning of her favor in a hundred scenarios, all having a common thread, reminiscent of the Scarlet Pimpernel. We would meet by accident in some exotic circumstance forcing me to concealed identity as a fop. Later, as my succession of valiant and noble deeds became slowly revealed to her, initial scorn would be replaced by amusement, wonder, worship, and then passionate love.

This image, albeit somewhat tarnished from disuse in recent years, still served as a standard for comparison among ladies of my acquaintance. Until now, it had never been seriously challenged. Suddenly, it seemed, I was being asked to reevaluate it in apposition to Suzie Small. What suffered most from this hasty comparison was my own self-image. Did my Ice Queen really exist? What fearsome Jabberwock had I slain with my 'vorpal blade'? What errant rival had I jousted from his saddle? At very least, Suzie deserved some explanation. I looked up at Mona, who was watching my inner struggle with interest.

"I think I'd like to borrow your car," I said.

Suzie lived only a few blocks from the Lodge in the middle of what was called the East Sector; a sea of identical, boxlike plywood bungalows, so new as to be yet devoid of lawns or shrubs. There were no garages, but the builder had provided paved areas between the buildings. I was having a little trouble making out the house numbers in the gathering dusk, when I spied her little red VW. The house was dark, except for a dim light in a back room. As I went up the path, I could see that the front door was open in the warm evening. I rapped smartly on the screen door and waited.

"Is that you, Betty?" asked Suzie in a tremulous little voice.

"Nay, forsooth," said I, huskily, sweeping off an imaginary cap and getting down on one knee. "'Tis I, Prince Robert of Ward. I've . . . er got this glass slipper, and I'm trying it out on all the local tomatoes. Care to give it a whirl? If it fits, you could be Queen."

There was a long silence. Then I heard her familiar little giggle. "Cometh inside, my Prince, whilst I slip into something more befitting a fitting."

I opened the screen and entered the dark room, but she had vanished. Somewhere, I heard a shower running. I slipped off my clothes and fumbled my way down the hall. It was a very small shower . . . barely big enough for two people standing very close together.

*   *   *

I was a little late getting to Ogle's office next morning. Even then, I only took time to stop by the Lodge to scrape off the whiskers. As I trotted from the parking lot to the tech area guard gate, I was conscious of a curious feeling of exuberance. It wasn't quite the light-headedness brought on by lack of food or sleep; it was something new and unfamiliar. I pondered the problem, vaguely, as I tendered my badge at the gate, and made my way up to Graves's office to return Mona's car keys that I realized what was different. Suzie was sitting there in a pink shift, toying aimlessly with her typewriter. She looked up and our eyes locked.

"Good morning, Princess," I said.

"Good morning, Prince."

An eternity passed. Then Mona's calm voice broke in: "I'm sorry to interrupt this tender moment, Sir Robert, but if you don't get over to Dr. Ogle's office muy pronto, all your fiefs may be forfeit!"

A note on Ogle's door advised that we were to meet in the small conference room, where I found him, together with Jeff and George Ellingwood. Calder was missing; his replacement was introduced as Brian Mason, formerly Meteorological Officer, Royal New Zealand Air Force, now,

Lecturer in Meteorology, University of Hawaii. "I got tired of playing games with the Weather Bureau," Ogle told me later. "They're only interested in making forecasts for the corn belt. So I went outside and picked up Mason. He got a PhD from UCLA: tropical meteorology. His thesis was on movements of the intertropical convergence in the western Pacific. He's exactly what this program has needed from the beginning."

Today's briefing, Ogle advised us, was essentially a final recap of the Operation Plan: the last chance to make changes before the major task force elements move out to the forward area. After today, he warned, everybody will be on the move for a month or so. Even communications will become difficult. "I have arranged with H&N for office space and message service in Honolulu. That will be my primary contact point for the next month. After that, it will be in the headquarters compound at Eniwetok. Feel free to use either office for messages, local assistance, or just a place to hang your hats between planes. Please keep me posted of your whereabouts after you leave home base."

Ogle leaned back in his chair to relight his dead pipe, and when that didn't work he got out the other one and began to fill it. I thought he looked tired. But I was no sparkling rose myself.

"There is another matter I should mention, before you learn about it second hand," he said. "As of this week, I have been asked to assume additional duties as Deputy Test Director. That fancy title just means that out at Eniwetok

I'll be worrying about all aspects of getting this device ready to shoot and making the appropriate measurements. My bosses will still be Stan Burris and Al Graves, and you guys will still report directly to me. I haven't decided yet exactly where we'll all be sitting at shot time, but I'll let you know before the dress rehearsal."

"Rehearsal?" I said. "Are we going to rehearse atoll evacuation?"

"In principal, if not in fact," said Ogle. "Up to now, every task unit has devised and rehearsed its own procedures, within the framework of the Op Plan. The dress rehearsal will be our first—and probably only—chance to try everything out all at once, in real time.

"Some day in late October, still to be announced, we'll muster everybody to his assigned station, and count noses to see if we've lost anyone. We'll turn on all the electronics and look for interference and cross talk. If everything works, we'll launch the aircraft and go through a countdown and firing rehearsal. Then we'll ask Scripps for a dummy wave report, etcetera." He looked at his watch, and I thought I caught the glimmer of a wink. "If we head over to the lecture hall right now, we might have time for a roll and coffee before the briefing."

As opposed to our initial briefing last May, today's meeting was strictly business; no welcoming address or introductory speech. Only project leaders and up—perhaps 40 people all told. The military was represented by the three task group commanders, General Burritt (Army),

Admiral Wilkins (Navy), and General Glantzberg (Air Force), and their aides—all in mufti. The rest of us were scientists and engineers from various laboratories assigned to the scientific task group, JTF 132.1, headed by Al Graves. The meeting was chaired by his scientific deputy, Stan Burris, who would act officially as the chief executive officer for Operation Ivy. Burris, Ogle had told me, was a nuclear engineer, and had been responsible for planning the Ivy operation since inception. Appropriately, he looked like an Ivy-League senior, handsome and solidly built, with regular features and a crew cut. He had a smooth, even voice.

"Good morning, gentlemen," he began. "This may be the last time we will all be together in one room until this operation is concluded. Before we get started, I wish to announce the appointment of Bill Ogle as Deputy Test Director for Ivy. His radsafe slot will be filled by Walt McConnell, who has already been running TU-7.1 for some time." There was a murmur and a spatter of applause, while he picked up his notes from the rostrum.

"This morning," he continued, "we will hear project status reports from all task units. Because we have so many agencies represented here, I would like each project leader to give his name and affiliation, the number of people he will be bringing out to the forward area, and their expected dates of arrival. This will let Security and Housing know when to expect you. Then, after you have briefly—repeat, briefly—described the project function and status, I would like a short rundown of work location and pre-shot activities in the atoll area." He gestured toward the large map of Eniwetok on the easel behind him. "And, I want everybody else here to listen carefully to these descriptions from the standpoint of possible conflict with his own activities. If you foresee any problems, sound off, and we'll make some arrangement to resolve them.

"As you will note from the revised Operation Plan, if you have had time to examine it, there will be ten task unit reports in addition to TU-1, Scientific Programs, which alone includes fifty-six projects distributed among eleven programs. If we allow five minutes per report, and have sandwiches sent in for a working lunch, we might possibly wind up by 1500. This would give Admiral Wilkins an hour or so to talk about pre-shot evacuation. If not, we've got all day tomorrow. Any questions? Okay, let's get busy."

To preserve chronology, Burris skipped over the scientific programs and took up first the reports of task units 2-6, dealing with the production, care, and feeding of the Mike device. Although the presentations were non-technical, as an engineer with an armchair interest in physics, I could appreciate that the design and production of all that hardware in a six-month time frame was a stupendous achievement.

People around the Lab had always referred to Mike as the "Super", a contraction of the "Superbomb" of Teller's conception, which had engendered in me a mental picture of a huge, torpedo-like object with fins on one end. Nothing could have been farther from the truth. Mike was not a weapon by any stretch of the imagination. Instead, he was a one-of-a-kind laboratory experiment that more resembled a locomotive boiler standing upright on stubby legs, with a forest of pipes and tubes protruding in all directions, like a patient in intensive care. Mike weighed seventy tons, and had been fabricated, piece by piece, among several divisions of the American Car and Foundry Company, none of whom knew what the others were doing. The pieces had already been shipped to the Pacific, and were being assembled and fitted with a host of contrivances to measure various aspects of his function and performance.

Mike's fuel was liquid deuterium, the heavy isotope of hydrogen, which must be stored at 450 degrees below zero to prevent boiling. The deuterium was produced at a cryogenic plant in Boulder, Colorado, shipped directly to Eniwetok as compressed gas in 50-foot cylinders. There it would be liquefied in a specially built refrigeration plant, and transported by landing craft across the lagoon in giant thermos bottles (Dewars), each aboard its own, special, 25-ton low-bed truck. Each truck, in turn, was equipped with its own refrigeration system for circulating liquid helium through the dewar housing in order to minimize vaporization loss of its precious cargo. Upon arrival at the test site, the trucks had pumps to transfer the liquid deuterium directly into Mike's cavernous interior.

When fueling was completed and Mike had achieved thermal equilibrium, the arming team would arrive in a motor torpedo boat to make connections and final adjustments to Mike's plutonium trigger, an atomic device located somewhere in the middle of things, whose function was to raise the deuterium to ignition temperature (about 100-million degrees). Lastly, it was the job of the firing party to simulate the electrical connection between Mike and the firing station, and to run through the count-down.

The firing line consisted of a 24-mile electric cable between the shot point and a bunker on Runit Island, with a radio link between this bunker and the firing station aboard the amphibious flagship, *Estes,* which would be stationed thirty miles away to the southeast.

It all sounded perfectly straightforward. But, to me, a former aircraft engineer, the whole aspect was staggering. And all this had been accomplished in eight months, starting from scratch!

The rest of the morning was devoted to the scientific programs, the majority of which were concerned with details of the explosion itself, and the remainder with military effects; such as, the resistance of various targets to shock waves and to thermal and/or ionizing radiation. It would be futile to attempt to recount here the thousands of individual experiments planned for Mike. Suffice it to say that this would surely become the most-studied scientific experiment in history. From the instant when the last firing relay clicked shut, a thousand automatic instruments and devices would monitor every conceivable aspect of his behavior. Of the 36 islets dotting the 84-mile perimeter of the atoll, all but three supported one or more collecting or monitoring devices. Dozens more were sprinkled in the lagoon itself, in the ocean outside, or on other islands as far away as Hawaii. And each device was the responsibility of some task unit, whose representative had initially conceived it, proposed it, built it, tested it, and shipped it to the forward area, where, in the days or weeks before the test, it would be installed or mounted at its approved location, connected to its own timing circuit, and cocked in readiness. After the test, its message would be retrieved, analyzed, reported, and documented in a timely fashion. For some, the results of all this travail would be known in the wink of an eye after the firing button was pressed; for others, it would be hours or days before the radsafe people okayed relevant areas for re-entry.

Most of the above experiments were relatively small potatoes in the grand stew, and were rather quickly disposed of. But two of them stand out vividly in my recollection, not just because they both entailed enormous effort and expense, but also because they both ultimately had a strong emotional impact on the outcome of the test. More than anything else, they engendered in me the feeling that Ivy was a risky operation.

The first experiment was an attempt to look into the heart of the explosion at very early times, to examine the kind and intensity of prompt radiation. Very simple, in principle. You just cut a hole in the outer bomb case and pipe the light produced when it goes BOOM to a battery of instruments and cameras situated in a bunker strong enough and far enough away so that it won't be destroyed by the blast arriving a few seconds later.

In practice, it was a bit more difficult. Instead of one window, there were six; far enough turned out to be almost two miles; strong enough meant concrete walls and roof eight feet thick and buried under 20 feet of sand. The light pipe was an elevated plywood tunnel filled with helium, eight feet square and 9000 feet long, sitting on 1800 posts set in concrete. Because Eluklab, the shot island, wasn't nearly big enough to accommodate the tunnel, it was necessary to connect it to two adjacent islands, (Drildrilbwij and Boken) by a two-mile causeway of dredged rubble. Then, to keep the expensive helium from leaking out through cracks, it was sealed into box-car-size plastic baggies. It would take about 4000 big helium cylinders just to fill up the baggies!

Under the previous op-plan, with a max-credible upper limit yield of 5-megatons for Mike, all the bunker instrumentation was arranged to be monitored and controlled from the bunker on Runit Island, fifteen miles from Ground Zero (GZ). The Runit bunker had been a shot control point during GREENHOUSE operation, and had several levels of protection, including a standby electric generator and sleeping quarters below ground. Now, under the new 100-MT Op-plan, and with total atoll evacuation mandated, it seemed that nobody had been able to figure a practical means of telemetering the necessary control functions to a remote, floating control station. The best that EGG could come up with was televised instrument monitoring to the *Estes*, which would permit stopping the test in case of instrument failure at any time between evacuation of the control team at midnight on D-1 and the scheduled shot time the following dawn. It seemed to me that a relatively modest experiment had now grown to such monstrous complexity that it threatened the whole operation.

The second big experiment was the one General Glantzberg had raised such a storm about during our last visit: the sampling of radioactive cloud debris by flying high-performance aircraft through the mushroom stem during the first few hours after detonation. Glantzberg gave us a little pep talk while his aide, Colonel Jack Parsons, was scribbling away at the blackboard behind him.

"When Mike was first upgraded to 100-MT," he began, "we thought at first that we might have to scrap the whole penetration exercise. The scale was just too damn big! It stretched everything to the limit and left no margin for error. So . . . I'm very happy today to express my appreciation to Colonel Parsons and his staff, who have come up with a plan which stretches everything to the limit, leaves no margin for error . . . and still gets the job done." He flashed his big smile and sat down amid applause, as Parsons dusted the chalk off his hands and picked up a pointer. He was a tall, thin, studious-looking man. With rimless glasses and black hair combed straight back, he more resembled a law clerk than a military aviator.

"General Glantzberg is really not overstating the case," he began in a soft, even voice. "What we are faced with is five different task units trying to fly about 29 aircraft missions in the same airspace within four or five hours, and all operating out of a single airstrip two or three hours distant. Twenty-two of these missions will be under my control, although, at shot time, only half of them will be up there—together with four photographic missions, two instrument drops, two shockwave impact tests, and a weather observer scouting for thunderstorm activity. Most of these aircraft will be flying instrument patterns with no visual reference, and will be vectored to their initial positions by two control aircraft . . . sort of orbiting control towers, holding station on the explosion cloud. While each task unit has been going through its own private drill at home, we won't have a chance to practice all together until the grand rehearsal in mid October.

"Our job, the mission of Task Unit 7.1.1, is to obtain radioactive debris samples from the Mike cloud stem. These samples will be flown directly to Los Alamos for radiochemical analysis, which should provide the most reliable estimate of total energy release of the Mike device. So this sampling mission is one of the most important activities of Operation Ivy.

"How do we plan to do it?" He turned to the blackboard, where he had drawn, at the left, a sketch of a fat mushroom cloud, together with a scale of altitude in feet. Along the bottom, there was a scale of distance in miles from the center of the mushroom stem. "This is our best guess of how things will look out there at H+90 minutes, which is the projected start time for our sampling operation. The Mike cloud will be centered about 400 miles from our operation base at Kwajalein Atoll, and will be drifting westward at ten to fifteen knots. We have assumed the stem to be about twenty miles in diameter and 50,000 feet high, and a mushroom cap 60 miles across, topping out at 100,000 feet. These figures are for a 30-megaton burst. If Mike goes bigger, nothing about this operation will change significantly.

"At this time of year, the intertropical convergence moves north to about ten degrees latitude, so we can expect multilevel stratus and stratocumulus clouds with intermittent thunderstorms as high as 25,000 feet, as I've indicated by this wavy line labeled 'cloud tops'. So, if the samplers approach the stem at 40,000 feet, they should have perfect visibility until penetration, and again after they emerge. The idea is to slice deeper and deeper, until we approach our radiation tolerance limit or run low on fuel."

Parsons put down the pointer, took a sip of water from a glass on the table, and waited for the murmur of voices to die down. He appeared outwardly calm, but I noticed that his hands were trembling. He had obviously been under tremendous strain.

"Everything about this sampling operation is geared to our choice of the F-84G fighter," he continued. "It was the only aircraft available to us capable of operating in clear airspace above 40,000 feet, and of withstanding the severe turbulence anticipated within the Mike cloud stem. Under these conditions, the F-84G burns 1200 gallons of fuel per hour, which, in terms of the distances and altitudes shown on my sketch here, means that each aircraft must be refueled twice during its mission.

"According to our Op-plan, three flights of four aircraft will depart Kwajalein at hourly intervals, commencing at H+30 minutes, and rendezvous with four KB-29 aerial tankers at 20,000 feet and 20 miles south of the cloud track. After refueling, they will climb to 40,000 feet, penetrate the cloud stem in pairs until down to 1500 lbs fuel reserve, and then descend to a second tanker rendezvous, farther southeast, before returning to Kwajalein.

"Now, of course, anybody familiar with over-water operation is going to ask how in blazes these fighters are going to find their proper tankers in all that empty airspace, where a plane cannot be seen farther than about three miles. The answer is that we will have a KB-29 control aircraft orbiting just above each tanker group, equipped with radar, three channels of voice radio, and a homing beacon. Their function is to vector the outward-bound fighters to the first tanker rendezvous, and then to a second rendezvous with a B-36H penetration-control aircraft orbiting at 40,000 feet. The B-36 will direct them when and where to penetrate the cloud stem. Coming back, they switch frequencies and hunt for the second tanker control. If they can't make the return connection before running below 1000 lbs of fuel, they head for the Eniwetok range beacon. The field should be open by that time. We'll also have backup navigation assistance from the destroyer *O'Bannon*, stationed below the second tanker group, and equipped with a radar tuned to the fighters' IFF frequency. The *O'Bannon* should be able to see the fighters 100 miles away, and give their positions to the control aircraft."

We sat there a moment, soaking this up. Then someone asked the obvious question: "What about radiation exposure?"

"Ah, yes," said Parsons, "we have been working very closely with Los Alamos on that problem since the beginning." He looked over at Walt McConnell, our new radsafe chief, who was sitting next to Ogle. "Do you want to respond to this, Walt?"

"Sure," said McConnell, rising to his feet and glancing at his watch. "We were going to cover sample recovery in our general radsafe presentation this afternoon, but this is a somewhat separate problem. We've got a few minutes before lunch, so we might as well wind it up now."

There were two main problems: pilot protection and sample retrieval and transport. They anticipated that the aircraft might be exposed to radiation intensities as high as 500R, which could be fatal to an unshielded pilot.

Accordingly, all twelve aircraft had undergone extensive modification. Exterior surfaces were filled, sanded, and polished to reduce particle adhesion. Fine-particle filters were inserted into the cabin pressurization ducts. Special instrumentation included an exterior radiation-level indicator, an interior accumulated dosimeter, an extra radio, and a homing beacon sensor. The pilot would be wrapped in a lead-fabric cloak. Lastly, as if that were not enough, the pilots had been granted special authorization for 20R of whole-body radiation exposure for this single mission, as contrasted to the 3.9R limit authorized for all other task force personnel during the entire Ivy operation. It was obvious that somebody wanted those radiation samples very badly.

The sample collectors were built into the front end of the two auxiliary wing-tip fuel tanks. When the pilot pulled a lever, air was admitted through a hole in the nose of the fuel tank, passed through a special fabric filter, and exhausted through slots. After the 'hot' aircraft landed at Kwajalein, it was supposed to taxi to a restricted wash-down pad, where technicians in exposure suits were to extract the filter cloths with long tongs and insert them immediately into lead cylinders. The aircraft were then to be washed down with hoses, after which the pilots would emerge, disrobe, shower, and be hustled off to sick bay to have their dosage films analyzed. Upon completion of the exercise, all sample cylinders were to be flown directly to Los Alamos for analysis.

There followed a good deal of discussion, mostly about radio traffic during the exercise, which would come at the same time that many helicopter flights would be mapping surface radioactivity so that the atoll could be re-entered and other vital data recovered. I found myself pondering the enormous amount of effort, training, and experience required to turn out a modern day fighter pilot, to which were now added the complex performance requirements of the present mission. Nobody had said anything about flying through the Mike chimney. But in my flying days I had heard numerous accounts of pilots who had ventured incautiously into ordinary storm clouds, only to discover hundred-knot vertical winds that flipped them around like leaves, and in some cases dismembered the planes themselves. The Mike cloud ranked with the biggest thunderheads. I had little doubt that the penetration team would earn its flight pay.

At the stroke of twelve, there was a knock on the door, and Buriss interrupted the proceedings to admit Mona and Suzie, pushing a large serving cart loaded with sandwiches. While everyone was stretching or straggling down the hall to the biffy, I followed Suzy back to Graves's office. Fortunately, there was no one else about, because we were instantly locked together, arms embraced, and hearts pounding. It seemed suddenly so very different to be kissing someone with much more than casual interest. She pushed me away and stood there, hands to her face. "My God," she gasped, "I don't know what's happening to me.

All summer I couldn't work because you weren't around, and now . . . I can't work because you *are* around."

"I know," I said in a choked voice. "Obviously we're going to have to find out what's going on. Look, I'm pretty sure we'll finish up today. Tomorrow is Sunday. Could we run off somewhere and sit on a mountain top?"

"Super! I know a perfect place. There's a little spring coming out of a cliff. You can see for miles. I'll make up a picnic basket . . . ."

"Wonderful," I said, hearing footsteps outside. "I'll call you as soon as we break up." It was Mona, so I said: ". . . just came in to sharpen a pencil . . . ," and slipped out.

I went back to the conference room and had just grabbed a sandwich and a cup of coffee when I noticed Ogle beckoning to me from the corner of the room, where he was standing with a slender, grey-haired man. "Bob, you've met Admiral Wilkins, I know."

"Yes, sir," I said, extending my hand, "although I'm afraid I didn't recognize you out of uniform."

"Well, Bob," he replied, taking my hand with a twinkle in his eye, "they often say: 'clothes make the man.' Please feel free to call me Bill, unless I'm wearing the shoulder bars."

We all laughed, and Ogle pulled out his perennial pipe pouch. "Bob, as you know, we're trying to wrap up all the loose ends today. Bill has made a point about re-entry into the lagoon after the shot. As Walt MacConnell will talk about later, the first people going back in will be a helicopter survey team from the carrier, *Rendova*. They'll be flying an airborne radiometer and plotting ground radiation levels all around the atoll, so that the data recovery people will know what they're up against.

"Another piece of essential information nobody seems to have considered is local wave damage to ground installations that might also be a factor in data recovery. We've been thinking it might be a good idea to have a wave man aboard that chopper." He paused to light his pipe, and then flicked the match expertly into a sand bucket ten feet away. "Don't volunteer unless you feel comfortable," he added. "That chopper may get a little warm, but we can outfit you with lead BVD's."

"What's the time frame?" I asked, reflecting that I was clearly the only candidate, but also conscious of the wave-effects decisions that would have be made early after shot time.

"If you're thinking about the wave reports," said Ogle, "we'll know if the atoll blows in half as soon as the *Horizon* reports in . . . surely by H+30 min. If we have a tidal wave, all bets are off. If we don't, we won't expect to hear from the outer island stations for three or four hours. If we start your survey as soon as we hear from the *Horizon*, you should be back in time to respond to any questions about distant waves." He paused to relight his pipe, and then added, "If it's any consolation, I'll be in another chopper right behind you. We'll be headed for Boken to salvage some film from that big bunker."

"Sure," I said, shakily, my awe and sympathy for the penetration pilots vanishing in a flash of insight. Now I would be right up there with them. Then the old grey cells started clicking. "It would be helpful if someone could take some comparison photos the day before, so that I could flip through them for reference as we go along. Then I'll be able to distinguish the old from the new."

"No problem," said Ogle. "I'll work out all the details. We just wanted to get it into today's presentation so that anybody needing your input can request it."

* * *

After the coffee break at 3:30, we heard reports from Holmes and Narver, and various units of the military task groups, from which I gleaned a few interesting tidbits.

There were around 12,000 people involved in Operation Ivy, about equally divided among civilians and the three services, all living in strictest segregation.

The Air Force contingent (TG132.4) was mainly based at Kwajalein, never to be seen and rarely heard from, although a rather acrimonious debate evolved over the crowded conditions there. In particular, it seemed, the airmen objected to sleeping in 12-man tents, to which they were not accustomed.

The Army (TG132.2) resided in a tent city on Medren, the southernmost islet of Eniwetok Atoll, and farthest from the shot site. They had their own mess, post office, and open-air movie, and a shooting range to keep them from forgetting their professional obligations. The Eniwetok airstrip was also on Medren, where all incoming passenger traffic passed through security verification and badging, and was then transported elsewhere by helicopter or STOL aircraft, which can take off or land in 30 feet.

The Navy (TG132.3), of course, lived aboard its own ships, now a substantial fleet, capable of temporarily absorbing all island-based personnel during atoll evacuation:

1. USS *Rendova*, escort carrier, fleet flagship and Admiral Wilkins's staff headquarters. The *Rendova* carried a mixed bag of military helicopters for intra-atoll and survey missions.
2. USS *Estes*, amphibious fleet flagship, headquarters JTF132 during Mike test. Also Mike firing and scientific command center. The *Estes* had a helo-pad astern.
3. USS *Curtiss*, seaplane tender, transported Mike to PPG, and responsible for numerous post-shot measurements.
4. USS *Oak Hill*, landing ship, dock, transported most small craft to Eniwetok, including 19 LCM's, 4 LCP's, and three 45-mph motor torpedo boats (AVR) for people in a hurry, such as the Mike firing party.

In addition to the above, there were four destroyers, two personnel transports, one cargo ship, three fleet tugs, two LST's, nine LCU'S, and a handful of miscellaneous support vessels.

All the rest of us civilians (TG132.1), scientists, technicians, and construction workers alike, were quartered on Eniwetok Island, just North of Medren, and south of the main ship channel. Eniwetok also contained the task force headquarters (except afloat), the cryogenics plant, and many technical support facilities. Other than aluminum barracks, there were few amenities; evidently the military required more diversion. I was soon to discover why.

In addition to physical separation, interservice rivalry was sometimes carried to ridiculous extremes. For example, each service had a completely different set of code names for every islet on Eniwetok Atoll. The army gave them male names . . . Elmer, Fred, George; the navy used the international phonetic alphabet . . . Alpha, Bravo, Charlie; we civilians called them by their native names. I never learned the air force code, but it was something different.

Jeff and I made our wave hazard presentation after coffee. There were many questions and quite a spirited discussion, but no serious objections; obviously, we weren't in anybody's way. Oddly, it seemed, we would have the only scuba diving facilities at Eniwetok, and there were several requests for diving assistance from other projects. Scuba was in its infancy during the early 50's, and the navy had not yet discovered its usefulness.

We next heard from Walt MacConnell about the revised radiation program. Walt was a stocky, furry Irishman, whose hair and bushy beard resembled rusty steel-wool. He had that friendly, no-nonsense approach to matters that made him seem instantly believable.

Walt explained that the greatest personnel hazard from radiation would be eliminated simply by evacuating the atoll. At shot time, the fleet would be clustered southeast of the atoll, upwind, and far enough away so as to be out from under the mushroom umbrella. Each ship would have its own radiation monitor, and, in case of unexpected wind shifts, be able to take evasive action. Aside from the aircraft sampling program discussed that morning, the primary mission of his group was to establish and maintain radiation exclusion (radex) zones for ships, aircraft, and (later) surface travel within the atoll, and to monitor and decontaminate personnel and equipment wherever there was a requirement for entering a radex zone before radiation had died down to safe levels. The radex zones were to be revised daily, or oftener if required, and one milliroentgen per hour was considered low enough for indefinite exposure.

Anybody who expected to stay in the forward area after D-1 was to be issued a film badge, to be worn on the same chain as his security badge. The film badge registered accumulated radiation dosage, and was to be turned in for processing before leaving the area. If you had to go into a radex zone, your badge would be examined immediately afterwards. If you exceeded the limiting exposure of 3.9 R, you were shipped home and required to take a physical within 90 days; if you exceeded 15 rems, they would give you a physical immediately, and you couldn't come back for a year. The special authorization for the penetration pilots of 20R was considered a lifetime exposure; i.e., they had used up their allowable career tolerance. Walt was a good salesman; he made it sound as if people were screaming to get back into this line of work.

During coffee, I noticed that people had gathered into little groups, talking earnestly and with much emphasis. There was an air of urgency and anticipation in the room. We were like an athletic team, after months of training and rehearsal, receiving last-minute advice in the locker room before charging out onto the field for the big game. Even Jeff had dropped his usually placid demeanor, and was in animated discussion with Walt MacConnell. I grabbed a doughnut and sidled over. Jeff brought me up to date in a sentence.

"I was asking Walt about the physiology of radiation damage in places like Nagasaki and Hiroshima, but he says that most of the casualties there were caused by the fire storms."

"Fire storms?" I asked.

"That's right," said Walt. He was eating peanuts from a small vending machine bag, popping handfuls into his mouth and chewing vigorously, so that his rusty beard bobbed up and down. "Because of the inflammable nature of Japanese cities, those bombs were set to detonate at the optimum height for thermal effects. Everything within a mile radius was instantly set on fire." He chewed thoughtfully for a moment and then spread his hands out, palms up. "When you get that big a fire started, it behaves like a small hurricane. The hot air explodes upwards, and cool air is sucked in along the ground at 50-60 miles an hour. The interior is like a blast furnace . . . hot enough to melt steel! Everyone inside is either incinerated, or dies from lack of oxygen or from being crushed by falling debris. The only people who sustained observable radiation damage were outside the fire storm."

"But, those inside must also have suffered radiation damage," I ventured.

"Oh, certainly," he replied, "But, that's irrelevant. If you're out to kill people, which we were, the surest way, given the uncertainty of those early devices, is the fire storm." He stopped to empty the bag directly into his mouth. "On the other hand, if you're interested in how to survive such an event, then you study the five per cent who only suffered radiation damage." I think both Jeff and I were taken aback by MacConnell's candidness. It was a viewpoint I had never heard expressed. But, before we could respond, Burris rapped on the desk with his pointer for us to continue, and we returned to our seats. I later raised the question with Ogle, who commented, flatly, that MacConnell was absolutely right. "I'm sick to death of hearing bleeding-heart liberals moan that we committed a national crime," he said. "It was a national decision to drop those devices, with the objective of killing as many Japanese as we could. To say later on that we didn't mean to do it is sheer hypocrisy." Sixteen years later Ogle's picture was on the cover of *Time*, featuring an article citing this quote, which caused a spike in *Time's* circulation.

Our last agenda items, of course, were the pre-shot evacuation and post-shot re-entry of Eniwetok Atoll. Admiral Wilkins started things off by reminding us that the decision to evacuate everybody to sea for one or two weeks, made only three months previously, had roughly doubled the Navy's commitment to Operation Ivy. Despite the demands of the ongoing Korean war, they had managed to borrow two 10,000-ton personnel transports from CINCPAC, as well as several fleet tugs, barges, and oilers. As a further precaution, two LST's were to evacuate all natives from Ujelang Atoll, 130 miles southwest of Eniwetok, and, if necessary, all work personnel from Bikini Atoll, 180 miles to the east, where preparations were already underway for the forthcoming Operation CASTLE (1954). Lastly, in the event of worst-credible circumstances, plans were made for temporary evacuation of the 5,000-odd air force and navy personnel on Kwajalein by combining all available air and surface transport.

The evacuation plan, as outlined by CDR Nichols of Wilkins' staff, seemed simple enough although, from the diversity of activities outlined in today's briefing, I could foresee all sorts of complications. All task group commanders were to provide the navy (CTG 132.3) with a personnel roster, together with an activity schedule for each individual through completion of the operation. Upon arrival in the forward area, each person would be given an evacuation card telling him when and where to report. It was hoped to fly all personnel having no post-shot responsibilities to Hawaii by D-7 days.

Mustering aboard of all others not concerned with the care and feeding of Mike was to begin on D-7 and be completed by D-3 days. Except for the *Horizon,* which would be standing by one of her deep-moored wave stations 75 miles northeast of Eniwetok, all ships were to rendezvous at assigned stations 30-50 miles southeast of the atoll to await further orders. Nichols closed by emphasizing the responsibility of each individual to muster aboard his assigned evacuation vessel. Failure to obtain a complete personnel accounting by D-1 could cause a test postponement. A hold of more than two days would probably require test abandonment until next spring. This constraint was governed by the difficulty of maintaining all essential elements of the operation in a constant state of readiness.

Our final agenda item, proposed re-entry procedure, was handled by Bill Ogle. He came forward, put one hand on the lectern, and stood there a moment. Then he began, speaking in a clear, low voice: "It's been a long day, and everybody here has been working very hard for a long time. This is probably the last time we will all be together in one room during this operation, so there's a very important point I wish to emphasize, particularly to the technical and military support groups. All our efforts . . . everything we do, right up to the instant the button is pressed, is just placing our bets in this casino. We've hedged our bets as heavily as possible. But, until the button is pressed, and the wheel spins and the ball drops, there is no payoff! Re-entry is where we go in to pick up our wins and losses . . . it's the most important part of the action." He paused for a moment, and paced pack and forth along the edge of the platform, pulling a pencil from his pocket and rolling it between his palms. Then he continued, still pacing.

"The difficulty about re-entry is that, while we have a scenario and a priority list, we don't have a schedule . . . the schedule will be determined by the Mike yield and the weather. And, in some sense, Mike will be making his own weather. In a thermonuclear explosion this large . . . reaching, perhaps, up into the stratosphere . . . we will have a thermal chimney sucking up warm, moist air from sea level. According to Dr. Mason, here, part of this air will be cooled as it rises, and the moisture will be precipitated as rain. So, anywhere beneath the mushroom umbrella, we can expect intermittent heavy rain squalls, bringing down a lot of hot stuff from the main cloud system." He stopped pacing and faced us again, as if he had forgotten we were there. I suddenly realized what was bothering him. He didn't have a pipe in his mouth, and couldn't concentrate. Evidently the same thought occurred to him. He walked back to his seat, retrieved his pipe pouch, and began to fill up. It flashed through my mind that if we were, in fact, all out there ready to push the button and Ogle couldn't find his pipe, we would all be in deep trouble.

His pipe going, Ogle outlined his scenario. "First priority is fleet safety. Our weather survey plane upwind of the shot site should know within H+10 minutes whether or not the mushroom stem is moving in the forecast direction.

"Second priority is tsunami waves. Our waves group tells me that only if the crater breaches into the ocean is there a likelihood of a large tsunami. The weather plane should also be able to see the crater and report its configuration by H+10 minutes. We can also expect direct wave measurements from the *Horizon* by H+25 minutes. If either the crater breaches or waves are recorded in excess of 10 feet high and one minute duration, we will alert the warning system in Hawaii and our wave observers on Guam, Wake, Midway, and Johnston Islands. Further action will depend on reports from these islands.

"Third priority is recovery of film canisters from Eniwetok, Runit, and Boken Islands before they are fogged by radiation. We can go after them by chopper with exposure suits, provided that rad-levels are down to 10R/hour, and that the decon station at Medren is operating, and the airstrip is cleared for further canister transport to Los Alamos. So, as soon as the *Rendova* is radsafe cleared, we'll launch a radiation survey chopper to sweep the atoll counterclockwise from Medren toward the shot site, until the local background exceeds 100mR. We'll repeat these surveys hourly until the canisters are recovered.

"Beyond this point, there is very little we can do until the airborne radioactivity has blown off downwind, and the lagoon surface water activity has degraded below 1 mR. Since the main entrance pass is upwind, and circulation studies indicate that the lagoon should flush downwind over the westerly reefs, we expect the region near Medren and Eniwetok to clear first. Then we can permit the fleet to reenter, and commence the job of cleanup and rehabilitation of living quarters on these islands. If all goes well, we anticipate that reentry should be possible by D+1 or D+2 days."

Ogle leaned forward and tapped his ashes into the sand bucket near his feet, and concluded with: "I guess that's about the ticket. If there are any questions, now is the time to speak." A dozen hands shot up, and the word 'rehearsal?' predominated. "Oh, yes," he said, "I knew there was something I forgot. We're planning to have some sort of rehearsal around D-7 days . . . on a not-to-interfere basis with the Mike get-ready. We will probably send the *Estes, Curtiss, Rendova,* and the *Horizon* out to their assigned stations, and run through a regular count down, with the air boys going through their drill upstairs. The object, of course, is to pulse the whole system . . . timing, arming, firing circuits, communications traffic . . . the whole bit.

We'll announce it a week or so ahead and pass out a mini-op-plan to everybody concerned. If you want to participate, put your chit in." He smiled, and added: "But you better hurry; I'm leaving for Hawaii in the morning."

Then the questions flew. I signaled to Jeff; we strolled out together and raced down the hall. As we checked through the guard gate, I heard the stampede coming. "Where you headed, Jeffo?" I yelled as we sprinted across the lawn toward the Lodge."

"Three guesses," he yelled back. "And you?"

"One guess. See you on the plane."

* * *

That night, over at Suzie's house, we had a love-in.

"It's an old Apache custom, but I've added a few modern embellishments," she said, mysteriously, as she ushered me her darkened bedroom, lit only by small night lights plugged into low wall sockets. "First, we take off our clothes and get into bed, and then I'll explain the rules." As I wrestled with a recalcitrant knot on my left shoelace, my eyes adjusted enough to make out a large pitcher and two martini glasses on a night table beside the bed. Next to it was a bowl full of sliced vegetables: celery, red bell pepper, olives, cucumbers, and several hard-boiled eggs.

"Ok," I said, pulling the sheet up and accepting a brimming glass and a stalk of celery. "What about the Apaches?"

"Well, everybody knows how ingenious they were at torturing prisoners, but this book I read claims that they were also great lovers—especially the squaws, who were trained from childhood. Anyway, when a warrior prince from one tribe wanted to marry a princess from a neighboring tribe, their relatives first wanted to find out if they were sexually compatible . . . or else very bad medicine would afflict both tribes. So, they—the relatives—would set up a tepee, all by itself, and equip it with a week's supply of food. Then the couple would go in and get to know each other. If they stayed all week, everything was fine and they could get married. If not, the warrior would come out early, and the princess would commit suicide." Suzie sipped her martini and crunched a radish noisily.

"Sounds like a crock to me," I said, handing my glass back for a refill. "The Apaches didn't live in tepees. Who wrote that book?"

"I got it out of the Los Alamos Library." She reached under the bed and retrieved a dog-eared paperback. It was entitled: *Heroines of the Indian Wars* by Clara Barnes.

"Aha," I cried, "a female author."

"Bastard!" She grabbed the book and hurled it across the room. Then she leaped astride my chest and pinioned my wrists with her strong little hands. Her eyes were little slits. "Now I'm going to make you eat those words," she gritted from between clenched teeth. We wrestled briefly in mock ferocity. By spreading my arms and bending my neck forwards, I could almost bite her pink nipples. This she evaded by twisting from side to side.

Finally, I lay back, feigning exhaustion. "I give up, how does your game go?"

She slowly relaxed, lying down full length on top of me, just fitting between my insteps and chin. I was conscious of her heart pounding in synchronism with mine. "According to my book, we're supposed to torment each other all night, without reaching climax until the sun bursts over the horizon."

"What a way to die!" I said. "Only . . . we don't have a week."

"I know," she murmured." Then, with growing intensity: "Nevertheless, before this night hath ended, Prince Robert of Ward, I shall make thee cry 'Uncle'."

"Uncle," I croaked, weakly. "Uncle . . . Uncle . . . Uncle."

I awoke dreaming there was an earthquake. Suzie was sitting on the edge of the bed, shaking me gently. "Wake up, Sir Robert, it's Picnic Day." I struggled to sit upright, and she handed me a tall glass of tomato juice with a slice of lemon perched on the rim. She was wearing corduroy shorts and a pale purple halter. Her eyes shone, her teeth gleamed; just bursting with health and vitality. "Come on, Sweet Prince," she cried, giving me a last shake. "Your breakfast awaits and it's a beautiful day." She bounced up, arms raised toward the sky, and pranced into the kitchen.

I had always thought of myself as rather energetic, but it usually takes a minute or two to get the brain in low gear, and a cup or two of Jo before I dare shift into high. She was something else. But, after a hot shower followed by a cold needle rinse, the mists had cleared, and I wandered into the kitchen. Suzie had fixed a large plate of sliced bagels, smeared with cream cheese and topped with smoked salmon slices. While I wolfed them down and guzzled hot, black coffee, she bustled around throwing things into a big wicker basket, humming snatches of something reminiscent of Madame Butterfly. I chimed in with a rousing chorus of Verdi's Di Provenza Il Mar Il Suol, and went back to the bedroom to hunt for my footwear. Five minutes later, we were in Suzie's little VW bug headed west into the Jemez mountains . . . still singing our separate songs.

We had barely left the outskirts of town and entered the foothills, when the pavement gave way to gravel, and then to rutty dirt. "Maintenance road for the water system," said Suzie, skillfully avoiding the deeper holes with water still standing from yesterday's rain. "Elsbietka loves rough going." I marveled at the way the tiny car seemed to wade through mud, sand, or rocks with none of the spine-shattering jolts common to American cars. The VW was a relatively recent import, but already was proving itself as a sturdy, all-weather, all-terrain vehicle.

For a mile or so the road ran up the bottom of a canyon, paralleling a small stream and large steel pipe. Then we came to a concrete reservoir, blocking the entire canyon. The road swung abruptly left, and climbed steeply in a series of short switchbacks, finally emerging from the pine trees onto a bare ridge, where it ended in a small parking area. "Now we walk," said Suzie. So we got out, and I fished the hamper from behind the passenger seat. It was circular, about a foot across, with a curved handle across the top; not exactly the ideal shape for trail hiking.

"How far?" I asked.

"Two miles . . . maybe three. We go up a bit, too. Shall I carry it?" There was a note of challenge in her voice.

"No," I said, "I'll pack the grub. But, this is my kind of country. There's a hard and an easy way to everything." I reached again behind my seat and pulled out the camouflaged marine poncho I'd seen when retrieving the basket. I spread it out on the ground, folded the hood flat over the neck opening, and proceeded to arrange the basket contents in a packet on the hood. Then, I folded the poncho diagonally, rolled it into a cylinder, and tied the ends together, forming a loop. Finally, I stepped into the loop with the knot at my back, raised the whole works under my arms, and flipped the packet over my head so as to rest on my back just below the shoulders. "Presto," I said, "instant Eskimo tumpline. Heap comfortable. Carry 50 lbs 50 miles. Ugh, paleface squaw savvy?"

Suzie, who had watched everything in silence, now walked around me twice, examining the arrangement in detail. Then she pulled my head forward and kissed me very gently. There was a new look in her eyes . . . something bordering on respect. "Heap good, Chiefy," she said, softly. "Now we mush, okay?"

The trail wound up a stony ridge, sparsely covered with piñon pines and junipers. The sky was cerulean, the air soft, but cool at this altitude, despite the bright sun. We climbed for an hour, and suddenly broke out on a broad ridge overlooking an enormous, mountain-ringed valley. Although I judged the opposite rim to be twenty miles away, its peaks stood out in sharp relief against the clear, blue sky. The interior slopes descended steeply to a level, grassy floor, about a thousand feet below our vantage point. In the center of the valley rose a cluster of low hills, heavily forested with conifers.

"The Jemez caldera," I exclaimed in astonishment. I had no idea it was so close to Los Alamos."

"Damn," she cried, "you've seen it already."

I pulled her close. "No, sweetheart, I haven't seen it . . . just read about it: a very famous geologic feature; the biggest recent volcanic crater in North America. I'm very glad you brought me here."

"It was my own very special place," she murmured, her face buried in my shoulder. "I j-just wanted to sh-share it with somebody special." Her shoulders began to shake, and suddenly she was sobbing as if her heart would break. I had a strange knot in my own throat, so I sank down, leaning against a handy boulder, and cuddled her up. She was obviously going through some kind of crisis. I was a probably a factor, but not the only one.

Finally, she sat up, wiping her tear-stained face with the back of one hand. "God, what a blubbery mess I am.

I didn't want things to happen this way. I wanted it to be a perfect day in my special place." She smiled a little ruefully. "I've really never cried like this . . . except when Daddy died."

"When was that?"

"Last March. He had a heart attack and died very suddenly. But I didn't even know it until his lawyer tracked me down three weeks later. No one even knew where I was." She was again on the verge of tears.

"You must have been very close," I said, trying to get her to talk it out.

"More than close. My mother died when I was born, so Daddy had to take care of everything. We weren't just father and daughter . . . we were partners! Daddy had a horse ranch in Napa county. We raised breeding stock for the racetracks, mostly in California. I learned to ride before I could walk. But I did everything else, from shoveling manure to riding time trials. Every so often, we'd just take off and go hunting or fishing."

"What about school?" I ventured.

"I went to school part time in Napa, but mostly Daddy taught me. He was English, and frightfully well educated." She was picking up little stones and carefully placing them in a circle. "We had a great big elegant English ranch house. There was a fantastic library with about a zillion books . . . many more than the Napa county library.

"When the war came, we expanded into wine grapes, and then Daddy insisted I go to college. It was the first time we'd ever been separated. We picked Berkeley, so that I could come home weekends. Belmont Park was in Richmond, and I could get gas coupons to drive our truck back and forth in the pretext of delivering horses to the track. Of course, I did that too, but not always." She looked up. "This is all pretty boring, isn't it."

"Go on," I said, "I'll tell you when I'm bored. Did you learn to play tennis at Berkeley?"

"Oh, yes. I had to find something vigorous to do or I'd just have exploded, sitting in classes all day. By the end of my junior year, I could beat all the girls and most of the boys in my class."

"I don't doubt it," I said. "Look at those muscles." I pinched her bicep playfully between thumb and fingers. She stuck out her tongue. Then we got to kissing, and it was some time before we were back on track. I asked her how she came to work at Los Alamos. She had taken one of the UC bulletins home and left it lying around. Her father had noticed the position announcement and suggested she look into it

She was interviewed at school and offered the job next day. She didn't want to leave, being still a semester short of graduating, but her father had insisted, saying that she shouldn't waste her life on a horse ranch. When she objected, he said he was dickering to sell the place and move to Ojai. In fact, he'd already bought a house there. She didn't know that he'd already had two heart attacks. Three months after she went to Los Alamos, he had the third one . . . and it finished him off.

"And then I came along," I said.

"And I blew it."

"Not exactly. You just sort of rearranged my concept of an ideal mate." She looked at me skeptically. I told her about my Ice Queen. The hollow cheeks. The long, blond hair.

"Mmmmmm," she said icily, "and what does the new model look like?"

"Well, let's see," I said, looking up at the sky. "she's about 5-2 or 5-3, brown eyes, short brown hair. Pointy tits. Fast left jab and right cross. No sense of humor . . . .". And then she was in my arms, and we were rolling around in the pine needles. "That's what I love most about you," I gasped. "The gentle touch."

We had our picnic at Suzie's spring. It was hidden away in a cleft, several hundred feet below the crater rim, at the head of a tributary canyon to the reservoir far below. Just as she had described it, a small, clear stream issued from a fissure in the rock face, and cascaded down through a series of shallow pools. The view was northeast, but 'forever' was just the peaks above Taos rising out of the valley haze 75 miles away.

We spread the poncho on a patch of grass beneath a scraggly piñon, whose bare roots scrabbled among the rocks. Suzie had put together a do-it-yourself lunch: a ball of fresh-baked sourdough, a slab of English cheddar, two cans of Norwegian sardines, a bunch of huge red grapes, and a bottle of Louis Martini Mountain Sylvaner. "Crikey," she exclaimed, pawing among the comestibles, "I forgot the cork puller.

"Crikey?" I responded, surprisedly. "You must have been reading the Bastables."

"Darling," she cried, flinging her arms around my neck "I knew we were kindred spirits. You're the only American I ever met who knows about the Bastables." Then she sat back, head cocked to one side, and surveyed me curiously. "You know," she said, "I really don't know anything about you at all . . . except that Jeff told Mona you were pretty bright."

"Really not so bright . . . but a pretty good memory," I said, getting out my knife and going to work on the cork. "I remember all sorts of trash . . . such as the phone numbers of my mother's friends in old Pasadena exchanges." I got the cork out in several pieces, and filled the plastic glasses. "To the Bastables," I said.

"And to all them blokes as says, 'crikey'," she replied in cockney.

I began slicing the cheese and opening the sardines, but her eyes were still on me, so I began a rather rambling account of my personal history. I told her about my scientist father, who taught chemistry at Cal Tech, and lived in his own private world; and about my socialite mother, who had her own house in La Jolla and divided her time between tennis and bridge, leaving me most of the time to my own devices. "I was a rather enterprising kid, always jumping off roofs with umbrellas, building man-carrying kites, and blowing up trees with homemade gunpowder. In retrospect, it's rather a miracle that I survived."

Then there was Stanford, where I studied engineering; and the war, most of which I spent working in the aircraft industry. "And so, you see," I concluded, "I had a painless and interesting childhood, but never realized my boyhood dream of sailing to the south seas."

"But, you are going there now, aren't you? Very soon."

"I guess you're right. Not exactly as I dreamed, though."

"Seems to me that your problem is just the opposite of mine," she remarked, pensively, tearing off a chunk of sourdough and dipping it into her wineglass, watching the red color climb until it was saturated before transferring it to her mouth. "I mean, perhaps I had too much parental love . . . and you didn't have enough."

"Maybe we're each just what the other needs," I said, speculatively.

"That's just what I've been trying to convey to you, Dummy!"

"Why don't we give it a whirl?" I said. "After all, we've already resolved the most difficult question."

"You mean, whether or not I can cook?"

"Exactly. Now all we have to find out is whether we're sexually compatible."

We were awaked from a postprandial catnap in the warm sun by the distant rumble of thunder, and could see puffy cumulus swelling up out of the Rio Grande valley to the east. By the time we had scooped up our picnic remains and made our way back to the ridge top, we could see that it was going to be a close race to the car. We covered the two miles downhill in about fifteen minutes, but the storm front won by a hundred yards, drenching us to the marrow before you could say: Rumplestiltkin. Instead of being cowed by the downpour, Suzie began dancing wildly around, flailing her arms, and chanting Indian-like whoops and howls, until a blinding flash of lightning and instant crash of thunder galvanized me into action. I grabbed her by the wrist, dragged her to the car, and shoved her inside.

"If you were supplicating the rain gods," I shouted above the roar of hail on the metal car top, "I think you overdid it."

"I was just trying to thank them," she explained, "but I must have used the wrong words."

The temperature having dropped forty degrees, we were both shivering violently. I dumped the poncho's contents into the picnic basket and wrapped it around us. Then we sat there, huddled together, teeth chattering, waiting for a respite. It was hopeless to attempt the switchbacks below us when we couldn't see the ground in front of the car. Suddenly, the rain stopped, as quickly as it had begun, and the sun poured down on the dripping forest. But, more was coming. Suzie fired up Elsbietka, and we sloshed back through the chuck holes, now brimming over, without further mishap.

We drove straight to the Lodge, with the idea of getting me dry clothes. Suzie had bought a steak and a bottle of Merlot . . . a last, quiet evening together. But it was not to be. There was a note from Jeff at the desk. Tomorrow's TWA flight to San Diego was canceled, as was Carco to Albuquerque. A car would be coming to drive us down at 5:30 this evening. We were booked to Denver at nine, with a connection to San Diego from Denver at midnight. The clock on the wall said 4:20.

"Time for a drink at the wet bar," I said, trying to hide my disappointment.

"No," she said, "I'll take a rain check. Will you write, this time?"

"Every day." I kissed her gently. "Besides, you're at the focus of things here. You'll know where I am every second."

PART IV

DEPLOYMENT

August-September, 1952

The rest of the summer went by in a blur, tempered only by Suzie's distant image. The day after returning to La Jolla, I had bought a packet of pre-stamped postcards, and made it a point of scribbling a few lines to her each night before I fell into bed. Other than that, my most notable recollection is our frantic effort to get the *Horizon* to sea on time, loaded not only with our own gear but with all the goodies required for the four-month geophysical cruise thereafter.

She had come out of the shipyard at the end of July, where they had been overhauling her dredging winch and installing a fallout wash-down system according to plans sent us by the Navy. The latter was simply an array of lawn sprinklers topside, all connected by ordinary garden hose to the ship's fire control system. Auxiliary fire hoses were hung on each wing of the bridge to rinse off areas of her masts and superstructure that the wash-down system couldn't reach.

The following week, we took her out off San Diego to rehearse the seamount mooring emplacement procedure, which was Bascom's responsibility. The objective was to anchor the ship by her dredging cable in 5,000 feet of water, and then to assemble over side in tandem and lower to the sea floor the following string of components:

1. A 1,200-lb anchor clump (we used four railway freight car wheels chained together);
2. 4,500 feet of high-tensile steel wire, only as thick as a drinking straw;
3. A hollow, steel sphere, three feet in diameter, weighing 440 lbs in air, but having a submerged buoyancy of 480 lbs;
4. 1,000 feet of half-inch Dacron rope, with a flag float on the end.

The only really hairy part of this procedure occurs during the last few hundred feet, when everything is hanging over side. The breaking strength of the steel wire is only twice the anchor weight. If it lets go, the steel float comes charging back to the surface liked a runaway freight, and can do some damage. However, we had previously deployed similar systems a number of times in relatively calm weather without incident.

On the day of the seamount trial, we encountered 22-knot winds and choppy, six-foot waves. When the *Horizon* was anchored, stern-to by her dredging cable, she rolled like a drunken alligator. We were all a bit apprehensive. But these conditions were not atypical of trade wind seas off Eniwetok, so we decided to proceed.

On the first try, the wire broke at the top, just as we were connecting it to the steel float. On the second attempt, it broke during the final lowering phase described above. The float flew thirty feet in the air. It didn't hit anything, but the mate, standing on the wing of the bridge, could have patted it on the way up. At this point, Hetzel decided that the special termination fittings, clamped by six bolts to the each end of the wire, were kinking it when the ship rolled. He filed the corners of the wire groove in the next set of clamps and, presto, everything went down like goose grease.

After attaching the raft and connecting the signal cable, we weighed anchor and steamed around all night, to make sure everything was working properly. In the morning, we came back, picked up the raft, and cut its mooring line. There was no way to get back the rest of system, but the float was rigged to admit water and sink after five or six days, so that it couldn't eventually bob to surface and become a menace to navigation.

On 10 September, the *Horizon* sailed on Leg I of Capricorn Expedition, ETA Honolulu, 1 October, and Eniwetok, 14 October. We all went down to see her off—not by way of celebration, but because we had just learned that Roy Halliwell, chief scientist for Leg I, had ordered a good deal of afterdeck cargo offloaded, including our six seamount spheres, sixteen freight car wheels, and eight lead turtle fairings. Roy knew nothing about Ivy, but only that this equipment was needed for Leg II, a joint exercise between the *Baird* and the *Horizon* in the Marshall Islands. The *Horizon* was overloaded, and lacked work space on her afterdeck, whereas the *Baird*, still awaiting her winch cable, would come later and be under-loaded. Let the *Baird* haul all this heavy stuff!

There was no answer to Roy's ignorance nor impeccable logic. I got on the horn to Los Alamos, and thence to H&N's shipping agent in Oakland. There was an MSTS freighter leaving the navy's Oakland Supply Depot on 4 September, ETA Eniwetok on 28 September. They could take our stuff if we delivered it before noon tomorrow. By 1500 hours, I had rounded up a 10-ton flatbed and driver, got the stuff loaded, and headed north. Jack Jensen was riding shotgun. I told him not to come back until the ship sailed.

Charley Black sailed with the *Hor*, as she was known affectionately. An apt nickname, I reflected, watching her backing down into the stream. With her faded white paint, streaked with rust from every hull opening, she resembled nothing so much as a heavily-made-up lady of the streets who'd been standing too long in the rain.

With the *Horizon* gone, Jeff went back to Point Loma until it was time to fly out to meet her at Eniwetok, and I was free to concentrate on the distant island stations. The wave recorders were long since finished, and one of them had been happily scribbling away at the end of the Scripps pier for several weeks. The shop had done a nice job. The whole unit, except for a length of two-inch pipe, available anywhere, fitted into a small suitcase. With his duffle and the suitcase, each island operator could travel and set up shop independently.

My plan was to launch them all at once towards their respective stations, go to Honolulu for the crypto course with the Wake operator, Ted Folsom, and his alternate, Ray Smith, and then to visit each station in rotation to make sure everything was on line. Johnston, Midway, Wake, Guam, and then on to Eniwetok via Kwajalein . . . 8,000 air miles the long way around. I wanted to arrive at Eniwetok by 12 October, just before the *Hor*. Allowing two weeks to wrap up the island stations, we should leave La Jolla the last week in September.

Next morning I called the island hoppers together and distributed our travel orders: a first endorsement and 36 copies. Except for a red arrow identifying the bearer, the orders were identical: a list of names and the message:

EFFECTIVE THIS DATE THE FOLLOWING-NAMED CIVILIAN PERSONNEL, OFFICER GRADE, ARE ORDERED TO PROCEED EARLIEST TO HEADQUARTERS FOURTEENTH NAVAL DISTRICT, HONOLULU, FOR FURTHER ASSIGNMENT ON REQUEST. ALL MILITARY TRANSPORT AUTHORIZED, CATEGORY F, PRIORITY 2B. SUBJECT PERSONNEL AUTHORIZED 200 LBS ACCOMPANYING HOLD BAGGAGE. HQ.CINCPACFLT.

I looked at the circle of bright young faces. "Very nice orders," I said, "a blanket authorization to travel via military aircraft, anywhere, any time, priority 2B—the same as a captain on official business or a senator on a junket. The military hates to issue orders like these, but we managed to convince them it was the only way of assuring the flexibility we need to get the job done. So, don't abuse 'em and don't lose 'em!"

Then I handed out their station assignments, naval ID cards, and letters requesting the various island commands to provide berthing and messing for two months, again in Officer Grade facilities, and local transportation, as necessary to carry out official duties. "We didn't shake dice to see who goes where," I said. "But there really isn't much choice. Only Guam has trees. Any questions?"

"Yeah," said George Price, who was slated for Johnston Island. "When do we have to leave?" George was tall and gangly, pimply and fearful. He was also married and had an expectant wife. I had put him at JI because he could get home quickest from there in an emergency.

"You just call the (naval) District Transportation Office in San Diego, and ask them when and where to report in order to get to Johnston by 1 October, priority 2B." Then I gave them all a list of cable addresses where I could be reached throughout the operation. We had gone over everything else a dozen times, so I just thanked them all for taking time from their studies to help on an important mission.

That evening, I wrote Suzie a long letter, signaling her in our agreed-upon code to direct future letters to our task unit's FPO address. Our late correspondence had flagged, and she was evidently down in the dumps. I suspected that things were pretty slow at LASL since most of J-Division had flown the coop. Part of my own delinquency was due to overwork. But there also seems to be a limit to what two people can write about, once the early rapture has been elaborated, and there is no other bond of long association. I wrote that I adored her (true), and thought about her constantly (not true), but that things were just going to have to hang fire until I could do something about them personally.

I walked to the corner and mailed the letter with somewhat mixed feelings about my own motivations. I seemed aware for the first time of a curious duality in my character; with no extraneous factors obtruding, I could delight in her company, and could visualize no serious obstacle to an enduring relationship. But, faced with the responsibilities currently embodied in Ivy, I found it convenient to put her temporarily on the shelf; to step through the mirror, as it were, and totally devote my thoughts to the problems of this other world. Was I so singular? I recalled Ogle's remarks about the high mortality rate of LASL test staff marriages. Much the same separations were incumbent on oceanographers. Perhaps what bothered me most was the twinge of guilt I felt in this subterfuge, like a boy playing hooky.

IVY-MIKE

On sudden impulse, I ran back to my apartment, dialed long distance, and gave the operator Suzie's home number. You couldn't direct-dial in those days; long distance was only for emergencies. She answered after five rings.

"Darling," I said, "I just wrote you a stupid letter."

"Robert, isn't that strange; I just wrote you a stupid letter. Will you forget my letter, if I forget yours?"

"Of course."

"I love you."

"Ditto."

It was a stupid conversation, but I felt a lot better.

Because of the crypto course, Ted Folsom, Ray Smith, and I planned to leave around 20 September. The trip to Hickam Field, Honolulu, is hardly worth recounting, except for its agonizing deliberacy: A day at the District Transportation Office, San Diego, to have our unbelievable orders validated; a two-day wait for a navy flight from North Island to Alameda; a bus shuttle to the Twelfth Naval District HQ for more validation; another bus to Travis Air Force Base near Sacramento; a two-day wait for a 12-hour MATS flight to Hickam; six days to cover what is now a five-hour trip! And, every carrier and command wanted several copies of our orders. We arrived at Hickam with only 16 left of the original 36. But an obliging yeoman in the DTO ran us off another ream on his ditto machine. We were beginning to get the swing of how the military operates; I wondered how long a priority 2D might have taken.

During the trip, I had ample time to take the measure of my companions. Ray Smith was an affable and gregarious lad of twenty-two, with a chunky body and a full black beard. He was in his second year of graduate study as a biologist, and was a little upset at being an alternate, having volunteered for the mission in hopes of studying the marine life at Wake. In retrospect, he might have prospered better than Ted Folsom, who was 41, and nearing the end of a six-year struggle towards his degree in physical oceanography. Ted was thin, and prematurely gray, with that perpetual air of puzzled bewilderment that characterizes the absent-minded professor. He planned to review German grammar at Wake, having twice failed the language exam. I had selected him because of his mechanical aptitude.

After a night in the transient BOQ, we reported to district headquarters, a three-story, yellow, wood-frame building with a full balcony around each floor. We ascended the steps to a central foyer furnished in tropical rattan, and presented our orders to the Officer of the Day, a youngish Lt. Commander in crisp summer tans. It soon developed that the command could find no record of our request for crypto training. The last class had just finished, and there would not be another for a month. At my request, the OOD telephoned the JTF-132 number Ogle had given me and explained our dilemma. After some discussion, he hung up and suggested we return to our quarters to await a response. "Someone is trying to pull strings," he said, looking at my aloha shirt, my tennis shoes, and Ray's beard. "But, I'm afraid there's not much we can do. After all, we're fighting a war in Korea."

We had no sooner gotten back to the barracks, when the phone rang. It was the OOD, sounding a tad more deferential. A special course was being set up for our benefit, beginning Monday morning, which was the earliest that an instructor and the equipment to be furnished us could be flown here from the east coast. We were to report to 1150 Sutter St., at 0730, with orders and security ID. Sutter St., it seemed, was one signal east of the Naval Station, off Kam highway. "Well, Gentlemen," I said, after explaining the circumstances, "This is only Friday. Why don't we get ourselves a hotel room in Waikiki for the weekend? This may be our last liberty for six weeks."

Ray jumped up and grabbed his duffle, but Ted was shaking his head. "I think I'll stay here," he said, somewhat wearily. "I can study German just as well right here—and a lot cheaper."

Because neither Ray nor I had been to Hawaii before, we decided to rent a car to tour the island. A few minutes on the phone sufficed to bring an agent to our door, from whom we negotiated a much-abused '46 Chevy coupe from Sailor Main's rental lot, just outside the Naval Station. We had our choice, $20 for the week, or $35 for the pink slip.

We took the week, and a greasy map, and were soon rattling happily along Kamehameha highway, past Hickam field, past miles of open country with the mountains to the north shrouded in perpetual cloud, past the Dole pineapple plant with its doleful aroma, and into the Honolulu waterfront. We swung around the Aloha tower, where the Matson liners dock, and where Kamehameha became Ala Moana Blvd, passed the Honolulu Iron Works, the Kewala basin, with its tuna boats marshaled in odorous array, crossed the Ala Wai bridge, and found ourselves in the heart of Waikiki. We cased the Moana (too big), the Royal Hawaiian (too fancy), and ended up in a charming thatched bungalow of the Niamalu Hotel: twelve cottages scattered among two acres of palm trees, where now stands the mighty Hilton Hawaiian Village.

After La Jolla, Waikiki Beach was a disappointment . . . consisting of little patches of coral silt, caught in crevices of a mile-long, disjointed, concrete seawall, against which Dixie cups and drinking straws sloshed gently in tepid water. By wading gingerly over sharp coral, a determined swimmer could eventually attain a depth where his knuckles no longer scraped bottom. We thrashed about for a while but, towards three o'clock, the clouds burgeoned overhead, the rain pattered down, and we beat a hasty retreat. After showering, we sought surcease from the downpour in the Niamalu's thatched bar, drinking rum punches and listening to a huge Hawaiian entertainer make a ukulele sound like a trio of five string banjos. It was very pleasant, sitting there, nibbling pupus and watching the rain dripping from the eves. Ray Smith was a fine companion . . . but I would have preferred Suzie

IVY-MIKE

Saturday, armed with a six-pack of cold beer and a box of rice cakes rolled in seaweed (sushi), we set out to circumnavigate Oahu, counterclockwise. Wending our way past the zoo, and the jungle-covered mansions festooning the flanks of Diamond Head, we soon came to a ten-mile stretch of two-lane road, running arrow-straight between rocky, cactus-covered hills and thorny acacia flatlands, and terminating in Koko Head, an ancient mini-volcano whose crater had breached into the sea, forming a beautiful, semicircular bay. Seaward, the basalt cliffs rose vertically from 60 feet of crystal-clear water. Shoreward, the bottom shoaled to a sandy crescent, girdled by cocoa palms.

Today, Hanauma Bay is a public park, with a paved road down into the crater. A favorite of diving clubs, it daily hosts upwards of 2,000 people. But on that Saturday, in September, 1952, as we walked down the steep rugged footpath, there was not another soul. Our circumnavigation forgotten, we spent the entire day in our private paradise, snorkeling among the coral reefs, diving into the underwater lava caves, and lolling in the shade, listening to the boom of surf against the rocks that guard the entrance.

Sunday, we made it all the way, although the road around the northwest corner of the island dwindled to a pair of rocky ruts. The high points were body-surfing at Makapu Beach, the tremendous sweep of the pali cliffs, rising 4,000 feet vertically from the coastal plain, and eating ice-cold pineapple, right out of the field, from a tiny roadside stand. On the way home, we stopped by the Naval Station and persuaded Ted to come back with us to Waikiki. "One last little fling in Paradise," I said. Little did I wot how prophetic those words were to become.

1150 Sutter St. proved to be a long, grey, one-story concrete building, with no exterior identification The building stood within a high fence, topped with barbed wire. There was a guard gate before the front entrance, and a parking lot outside. Early as we were, the lot was half full. We parked, and identified ourselves to the guard, who announced our arrival over his intercom. After a few moments, a familiar figure strode out to meet us . . . Major Frank Davis, General Clarkson's adjutant. "Bob Ward!" he exclaimed, extending his hand "Good to see you again." We shook hands, and I introduced him to the others. Then he took us through the gate and up the walk to the building. "I'm really sorry about your misfire at CINCPAC," he burst out as we entered the foyer of the building and approached a reception counter. "Somehow, your course requirement completely slipped through the cracks. Luckily, we were able to repair the damage without too much lost time, eh? Your instructor's waiting outside, but first we've got to get you all signed in and badged."

"Just where are we, Frank?" I asked, as we produced our ID cards and signed the visitor register.

"Sort of a task force annex. Mostly to assist people in transit, like yourselves. Here are your temporary badges. You can leave them at the gate and pick them up again tomorrow; they're good for the rest of the week." He led us out a side door, where an army sergeant, who had been leaning against a jeep, sprang to attention. He was wearing paratrooper fatigues, and packing a 45 automatic in a side holster. "Meet Sergeant Lawson," said Davis, returning his salute, "He'll deliver you back to the gate and pick you up in the morning. Sorry, I can't invite you all in for coffee. This place is mostly out of bounds, unless you've got the Pope's blessing." He winked at me, and waved goodbye as we clambered into the jeep and drove away.

After passing acres of apparently empty storage buildings, we pulled up before an isolated concrete dugout, half underground. A sign read: DANGER EXPLOSIVES. Lawson leaped out and fitted a key to the massive padlock. "'Ain no powder in yere," he grunted, as he swung the massive steel door open and flipped on a light switch. "But this area is drah, prahvet, an' seecure . . . An' thet's all the book requars 'thin a guarded compoun'." Sergeant Lawson was tall, thin, and wiry, smooth-shaven and bristle-haired. He had hash marks above his elbows, and squint-lines radiating from the corners of his pale blue eyes. I judged his accent to be Southern Appalachian.

Inside, the bunker was completely empty, save for a wooden table and four chairs. On the table rested two metal boxes, covered in leatherette, with snaplocks and recessed handles. Sergeant Lawson unsnapped the cover housing the first box and set it aside. It contained nothing but a stack of papers and pamphlets, about 10 inches high.

"Rules an' regalations," he commented, unsnapping the second box. It contained what appeared to be a small, portable typewriter, except that the platen was twice too large. There was a roll of paper tape at the left end, and the tape ran horizontally across the striker plate and emerged through a slot at the right side.

"Thar she be," said Sergeant Lawson, reverently, "the KQS-8 code ENcryptor-DEcryptor. Taken us through all o' the last war, and most o' this'n 'thout no compromise." He tapped his knuckles on the table. "Uncle Joe (Stalin) 'd give his left testacle t' borry one o' these fur a day er two."

"Looks remarkably simple," said Folsom, intrigued by any unique mechanical contrivance.

"Easy ez apple pie," said Lawson. "C'mon, try her out."

Ted seated himself at the table and composed a rapid hunt and peck message. As with any typewriter, the keys flipped up and the platen rotated, but the message appeared, instead, on the tape strip issuing from the slot. And instead of sensible English, the tape contained nothing but five-letter groups of gibberish! "It's just a converted teletype machine," he chuckled, "but, somehow the message gets scrambled inside. See, the tape is gummed, so that it can be cut up and stuck on a standard message sheet."

"OK, Sonny," said Lawson, tearing off the tape and flipping a toggle lever at the side. "Now, jes' type in whut jes'come out." He held the tape so that Ted could read it while he, somewhat more tediously, copied the gibberish.

IVY-MIKE

I watched the new tape emerge: it read, Four score and seven years ago.

"Fascinating," I cried. The fourth letter in the first two words is "r" in the uncoded version . . . but not on the coded tape!"

"Rat on, Sonny. This 'yere machine resets the code ever' key stroke. See . . ." He flipped the toggle to encrypt, and typed in a string of e's. The issuing tape contained a string of random letters, again in five-letter groups.

Then he stood back and lighted a cigarette. "Why'nt y'all give it a try? They's coffee 'n rolls 'n the Jeep. Thin we'ns kin git down to whut ah come all th' way from Fort Benning ta larn yew."

With the aid of the manuals, and Sergeant Lawson's patient direction, we spent the day learning how the KSQ-8 operated; how to set the code of the day, the week, and the month; how to assemble and disassemble all its bits and pieces; how to diagnose and repair its illnesses.

On Tuesday, we tackled the more-formidable mountain of paperwork that accompanied its use. In an unguarded area, the machine must be stored in a safe, together with its documentation. When out of the safe, an armed guard must be present. A log must be kept of all message traffic. In case of malfunction, sixteen agencies must be notified by priority messages. The unit could only be replaced by an armed courier.

But the most stringent regulations concerned the question of compromise; that is, disclosure of the machine or its code books to unauthorized persons. Intentional disclosure was tantamount to treason, punishable in wartime with the death penalty. Accidental disclosure could bring life imprisonment. Under threat of disclosure, the machine was to be destroyed. There was a destruction manual detailing approved methods; the unit was equipped with batteries and thermite destructors that, when activated, were designed to melt it to a puddle. Other methods included burning it up with an acetylene torch; driving a tank over it; or smashing it to powder with a sledge hammer. In any case, these actions were to be reported by radio and followed by written reports in five languages to all NATO countries.

To Sergeant Lawson's evident delight, we completed the course Tuesday evening. Frank Davis would arrange to have Little Mollie, as we had dubbed her, couriered to Wake and delivered to the Island Manager, who had a safe and a firearm with which to guard her until Ted Folsom's arrival. "Sure am glad you college boys takened to Mollie so quicklike," he volunteered as he dropped us off at the guard gate. "Might git home fur the Worl' Series opener. Take keer."

Next morning, Wednesday, 30 September, a little hung-over from too many Mai Tais, we drove out to the District Transportation Office and filed for our disparate destinations. There was a C-124 leaving for Wake at midnight. It was a huge, slow cargo aircraft, but our orders applied to anything that flew. Ray was booked on a flight back to Travis Thursday morning, and I could catch the daily Kwajalein shuttle to Johnston Island at 1500 hours that very afternoon. Despite the delay in getting to Hawaii, we were almost exactly on schedule.

* * *

I dropped the troops off at the transient BOQ, and drove back to 1150 Sutter to give Frank Davis a short progress report for Ogle. This time, I was invited inside, and found, as I had suspected, that this long, gray building housed, not only the JTF-132 Honolulu headquarters, but also the branch offices of the Atomic Energy Commission and Holmes and Narver. "With the war going on, we try to stay out of CINCPAC's hair as much as possible," said Davis. "In fact, only the top people over there even know we exist. So, if you run into future problems, give us a buzz here before you bother them. We have some ways of cutting red tape that they don't know about." Then he introduced me to Colonel "Mike" Jacobs, who would be General Clarkson's Honolulu deputy throughout the operation.

Davis, himself, was headed west in the morning to join Clarkson, who had been at Eniwetok since 16 September. I mentioned our travel schedule, and wondered whether he'd be going by way of Wake or Johnston. "I'm not sure," he said. "There's supposed to be a typhoon somewhere between Johnston and Kwajalein, so I suppose we'll detour through Wake."

"Maybe you could give Ted a lift," I said. "It's 12 hours in a C-124, and pretty cold in the cargo section."

"I'm hitching a ride myself, with General Wise. He's got a load of brass on board, but we can probably take Ted if there's room. How do I reach him?" I gave him the BOQ number, and thanked him again. Davis was one of those rare, resourceful aides, always two steps ahead of his job. He would go far.

I had barely time to drop off the car. I don't think they expected to see it again; transient military often just abandon rented cars in the bushes; and ran into the BOQ for my duffle, before reporting to the Hickam terminal. Ted was out for a walk, so I asked Ray to track him down and chain him to the bed until Davis called. Fortunately, the duty driver was on his toes, and we made it to the terminal as they were calling my name for the last time. Because of the typhoon, they had advanced the flight an hour.

The equipment was R-4D (Douglas DC4), and took three hours to cover the 750 miles to Johnston. Out of my small porthole, I first saw only a long, thin stretch of coral reef, trending southwest, and upon which enormous breakers pounded endlessly. Then, as we made our descending turn onto final, I caught a glimpse of a small sand bar . . . and nothing else! This impression was hardly altered after we had taxied a short distance to the small terminal, and I stood again on terra firma; Johnston was an airstrip, a dozen cylindrical fuel tanks, and a handful of Quonset huts. Except for flashes of foam, the barrier reef was invisible to the northwest.

All of us passengers crowded into the tiny terminal as a truck drove out to refuel the plane. Johnston was an Air Force base. I presented my orders to the duty Lieutenant, who asked me to stand by until the plane had refueled, reloaded, and taxied away, leaving only three of us in the terminal. Then I inquired about George Price, whom I had half-expected might be on my own flight. "Price," mused the lieutenant, who looked 21, and had a shadow of a reddish mustache. "Tall kid? Pimples?"

"Right, fits his description."

"He came in two days ago, Sir. Got a message yesterday. Something about his wife. He flew out this morning . . . Sir. Would you like to ride up to the Colonel's office, Sir? He might have left a message."

The Lieutenant was right. George had left his wave recorder kit (thank the Lord), and a short note. His wife had gone into labor a month early, and he felt he must leave. He hoped that I would understand, and know what to do. I glanced at my watch; it was 1830 hours, Honolulu time. "Have you got voice transmission to Honolulu?" I asked.

"We have a MARS station, Sir. The enlisted personnel use it to make personal phone calls anywhere in the States. They can patch you into Honolulu telephone, if there's a ham listening."

"How about sending a priority TWX?"

"Have to get the CO's OK. He's at the O-Club." I opted for the TWX, and fired off a message to HQ-JTF-132, requesting they intercept Ray Smith and divert him to Johnston on the earliest flight, and to advise me of his schedule. Then I joined Colonel Abel and Lieutenant Sparks in a few drinks over shuffleboard.

By the time Ray arrived on the Thursday shuttle, I had picked out a site for the recorder at the end of a small loading dock, and had the local machine shop cut and thread a 12-foot length of 2-inch pipe. They also made up two U-straps for bolting the pipe to the dock timbers. While these activities were underway, I walked around the island—a leisurely two-hour stroll. There was no lagoon, in the ordinary sense; the bottom simply sloped seaward very gently in all directions, but so gradually that waves were entirely dissipated before reaching shore. The shallow area between the island and the barrier reef to the west was choked with coral heads, separated by a myriad of meandering passages. The water was unbelievably clear and, even close to the loading dock, swarmed with many kinds of fish. Ray would have a field day.

When I met him at the gangway, he was grinning from ear to ear. "Looks like you lucked out, after all," I said. "Did Ted get off on the General's plane.?"

"Did he ever? Major Davis phoned and asked him to be ready about 8:30pm. Right on the dot, an air force limousine picks us up—I went along for the ride—and whisks us straight out onto the field and up to this monster jet, a DC7 conversion, I think, and off they went. But that's not all. This morning, when I went over to change my reservation to Johnston, everybody was talking about the monster typhoon that had just hit Wake Island. The jet made an emergency fuel stop, dumped Ted off, and then got the hell out. Now, Wake is blacked out . . . No radio, No Loran . . . Nothing."

We walked to the baggage cart and retrieved his gear, while I reflected the best course of action. "Well, as you've probably guessed, Price bailed out with baby problems, but I've got everything ready to go here. We can install your recorder in the morning. Let's stroll up to Communications and see if there's any news about Wake."

But there was nothing until Friday morning, when the Colonel was handed a dispatch as we were seated together at breakfast. He passed it around. Wake had been clobbered. The control tower and Loran antenna were down. Most buildings had suffered damage, including the power plant. The navy was flying in tents and food. Only daytime landings were permitted until the runway lighting was reestablished. Poor Ted, I thought, he's in a disaster area. I'd better get out there as fast as possible and give him a hand. I wondered how Ralph Myers was making out at Midway. If everything was OK there, I might skip Midway and go directly to Wake. John Knauss had planned to go out to Guam a little early, 'just to see the sights.' In any case, there should be messages waiting for me in Honolulu. Everybody had expected us to take a week for the crypto course. "Let's get rolling," I said to Ray. "I've got to catch the shuttle back to Hono at 1400."

With a little extra muscle from two air force mechs, we had everything buttoned up and operating by noon. There was something nice about working in a place where the most remote facility was about 100 yards away. We even had time for a swim before we saw the shuttle on final, and strolled down to the terminal. "I'm going to alert Peterson to stand by to replace you here if Ted's in trouble," I told Ray. "After all, you're the only alternate who can operate Little Mollie."

"Fine with me," he replied. "That way, I'll get to see two islands."

I got back to Hickam at 1930, but Sutter St. operated around the clock. There was only one message . . . from Knauss, on Guam. He was in operation and awaiting further instructions. Good on him; but I kicked myself for not launching the troops earlier. Who would guess that it would take a week to get to Hawaii; that Price's wife would hit the jackpot a month early; that a typhoon would clobber Wake? And still no word from Folsom . . . or from Myers at Midway.

It was Friday night, and District Transportation was closed. But I had orders good on anything, flying anywhere. I wandered around the huge barn of Hickam terminal, which must have seen earlier duty as a dirigible hangar, until I found Flight Operations, the office where pilots file their flight plans and collect the latest weather information. I showed my orders to the non-com behind the counter and explained my problem. "Nothing till Monday outa here," he mused, scanning the chalkboard on the wall behind him. "Lem'me check with Barbers Point." He dialed his counterpart and relayed my question, reading from my orders. Then he hung up, smiling. "Hey, Buddy, you're in luck. Barbers has a pax-cargo flight, Midway-Wake-Guam, scheduled for 0400 tomorrow morning. The navy's always happy to oblige people with CINCPAC orders."

"Great," I said. "How do I get over there?"

"Hell, your ID says you have equivalent rank of Commander. Just call the OOD at the Naval Station and ask for transport—pronto. Here, I'll be glad to phone for you."

About an hour later, after a 25-mile circumnavigation of Pearl Harbor, the duty driver duly deposited me at the Operations Office, U.S. Naval Air Station, Barbers Point, where they logged me in and told me to report at 0300. On my way to the BOQ, with view to catching a few hours sleep, I chanced by the O-club and remembered I hadn't eaten since leaving Johnston. The dining room was closed, so I wandered into the bar; and there on a stool, clad in shorts and aloha shirt, sat the missing Ralph Myers.

"Dr. Livingston, I presume," I said, pounding him on the back. Myers coughed, and flung out an arm to keep himself from falling off the stool. "My God," he spluttered, finally recognizing me, "I didn't think you'd be along for another week."

"You're on tonight's flight, I take it?"

"Yes. In fact, I've been on it since San Diego. The navy has one flight a week that goes straight through to Guam, via Midway and Wake. In fact, we've been sitting in this God-forsaken place for two days, because of the hurricane . . . er, typhoon. Otherwise, I'm sure the station would have been running by now."

Myers was a chubby, Jewish mathematician from New York. Very bright, but not very worldly. "You buy that outfit here?" I asked, looking at his white, hairy legs. He nodded, so I added: "I hope you have a warm jacket. Midway's at 28 degrees latitude. The weather's more like San Diego than Hawaii. It might get pretty chilly by November."

Then I eased up, ordered a sandwich and a beer, and brought him up to date on the overall situation. As far as I was concerned, the train was now back on track, and my only real concern was how Ted Folsom was making out at Wake. I would continue on the same flight, and only utilize the refueling stop at Midway to help Meyers select an appropriate instrument location.

We had another drink, and I learned a little of his background; about as different from mine as I could conceive. He had been raised by German refugee parents in the lower East Side, and attended New York University. He probably would have stayed there indefinitely, happily making chicken tracks on blackboards, had he not attracted the attention of Henry Engels by his Master's thesis: The Statistical Properties of Wind Waves at Sea.

Henry had invited him to La Jolla for summer study, and then persuaded him to stay on to finish his PhD. He was one of the few people I knew who never adjusted to our raucous western living, or having to drive ten miles to San Diego to find a kosher deli. He would get his degree in January, and was headed straight back to NYU.

In contrast to all military tradition, our flight departed on schedule. There were only five of us passengers, seated on folding canvas benches along one side of the aircraft, near the cargo door. The remainder of its cavernous interior was crammed with crates and boxes, all secured against movement by webbing straps hooked into pad-eyes in the flooring. Most of the cargo was food, bound for Wake. We used every foot of runway getting off, and even after reaching cruise altitude, the thunder of the engines made conversation impossible.

I fell to musing about our island destinations: Midway and Wake, two stepping stones to the orient; both vital to Japanese military conquest; both bloody battlegrounds of World War II. Except for the brilliant destruction of their carrier fleet during the Battle of Midway, the Japanese would have had a clear path for land-based bombers all the way to Hawaii.

We landed at Midway Island at 0730, local time. The pilot advised us continuing passengers that we would only be on the ground two hours, because he wanted to arrive at Wake before darkness closed out the still-unlighted runway. Fortunately, everything moved like clockwork.

The Island Commander, a Coast Guard officer, put a jeep and driver at our disposal; we found a nice spot on the harbor seawall for the recorder; and even had time to visit the plumbing shop and order a piece of pipe cut and threaded. I got back to the plane with minutes to spare, and paused at the top of the gangway. It was raining, and a bit chilly. Myers looked a little disconsolate, standing there, now clad in a plastic raincoat and pith helmet over his Hawaiian garb. Beyond him, I could see a nice stand of ironwoods on a low hill. Evidently I had been wrong about Guam being the only island with trees.

Seen from the air, in a chance-ray of the setting sun, shrouded in bands of dark clouds, Wake Island resembled nothing so much as a green horseshoe, covered with thorny scrub. The white scar of the mile-long runway occupied half its southern limb, and a couple of dozen buildings were scattered along the taxiway and hardstand of its northern limb. The shallow lagoon, a paler green, was enclosed westerly only by a stretch of flat tidal reef. Unlike Midway, which lies at the end of a 1200-mile chain of reefs and ledges trending northwesterly from Hawaii, Wake is totally alone in the vast openness of the North Pacific.

The pilot made a complete circuit of the island before coming in to land from the west, and I could see white patches where graders had been at work, scraping sand driven across the runway by wind and waves from the typhoon into piles along the apron. But the devastation only became apparent after we had rolled to a stop and emerged from our aluminum cocoon. The right half of the two-story, wooden terminal building, with the control tower above it, lay in wreckage, hastily shoved aside by bulldozer. The stumps of a dozen spindly palms gave mute testimony to the wind strength. And the windows of every structure visible gaped empty, or were patched with plywood. Pools of water stood everywhere.

At first, there seemed no sign of life. But then a forklift emerged from the open door of a Quonset hut alongside the terminal, with two men riding on a pallet; they commenced offloading the aircraft. Next, a pickup truck came splashing down the road, and two men got out. One of them was Ted Folsom, still in the same outfit I'd last seen him wearing in Hawaii. The other was a small, stout man in shorts, long socks, and a faded aloha shirt.

"Bob Ward," said Folsom, stumbling forward. "Saw your name on the manifest. Thank God you're here. Meet Mr. Mussen, Island Manager."

"Doctor Ward, is it? Howd'ya do," said Mussen, giving me a limp handshake. "Do you have any idea what a crisis your er . . . code machine has precipitated on this island?" I shook my head, but before I could comment, he rushed on, the words spilling out in a torrent . . . "Crisis, yes, a bloody crisis! . . . the damn thing arrived a week ago . . . armed courier . . . insisted on putting it in my safe . . . had to take everything else out . . . sign bloody receipts and promise to guard it night and day with my pistol . . .

only weapon on the bloody island." Mussen sputtered to a pause, and wiped his face with a large handkerchief... "And when the bloody typhoon knocked down the terminal, it destroyed half the files that had been in the safe." He didn't have a British accent; I wondered where he'd picked up his affectation for "bloody".

"I'm very sorry about your safe and the loss of your files," I said. "Perhaps if we went inside and sat down somewhere I could explain our mutual predicament."

Mussen took us upstairs into the undamaged section of the terminal, where he'd established a temporary office across the hall from Operations and Weather. The place was a mess; windows boarded over and boxes of water-stained papers stacked along the hallway. His controversial safe, standing in one corner, looked scarcely large enough to contain Li'l Mollie and her case of instructions and destructions. Outside, I could hear the hum of an auxiliary generator that was evidently supplying temporary power to the building. Seated at his desk, chin supported in on hand, Mussen had obviously been under heavy strain; Folsom didn't look much better.

Within the limits of the security instructions I had received, there was some latitude allowed in discussing emergency procedures with public officials. I explained to Mussen, and to Folsom, who knew scarcely more, that the United States intended to detonate a large atomic device in the Western Pacific later in the month; that everything connected with this test was top secret, and would not be made public, except at the President's discretion; that the measurements conducted at Wake were an essential part of this experiment, and required very limited, but high-priority, message traffic. Hence the requirement for a code encryptor; all teletype traffic was transmitted over telephone cables which, because of the Korean conflict, had largely been preempted by the military. Only coded traffic could assuredly be prioritized to the Pacific Task Force. "So," I concluded, "if you can live with this situation for a month, we should be out of your hair."

"I can live with that," said Mussen, rotating his wedding band with the thumb of his left hand. "I appreciate your confidence and apologize for . . . blowing my top. In reality, this island is just an aircraft gasoline station. We're at the end of the line out here; I rarely get any explanation for the instructions I receive. The safe business was just the last straw." It was very hot and damp in his windowless office; he mopped his face again and stuffed the handkerchief into the pocket of his voluminous shorts. "But, as Mr. Folsom can better explain, there are certain other problems still to be resolved."

I looked at Ted, who had been sitting backwards in his chair all this time, with his arms wrapped around the seatback. "Transportation," he said. "The only practical site for our instrument is four miles away from here, on the other side of the island . . . in the boat basin . . . out beyond the aircraft runway. There's no habitation out there. In fact, now that they've gotten the sand cleared off the runways, there's nobody even working out there! Everybody is living in tents, over on this side. Even the cafeteria is a tent. Mussen's truck is the only utility vehicle still running. So, right now, even if we had the instrument installed and operating, there is no way I could keep an eye on it, regularly, except by walking."

I looked at Mussen, who was twiddling his ring again. "I might get a motor-scooter flown in here for Ted, if you could manage to get us over there and back for a couple of days . . . you know, drop us off with a sandwich and coffee?"

"I think we can manage that . . . might have to send you over in the dump truck." He managed a weak smile.

"OK," I said, jumping up. "Let's get Li'l Mollie out and pulse the system."

I spent that night in a twelve-man tent, with Folsom, and the passengers who had arrived with me that afternoon. During dinner, Ted had given us a rundown of the devastation wrought by the typhoon. To begin with, the wind and huge storm waves had come out of the south, which is normally the protected side of the island under the prevailing northeast trade winds. The wartime Japanese garrison had fortified the island by bulldozing sand and coral rubble into a continuous dyke, 20 feet high, just above the normal high tide level, and digging slit trenches all along its top. The storm waves had removed large sections of the dyke, spreading the material over the airstrip behind it in layers up to four feet thick.

All heavy supplies were brought in by ship, which normally moored to two permanent buoys on the south side, and adjacent to an old reef channel that had been enlarged by dredging. The channel terminated in a dredged basin, blocked off from the interior lagoon by a rubble dam. Ships were unloaded onto lighters, which ran up the channel to the basin, where there was a crane to get the stuff up onto the dock. Typhoon waves 60 feet high simply obliterated this system, which had existed since before the war. They tore out the buoys, filled the channel with rubble, breached the dam, and sank all the lighters. The island was just back to conditions that had existed before man ever set foot there . . . with no means of supply, except by air . . . after the runway was cleared.

Next morning, we procured a length of pipe from the plumbing shop, one of the few buildings to have escaped much damage, and were dumped off at the boat basin by the dump truck . . . just as Deadly Dudley (Mussen) had promised. We found an undamaged section of loading dock, and within two hours had nailed the pipe to the dock timbers, and the recorder was scribbling a muted tide trace, while waiting patiently for the waves from Mike, which would be originating only 460 miles to the south.

We had just finished the sandwiches and canned peaches thoughtfully provided by the harassed Filipino cook, and were preparing to do a little boondocking—the exploration of buried Japanese fortifications, most of them untouched since the war—when Dudley Mussen roared up in his truck and whirled to a stop in a cloud of dust.

"You've gotten a reply to our coded TWX?" I ventured, before he could open his mouth.

"Reply!" he roared, shielding his eyes from the blazing sun. "We've got fifteen bloody replies . . . and more coming in every few minutes. It's our job to service 45 flights a day through here, and we can't afford to have the radiomen tied up like this."

"Looks like the 'system' has discovered Wake has a code address," I said. "Well, we're secured here. Let's go and see what they want."

Once we got Li'l Mollie set up with the code of the day, it took us only about two hours to catch up with the incoming traffic. I had been right; many of the messages were routine inquiries that should have been sent through unclassified channels to FAA, Honolulu. People were just using us as a shortcut to getting quick responses. But there was another group of "INFO" copies to Wake, addressed to military commands in Korea, Japan, and Hawaii. Apparently our code group assignment had appeared erroneously on somebody's master list, since there was no evident reason for sending copies to Wake. Obviously, something had to be done to shut off the information stream.

I fired off a coded message to Sutter St., explaining our dilemma, and stating that we would not decode any further traffic unless proceeded by the code group:

ZZZZZ. I also asked for acknowledgment of our previous request (Folsom's motor scooter) and the present message. Mussen, having long since departed, we locked Li'l Molly and the pistol in the safe, and told the radio operator to buzz us in the FAA bar if our special code came through.

The reply came rather quickly. It read: ZZZZZ YOUR 042022Z AND 051616Z ACK. TRANSPORT EN ROUTE. END. The coded traffic continued all night, but tapered off toward morning. I burned the whole bunch, and that was that!

Monday was my birthday, October 5th. I was three days ahead of schedule, and the weather was lovely. Locals say that, give or take a typhoon every ten years, Wake has the world's best climate: usually between 75 and 85 degrees; 30 inches of rain, evenly divided; and always a cooling trade wind breeze from the northeast at 10-15 knots. I decided to play hooky and go skin diving. Ted was sunburned from yesterday's exposure, so I volunteered to go out to the boat basin and change the recorder chart, which had to be done every 24 hours.

At breakfast, I discovered that there was a salvage crew going to work on the lighters, so I hitched a ride on their truck-crane. Most of the crew were Hawaiians, keen divers, and familiar with local conditions. They worked from 0730 to 1500, without lunch. If all went well, they would take me diving around a famous wreck, the *Suva Maru*, which had been torpedoed early in the war as it attempted to run our blockade of Wake. She was the last supply ship to reach the island, and by the end of the war, 1700 of 2500 survivors had starved to death.

Wake had had three ship lighters before the typhoon, all of them navy Mike Boats: rectangular steel boxes, with a boxlike conning tower aft and a bow door that could be lowered as a ramp. Two of the lighters had sunk at dockside, but the third had been stranded on shingle at the far end of the basin—almost clear of the water. She had a gash in her bottom, but the crew had already ascertained that her screws were undamaged and her diesel engines could be started. Today's objective was to weld a patch over the hole, and lift her with dock-cranes into a cradle, where she could be worked on.

As the crew was wrestling with the lighter, I walked down the boat channel towards its entrance to the sea. To my left was the fuel farm, a dozen huge storage tanks, into which aviation fuel was pumped from tankers, tied up to the mooring buoys. Fortunately, most tanks had been nearly full during the typhoon, and suffered only minor dents from rubble tossed around by the waves. But two empty tanks had been floated right off their foundations and transported half a mile across the open land behind the dike.

I was similarly appalled by the damage to the mouth of the entrance channel. Huge concrete blocks, each weighing several tons, and each with its integral ring-bolt, whereby it had once been carefully placed so as to smoothly armor the channel against wave attack, had been scattered over acres of ground. Somebody would have a bit of work setting things right!

But today, the sea was calm as a lake. I slipped on my fins and faceplate, slid off the reef into crystal water, and paddled straight out. I was suspended over an immense, sandy meadow, gently sloping seaward for about a thousand feet, where it curved downward and plunged out of sight. Half a mile eastward, I could see a ship's bow wedged against the reef at a steep angle, while the stern half was under water . . . probably the *Suva Maru*. With nothing more to see in this wasteland, I swam back, coming presently upon an array of three huge anchors, spread-eagled like a claw. A massive chain from their apex stretched shoreward. One of the ship-moorings, but the buoy was nowhere to be seen. At least the lighter crew would be happy to know that the anchors were intact. Normally, one would have expected these waters to abound in fish, but I saw only a few fleeting shapes. Had the typhoon somehow alarmed them? More probably, it had scoured the reef of food, and the fish had simply moved around to the leeward side of the atoll. It was an eerie landscape.

Meanwhile, back in the basin, the salvage crew was having its jollies. They had got the lighter out and suspended over its cradle, when the truck-crane toppled sideways. Now they were righting it with the another crane, but its boom was bent. Back to the barn for repairs. I told them about the anchors, and the absence of fish. One of them said: "Boy, you lucky shark not deh. No fish, he eat you wikiwiki." They all laughed, and I shivered, inwardly. Ten years later, one of my own diving team was to be severely mauled near that same location.

Back at the tent, I found Ted despondent. His "transport" had arrived. It was a bicycle—a girl's bicycle with a basket on the handlebar. It still had the Sears tag attached. I wondered whose slush fund had been tapped for $26.50. "Cheer up," I said, squeezing his shoulder. "Ten knots, 40 minutes per trip . . . it's a lot better than walking."

He looked at me sourly. "Better get your stuff together. The plane's still on the ground while the crew eats. You're booked out to Guam at 1800."

* * *

Having sent a message ahead, John Knauss met me on arrival at NAS, AGANA, GUAM. The sun was just rising, and I had a vision of trees, and mountains swathed in jungle, as he whisked me in his personal Jeep up the slopes of Mt. Lam Lam to his fancy digs in the Senior Officers BOQ, at COMNAVMARIANAS. We breakfasted on linen, set with silver service. John was obviously already well-adapted to primitive island living. But, he was 'to the manner born'; the only son of a Connecticut banker, Harvard-educated, and smooth spoken; a navy veteran, he would prosper in most any military environment. Why he had chosen science was a mystery, but he went on to become the Dean of Oceanography at an Eastern college, and probably entrances his adoring grandchildren with tales of roughing it on Guam.

After breakfast, we rattled 25 miles over rough roads, through a tunnel of dense greenery, and down into picturesque, uninhabited, Ylig Bay, where his recorder was bolted to a piling, some distance from shore. Of course, he had a dinghy there, in which he was normally rowed out by his driver, who also held an umbrella whilst he changed charts, if it were raining.

And how did he manage all this? "Well, Old Boy, the Navy looks after its own . . . You remembah, ah . . . I went through Hahvahd in the V12 program, and was commissioned during the wah as an aide to Admiral Bennett, the first Chief of Naval Research. In fact, ah . . . that's how I first became interested in oceanography." Sitting there, in his dinghy, in the rain, if he had pulled out a snuff box and offered me a pinch, I shouldn't have been the least surprised.

Having applied for entry to the Pacific Proving Grounds, via Eniwetok, I cooled my heels for two days waiting for a flight. Not altogether wasted, albeit; Guam is a fascinating island. It's the kind of place you'd go to if you wanted to film King Kong. The northern half is surrounded by a barrier reef, with a shallow lagoon inside, from which limestone cliffs rise vertically to a flat plateau about 600 feet above the sea. The cliffs are so festooned with creeping vines as to almost completely conceal the rock beneath. And at their feet is a dazzling array of small pocket beaches, fringed by cocoa palms, and studded with offshore rock mushrooms with leafy crowns.

Most of these beaches are inaccessible, except by boat, and because of military facilities above, most are out-of-bounds to all but mad oceanographers holding Secret clearances. John and I spent the time playing Robinson Crusoe, where no human foot had printed the sand since the war—and perhaps long before. In childhood, most of us dream of such places. Most of us never find them.

* * *

On Friday, 9 October, I sneaked into Eniwetok by the back door; that is, by bumming a ride on a P2V patrol plane that was delivering photo films to JTF-132 headquarters. By this unwitting subterfuge, I escaped a half-day of briefings on security, VD control, radiation safety regulations, etc. At first, Security wanted to send me back to GO, or to JAIL; but an appeal to higher authority brought a stern lecture, a black ID badge, replete with an unflattering full-face photograph, and a film badge to check radiation dosage.

The airport and security office were on Eniwetok Island, the largest of some 38 sandy islets dotting the rim of Eniwetok atoll. The islet also supported acres of tents, housing the 1,200-man army cantonment of TG-132.2, an outdoor movie theater, a softball diamond . . . and no trees. Transportation to adjacent Parry Island, home for us 1,800 civilians, and Headquarters, Joint Task Force 132, was provided by a fleet of tiny L-13 "grasshopper" aircraft, carrying a pilot and three passengers. Our plane took off at 25 knots. Considering that the mean trade wind speed in these parts is about 22 knots, the plane could make very little headway across the atoll, and was limited to flying north and south between these two islands. For longer flights, they used helicopters or DC-3's.

From the air, Parry Island, four miles distant, offered little to commend it over Eniwetok. There was a fenced, central compound, several large buildings, and the whole rimmed by rows of aluminum barracks. To the north, the next island (Japtan) was shrouded in the dark tendrils of a rain squall. Eastward, the surface of the lagoon was cluttered by a vast array of ships and boats, comprising the 5,500-man navy contingent of TG-132.3, while 450 miles to the southeast, the 2,500 air force minions of TG-132.4 shared the limited facilities of Kwajalein Naval Station.

Shortly we entered the squall itself, the sky changing instantly from bright sunlight to somber darkness, while rain of unbelievable intensity hammered the little aircraft. The pilot turned into the wind as we settled toward the short runway, looking out the side window at a flight signalman, and landed, at 5 mph. I sat there for a moment with the door open, waiting for a lull in the downpour.

The pilot said: "might as well run for it. That's Murphy's Second Law . . . It's impossible to stay dry on 'Wetok." So, I ran—and got drenched.

We passengers had no sooner collected in the hutment to await the shuttle bus to the billeting office, when the rain stopped and the sun burst forth. Within seconds, the water had soaked into the crushed coral, and the roadbed was steaming. Aside from the squishing in my shoes, there was little sign of the deluge.

However, the first thing to appear was not the shuttle bus, but a jeep, caparisoned in plastic side curtains, and driven by the ubiquitous Major Davis. "Greetings to the Pacific Proving Grounds," he beamed, jumping out and grabbing my soggy suitcase. Davis, somehow ignoring Murphy's Law, looked as fresh and crisp as ever. "I've come to get you settled in," he said. "You're invited to cocktails and dinner at the Flag Mess . . . in 45 minutes."

"How did you know I would be on that grasshopper?" I asked, as we jounced over the corduroy ruts along Main Street.

"We keep a pretty tight rein on our principals," he replied. "Dr. Knight and Mr. Jensen are arriving tomorrow, but the *Horizon*'s not expected until Tuesday. They've been held up by the typhoon. I understand they took quite a shellacking west of Johnston Island."

That was something I'd never thought of. If Halliwell hadn't forced us to ship the heavy buoy components separately, they could well have been lost overboard in heavy weather. I wondered where the stuff was now. Jensen should have the lading bill. I put the question to Frank. "Could be anywhere in the warehouse area," he said. "We don't do anything by paperwork out here. Your gear should have been color coded by paint before it was shipped. You just wander around and look for it."

We came to Billeting, and I signed my life away for two sheets, a pillowcase, and a threadbare towel. Then we bounced another couple of blocks, and he let me out before Building 131, one of a seemingly infinite row of identical aluminum barracks. "I've got a few more errands to do," he said. "Just ask anybody where the Flag Mess is . . . It's only a couple of hundred yards." As he drove off, I saw another black cloud bearing down. There was a flash of lightning, and the smell of ozone. I could hear the roar of rain on the metal roof as I scuttled inside the open doorway.

The one-story barracks was divided lengthwise by a central hall. There were four rooms at each end, and each contained four double bunks. Centrally, there were washrooms and toilets on one side, and a common area opposite. And all of these spaces were simply divided by head-height partitions, giving way to open common space beneath the gabled roof. There were no doors on the building, nor screens on the windows, which ran continuously along both sides. But the gabled roof overhung the walls by four feet; with metal shutters that could be let down to keep out the rain.

Our TU-7.3 room assignment was at the far end. As I passed through the foyer, there was a poker game in progress . . . five men seated around a sheet of plywood elevated on concrete blocks. They nodded as I went by, but without interrupting their game. The far doorway let directly out onto the beach shingle above the fringing reef. We were at the downwind edge of the atoll, and a fresh breeze blew implacably through the building; salt stalactites from the wind-whipped surf had formed horizontally on the door and window frames. But, with all the wind, the spray, and the rain, the temperature hung near 84 degrees, which was the temperature of the sea, and it would have been oppressively hot inside without it.

I threw my duffle on a lower bunk, stripped off my wet clothes and hung them on the metal bed frame, and went down the hall to shave and shower. It was the end of the day shift, and people were straggling in from work. The poker game had grown considerably; it was penny ante and nickel limit. There was a bottle of scotch on the table, and it was being passed around. I declined the invitation to join, but said I'd be back later. I put on my last clean shirt, new, khaki-drill trousers, wet tennis shoes over dry socks, and ventured forth into the warm, wet air. The Flag Mess was only two blocks up the beach from our barracks, and just across the street from the fenced headquarters compound. There was a large lounge in front, furnished in tropical rattan, and a smaller dining area to one side. But inside, I found only a sprinkling of people, almost all in khaki shorts; the military wore open-necked, short-sleeved khaki shirts, while the civilians favored Hawaiian prints. I recognized General Clarkson and several of his staff.

I spied Ogle in a corner, talking to Jack Clark, waving his bulldog for emphasis. He beckoned me over, and managed to catch the steward's eye to reorder drinks. "Hail, Theseus returns from Crete," he smiled, with a twinkle. "We've been following your peregrinations with interest. Are your sails black or white?"

"Don't jump off the cliff," I said. "Everything's white but my laundry. This is my last clean shirt."

"Rather nifty how you ended your coded traffic problem. Did you know that ZZZZZ is the code preface for: 'Air Attack on the White House'?"

My jaw dropped. "Of course, coming from Wake Island, nobody believed it," he went on, "but it gave the CIA quite a shock. They wondered how you learned it. Anyway, can I take it that all island recorders are operating?"

"Bill is kidding you," said Jack Clark, kindly, ". . . I mean, about the White House code."

"He probably feels safe from all rebuttal in his new sinecure," I jibed. "Who else would send a girl's bicycle to a guy like Ted Folsom? He took it as a personal insult."

"Girl's bicycle?" asked, Ogle, puzzled. "I just suggested Frank Davis send him the quickest, cheapest thing that would get him across five miles of flat island twice a day."

The steward came by ringing a little bell, and we all straggled in to dinner. There were only about fifteen of us at a table set for forty. General Clarkson went to the head of the U-shaped table, and seeing us approaching, suggested I sit at his right. "Major Davis has kept me abreast of your progress, young man," he rumbled, "and I'm most anxious to know the present status of Wake Island. General Wise had a very brief, but pessimistic view of it when he dropped off your man . . . Folsom, was it?"

Astonished at his memory for details, I briefly recounted my impressions. "The biggest job will be dredging the channel and rebuilding the dam, so that ships can be offloaded. Right now, the island is completely dependent upon air supply. I don't think fuel is a problem; the fuel farm is relatively undamaged, and they should be able to bring in tankers as soon as the moorings are re-established."

"So, nothing can be done about that before our test. How about the runway? Any serious damage? You understand, Wake is our first alternate aircraft staging base, in the unlikely event that we should have to evacuate Kwajalein."

"They've cleared the runway of sand, Sir. To the best of my knowledge there is no serious structural damage. But salt water evidently shorted out the underground runway lighting cables. I believe the island manager has requested emergency surface cables, but there is some problem about laying them . . . the cable truck is disabled . . . I'm afraid I don't know the details."

Clarkson thanked me, and turned to his aide: "Frank, we'd better ask General Glantzberg to verify the lighting problem, and see if he can expedite delivery of a cable truck to Wake, if necessary."

And that was that . . . no fuss . . . no muss. Just fly in a cable truck!

The rest of the dinner discussion centered around the weather. According to Ogle's new meteorological advisor, Dr. Brian Mason, the Intertropical Convergence—in effect, the climatic equator—had moved northward earlier than expected this fall, leading to increasingly unsettled weather, and frequent, heavy rain squalls. With the test only three weeks away, these intermittent downpours were having a serious impact on preparations. Back in the ZI, or Zone of the Interior (militareze for Continental U.S.), an inch per hour is considered heavy rain. Out here, we were getting four to six inches per hour. True, the squalls rarely lasted more than an hour, but when it was coming down, everything stopped; all digging; all concrete pouring; all welding; all radio transmission . . . You just got under something . . . and waited.

Worse yet, the experimental conditions under which the test was to be conducted required at least 24 hours of "normally stable" weather, centered on shot time. The test 'window' was November 1-3, as authorized by the incumbent president. The prospects for good weather appeared increasingly gloomy.

Back at the barracks, I found the poker game still in progress. In fact, as I later learned, it never stopped. Working three shifts around the clock, there were always enough people around to keep the game going. Similarly, with beer 10 cents, and Johnny Red $1.25, there was always enough liquor handy. I bought a dollar's worth of chips and played a few hands. Then I checked out by returning my stack and entering the balance in a tattered notebook. Rolled in my single sheet, I thanked providence for a weather bunk, where the sound of wind and surf drowned the strident voices of the players.

Day shift started before dawn; I was roused at 0530 by a single long siren blast, followed by a gravelly voice intoning: "Attention. Attention. This is Mahatma. Today is D-22." I scrambled into my shorts, tee shirt, and tennies, standard wear for the tropics, and followed the crowd through inky darkness to the mess hall.

And there, in two rapidly moving cafeteria lines, stood the most motley collection of humanoids that ever affronted my jaundiced eyes. Short men, tall men, thin men, stout men, clad in garments of every color and description, some shaggy, some trim, some bare and some tattooed, but all burned to the deep bronze that the tropical sun bestows, they moved their trays forwards, slashing, jabbing, and shoveling from a seemingly endless array of food trays.

And what food! Pork chops, lamb chops, beefsteak, sausages, eggs to order, corn bread, black bread, white bread, pies, cheeses, and tall, stainless coffee dispensers, milk dispensers, tea dispensers. Holmes and Narver had long ago discovered that the one way to keep men working under impossible circumstances is to provide endless quantities of good food. And it was all free. No cashiers interrupted the steady flow of food onto trays, trays to tables, and thence into the capacious stomachs of men to whom mealtime was the high point of the day.

Ahead of me, a bearded giant, with arms as big as my thighs, speared eight pork chops onto one plate, and filled another with pancakes, ten high. "Why so much?" I asked. "Can't you come back for more?"

"Don't worry, Buddy. This is just the first course. I'll be back."

We sat down together at the end of a long table with built-in benches, and I watched him plow through three courses, while I toyed with my bacon and scrambled. He was Stan Chambers, heavy equipment operator, ex-cornhusker from Keokuk, Iowa. He had signed a three-year contract with H&N, at $18,000 plus overtime, plus room and board . . . and no income taxes. When it was over, he would go home and buy the farm he lived and worked on. He showed me the photo of his husky wife and the three not-so-little cornhuskers. How few of us, I thought, have everything so beautifully figured out. In La Jolla, it would take half my wages just to buy him breakfast.

A gray, ragged dawn was breaking as I came out of the mess and headed for the administrative compound. More rain, I reflected, proffering my badge to the army guard at the gate, who carefully compared my face to the photograph before handing it back. Task Force

Headquarters occupied a windowless, aluminum building that was partially air-conditioned, for the preservation of records, if not its occupants. It contained offices for members of the headquarters command, as well as office or desk space for leaders of the eleven scientific task units under Task Group 132.1, of which I was one; namely TU-7.3. As it turned out, all of TU-7 (Hazard Evaluation) was in one office. As Deputy Test Director, Bill Ogle shared an office just down the hall with Stan Buriss, Commander TG-132.1.

I had agreed to meet Ogle at 0700, but found him there a half-hour earlier, puffing on his pipe, and scribbling furiously on a yellow pad. "I rarely eat breakfast," he remarked at my inquiry. "There's a coffee machine on duty here 24 hours a day, and that's all I need in the morning. Can I presume from the messages in your basket that everything is functioning on the outer islands?"

"I'm afraid I didn't see them. There was no one in the office. In fact, most of the offices along this hall are empty."

"Well, all these fancy offices were requested months ago for any one who put in a chit. I think you'll find that the program officers are scattered all over the atoll hooking up their experiments, or sitting in their instrument trailers. We do have a weekly get together, Monday mornings at 0800. You should run down Walt MacConnell, though. He's got a bunch of muster papers, etc. for you to sign.

"But the reason I asked you to show up this morning concerns the post-test wave-inundation survey we talked about last August. Remember?" I nodded, and he continued: "I've got a chopper laid on to go up to Boken, near the shot site. It occurred to me that it might be useful for you to come along and mark a chart where you'd like photos taken for pre-test comparisons. You'll be back in plenty of time to meet your people coming in from Kwaj."

"Fine," I said, "Can you get me some binoculars?"

"I'll see what I can do. Meet me at the Helo pad in front of this building at 0930."

The chopper was twenty minutes late; it was the binoculars. The captain of the light carrier, *Rendova*, Admiral Wilkins' flagship, had steadfastly refused to part with either pair of the bridge set; Wilkins had loaned his own pair to Ogle. You couldn't really fault the skipper; such commodities were essentially irreplaceable in present circumstances.

The HL-15 machine carried a pilot and copilot in the cockpit, and a crewman and up to four passengers as cargo. Ogle had arranged for us to sit in the open doorway, wearing May Wests, and strapped to the overhead. We had helmets with intercom communication to the pilot. He had also brought along a clipboard holding a folded chart of the atoll, and a grease pencil for marking photographic locations.

It was my first helicopter flight. There was no sense of vertical motion during liftoff. Instead, the ground seemed suddenly to fade away and shrink in size, as does the image in a zoom lens, and then to tilt crazily as we banked to circle out over the lagoon.

By far the largest object bulking on that dwindling panorama was the two-story cryogenics plant, within which thousands of gallons of deuterium, hydrogen, and nitrogen were compressed and liquefied to fuel and refrigerate Mike's cavernous interior. Nowadays, there are much bigger plants to fuel the giant space rockets. But, prior to Mike, "liquid air" was almost a laboratory curiosity; a means of deep freezing frankfurters so that they could be shattered into bits in high school science classes. And now, this huge plant, and all of its highly specialized machinery, had been designed, built, shipped to the Mid-Pacific, and assembled in nine months—just for this one test!

According to instructions, our pilot stabilized our flight pattern at about 500 feet altitude, and heading northward over the lagoon about 200 yards from the atoll rim. From where we sat, with our feet dangling into space, I could make out every detail of this half-mile strip of coral, curving to the horizon in both directions. The weather had improved somewhat since breakfast; the puffy cloud lines were now separated by patches of brilliant sunlight, that produced corresponding coruscations in the shallow water over the reefs below.

A quarter mile north of Parry Island, and separated from it by the only deep ship channel into Eniwetok Atoll, we came to the islet of Japtan. In the interests of native tradition, and current recreation, Japtan had been preserved as a park, with all natural vegetation undisturbed. And indeed, it was so thick in the central parts that I could not see the ground with binoculars.

For the next six miles, we flew along a continuous stretch of tidal reef, across which shallow water flowed steadily into the lagoon from the impetus of breakers pounding the reef edge from outside. In all of this stretch there were only three small sand islets, each devoid of trees and exhibiting evidence of preparations for the forthcoming test.

The fourth islet on my chart, called Runit, was about the size of Parry, and showed signs of extensive renovation. There was a large, concrete bunker complex, an airstrip, and a tent encampment. A bulldozer and a grader were putting the final touches on a rubble dike, circumscribing the bunker, which itself was covered by about three feet of gravel. At Ogle's request, we circled the area, and landed on the apron beside the airstrip. We jumped out, and Ogle began stuffing tobacco into his pipe. "This is one of our primary instrument stations," he said, walking towards the bunker. "It was also the firing station for **GEORGE** shot of **GREENHOUSE** operation last year. GEORGE was about five miles up the line from here, so everything in between was pretty heavily instrumented. We're using as many of those old stations as possible for Mike, even though it will be seven miles farther away. Anyway, I've asked H&N to throw up this sand dike as further protection against waves, because many of the instruments are below ground. This damn building goes down two stories—right to sea level."

We showed our badges to the ever-present soldiers guarding the access, and entered the bunker through a heavy steel hatch, somewhat resembling the door to a bank vault. Ogle explained that, as a former firing station, the entire building could be hermetically sealed against outside influence.

Inside, the main control room was ablaze with lights, and as crammed with instruments as the cockpit of a modern jet. A dozen scientists and technicians were stringing wires and twiddling controls. Ogle led me to one wall, where two steel pipes arose from the concrete floor and entered a locked steel box. The sign above it read: FIRING CABLE: AUTHORIZED ACCESS ONLY. He tapped the box with his knuckles.

"This is the cable by which the detonation sequencing instructions come from Parry Island to the Mike device," he said. "There are two knife switches inside this box. Each can be padlocked open or shut. The cable comes ashore at seven islands, and enters identical switchboxes. When the firing party comes out in late afternoon on D-1, after the atoll has been evacuated, it will go ashore at every island and lock the switches open. Then, after they have armed the device, they'll come back the same way, checking each piece of cable for continuity, and locking the switches shut. Finally, they'll go aboard the *Estes* and join the rest of the fleet outside the atoll."

"But, I thought you said the device was to be fired from the *Estes* at sea," I reflected.

"It is. The electronic sequence timer on Parry will be initiated by a radio tone-pulse signal from the ship. It's my job to push that button."

"What if you change your mind after you've pushed the button?"

"I've got another button. I can stop the firing command; but, I can't restart it. Considering our short time window, we'd probably have to abort the test."

"And why are you telling me all this?"

"Just for backup. The sequence timer runs for fifteen minutes; it not only fires the device, but it also starts a huge battery of instruments. Some of these instruments are considered essential, and can stop the test themselves if they should fail. You'll be standing beside me, in radio communication with the *Horizon*. If you don't get a final OK from the *Horizon* that the seamount recorders are working by the time we start the countdown, we may want to stop the test."

We had coffee in the mess tent on Runit, and I learned that the camp had supported 250 people for the past six months, although it was now down to three dozen or so. The tents were not worth salvaging, and would probably be incinerated by the Mike fireball, only 12 miles away.

Flying on around the atoll, we passed some seventeen small islets, of which the southern half were largely denuded of vegetation, and also considered uninhabitable because of lingering radiation from the GEORGE test 18 months previously. At the end of the string, we made a brief stop at Enjebi, about a mile square, and supporting an abundant growth of palm trees. Here another dike had been built around an instrument bunker, but I was dubious of its survival from wave action only three miles from the shot point.

Our last stop, and the focus of Ogle's attention, was the instrument complex associated with the shot site itself. As I later learned, most of this instrumentation was designed to take a quick, early peek at various aspects of the Mike explosion. This involved special cameras that could shoot a million frames per second, but which only ran for a thousandth of a second, etc.

But the drawings Jeff and I had examined many months ago hardly prepared me for the incongruous appearance of the complex as we approached it from the air. The Mike device was housed within a six-story metal box, sitting dead-center of Eluklab islet, a flat, treeless expanse of coral as big as the Rose Bowl. Eluklab, in turn, was joined to its twin neighbor, Bogen islet, by a two-mile causeway of crushed rubble. And supported above this causeway on concrete piles was the eight-foot-square plywood tunnel described in the Op plan. It connected the Mike housing with a four-story concrete bunker in the center of Bogen, which housed the Gamma ray detectors.

Halfway along the causeway, and somewhat to one side, were the remains of a third island, Teiteiripucci, which had evidently supplied the construction material. This last island also supported a tent encampment for 500 workers, vehicle parking, and a loading ramp extending into the lagoon. An LCU was parked at the ramp, in the process of offloading two large tractor-trailers. "We're just in time," commented Ogle, peering out the chopper door. "They're about to commence the third practice fueling of Mike. If we land right now, we should be able to beat them to the punch."

We set down on a pad at the side of the building, and walked around in front, where doors forty feet high had been rolled up. Several men were waiting for the fueling trucks to arrive. "Meet Harold Agnew," said Ogle, pumping the hand of a tall, thickset man of pleasant countenance. "He's Mike's chief cook and bottle washer . . . probably the only man out here who knows every nut and bolt."

"I take it this isn't the production model," I said, gazing up at the monstrous structure looming above us. More than anything else, Mike reminded me of a locomotive boiler, up on end, with dozens of tubes and pipes running in every direction from his cylindrical midsection.

"No," laughed Agnew, "Mike's one of a kind. Unless a lot of us have guessed wrong, we'll probably never build another."

"Don't tell the air force that," chuckled Ogle. "They're already designing a bomber that will carry Mike, and cryogenic tankers to fly liquid hydrogen and nitrogen all over the world. OK if I check on some shroud fittings that should have been installed this week?"

"Sure," responded Agnew "Just as long as your whirligig is off the pad when the fuel trucks arrive. They hate dust . . . and this is a timed exercise."

While Ogle was gone, I mentioned my early engineering training, and said I could well appreciate his problems designing a complicated metallic structure that could withstand the thermal shock of being filled with liquid hydrogen at 450 degrees below zero. Even at 40-below, steel becomes brittle as glass.

"We've had our moments," he agreed. "But out here the humidity is so high we've had to evacuate the system before filling, to prevent frozen moisture from plugging the valves. The first fill took four days. Now, we can do it in two . . . and keep her full and ready to go for 24 hours, by topping off every few hours as the gases boil away. All liquid levels can be monitored both here and in the Runit bunker. If they haven't changed by the time we get back there, we'll have to assume things are AOK when we fire Mike from the *Estes* three hours later."

Agnew walked out to meet the first of the giant trucks, bearing its 500-gallon thermos bottle of liquefied gas, fuming and sweating in the warm, moist air. I stood well back, gazing at the monstrous apparition; some chance arrangement of appurtenances gave Mike the appearance of a malevolent Baal, gazing from his steel temple over the placid lagoon; a miraculous contrivance of the human brain, ready at the touch of a remote button to transform himself into a supernova, hotter than the sun, in which the very elements are sundered and reborn, as they were during the creation of the universe.

Airborne again, Ogle directed my attention to a white line across the islet just east of the Cab, as Mike's house was named. "That's Jeff's line of wells," he said. "They're cased in five-inch pipe down to sea level. If you're over this way in the *Horizon*, you can go ashore at the camp and request a vehicle to drive out here. Otherwise, there are shuttle flights morning and afternoon from Parry. We'll stop at the camp for lunch, and then head back."

Like Runit, Teiteiripucci camp was now nearly abandoned. However, I could see a crew of men with a large truck, furiously handing up and nailing aluminum panels on the roof of the wooden box-tunnel. "Rain leaks," commented Ogle, noting my interest. "That remarkable construct is the brainchild of Ernie Krause. It was supposed to be a 'quick and easy' experiment to monitor prompt gamma emission. The gamma pulse is all over long before the fireball arrives. The problem is to record it from far enough away that the bunker can survive the fireball, but not so far that they are absorbed by the atmosphere.

"Well, Boken was as far as we could go without running out of real estate, so, the simple-minded solution was to build this wooden tunnel and fill it with helium, which has a very low gamma absorption." Ogle rolled his paper napkin into a ball and made a perfect two-cushion shot into the corner basket. Then he got out his pipe case and began to fill it.

"The idea was to contain the helium in giant, plastic baggies that just fit inside the box, and to inflate them one at a time, beginning about October first." He lighted up, and looked off into space. "Anyway, they finished the bunkers in August. They finished the box in September. But they've run into some problems. The plywood was rough, and nails were puncturing the baggies. So, they lined the box with building paper. But the roof leaked, and the paper wasn't waterproof. Now, they've flown out 6,000 sheets of aluminum roofing to stop the leaks . . . but, at the present rate of inflation, the baggies won't be ready until D-1 . . . assuming no further problems." He sighed, and got up to carry his tray to the dishwasher.

"You make it sound as if you were in some way responsible," I said.

"I am. The wooden box was my idea."

The rest of the trip was as uneventful as Ogle was uncommunicative; I couldn't tell whether it was concern about the Krause box or the telephone call he had received during lunch. It took the better part of an hour to circumnavigate the eastern half of the atoll, and there was one stretch of five miles broken only by a single, lonely islet. At the southern edge of the atoll, there were five more islets, plentifully wooded, and then a four-mile stretch of deeper reef, the South Pass, before we arrived back at Eniwetok and Parry Islands. In all, the 70 miles of reef enclosed 250 square miles of water—an inland lake in the middle of the ocean, impossible to see across, even from our cruise altitude of 500 feet.

We were met by an anxious crew of scientific types. Ogle excused himself and huddled with them in his office, while I went off to track down Walt MacConnell. I found him, strangely enough, at his desk in our TU-7 office, drinking coffee and popping peanuts, while studying a thick report.

"Heard you were here yesterday," he said, pumping my hand. "These two desks are for you and Jeff Knight. Got quite a load of mail." He opened a filing cabinet and drew out several packs of letters, tied with string, and a sheaf of teletype messages. "All the TU-7 mail is brought over here, so don't bother waiting in line at the mail room."

I sat down and went through the TWXs first. The top one was from the *Horizon*; she was having injector problems and running slow; ETA Eniwetok 15 October—three days late. She anticipated one or two days for engine overhaul and trials. Obviously, we would have to find an M-boat or something else to set the turtle fairings in the meantime.

The remaining messages were from the island stations. Each read like a weather report, giving coded wind and wave height information. Sent on a daily basis, the wave data we sought on D Day could be incorporated without novelty. The message receipt time was a test of transmission reliability. Everything was running smoothly, except that there were no messages from Midway. Of all places, I would have thought Midway the most reliable. On Walt's advisement, I walked next door to the communications building and fired off a TWX to Ralph Myers requesting immediate acknowledgement. I was told not to expect a reply before morning, so I went back to the office and began to sort the mail.

Most of it was for the *Horizon*—but there were six letters from Suzie. As I opened the first, I heard the patter of an approaching squall. "I better get back to the barracks to meet my guys when they come in," I told Walt, stuffing the letters into my pocket. "But tomorrow morning I'm going to need a little help rounding up these items." I handed him a list, upon which I had scribbled: Jeep, forklift, truck (2-ton), M-boat (3-days), workshop (12'x20') with 8-ft bench. "Can do?"

"I can loan you my jeep and an expeditor," he said, squinting at my list through the bottom of his bifocals. "That should get you started. But we'll have to put in a chit for the M-boat . . . probably Monday before you get it."

"Great," I said, then: "Where's the laundry? I'm totally out of clean clothes."

"Don't bother. They take a week and mangle things. There's a commissary next to the mess hall, where you can buy soap, and a free coin-op just around the corner. It's a waste of time trying to dry anything out here."

I made the commissary before the deluge, bought soap, six-packs of undershorts, T-shirts, and a plastic raincoat in which I sallied back to the barracks undeterred by the elements. Having dumped these acquisitions on my bunk, I maneuvered one of the poker gang into parting with a bottle of Johnny Red, since the liquor locker was only open Tuesdays from 1300-1500. A tepid (solar-heated) shower,

IVY-MIKE 271

dry undies, and a snort of the Red having brightened the spirit considerably, I had just settled into the bunk to savor Suzie's salutations, when in wandered Jeff and Jack Jensen, soaked to the skin.

"Soldiers of Scripps, I salute you!" I shouted above the roar of the rain, springing up and clutching my fist against my breast. "Jeffrey, you've been here before. Didn't they tell you about raincoats?"

"Must have been the dry season," grinned Jeff. "I don't remember anything like this."

"If this is the tropics, you can have my share," grunted Jensen, fishing a soggy pack of cigarettes from his breast pocket. He threw them on the bed, and fumbled in his duffle bag, extracting first their linen, and then a crumpled carton of Luckies. "At least the sheets are dry," he muttered, opening a fresh pack and lighting up. "Phooee! Seems like we've been setting on planes for four solid days."

"We saw Ray Davis at Johnston," said Jeff. "In fact, we had a pleasant evening with him and his new girl friend . . . at the Officers Club. He seems to have adjusted nicely to island living."

"Girl friend?"

"The Colonel's secretary," said Jensen. "Civil Service . . . lives with the school teacher. "She's a real knockout . . . keeps the whole base humming."

"Sonafabitch." I said, recalling my own social peregrinations at Los Alamos. "Well, as long as he does his job, I couldn't care less where he spends his spare time. Why don't you guys shower and put on dry clothes? Then we can splice the main brace before we go for chow. That's one outstanding thing about this island . . . the food."

MacConnell was as good as his word. By the time we showed up outside the HQ compound, Sunday morning, his Jeep was waiting, with a wizened, little H&N clerk named Sammy. Jensen had misplaced the cargo ship's manifest, but it didn't take long to spot the big steel spheres for the seamount moorings lying within a fenced area behind the H&N warehouse. Fortunately everything else was nearby, except for a couple of boxes containing our diving compressor, tanks, weights, and hand tools. These we found in the warehouse itself. Jeff's tide-well recorders were still on the *Horizon*, and not due in until Thursday.

Sammy also found us an unused office in the warehouse containing a desk and a telephone. I called MacConnell, who said we could have an M-boat plus three crewmen for three days, beginning Tuesday. Would that do? We agreed that it would take us that long to check out all our diving gear and muscle everything down to the dock. By lunchtime, Sammy had found us a workbench, a forklift, and a truck.

Placing 800-lb slabs of lead on the bottom of Eniwetok lagoon in a rainstorm is not a romantic job. Armchair travelers who are enraptured by the coral islands of the South Seas, the kaleidoscopic array of flora and fauna that enliven the pages of the *National Geographic*, or the televised adventures of Jacques Cousteau, should experience the joy of sitting in the bottom of a roofless steel box-boat, pounding through choppy whitecaps, while the wind hurls gobbets of rain horizontally, meanwhile attempting to wriggle into clammy wetsuits and all of the manifold paraphernalia that permits a shivering, naked, male access to an environment where he clearly does not belong.

Our scenario called for placing six turtle fairings at two-mile intervals on a line between the Mike Cab and the Eniwetok air-control tower, being guided into position by the traffic-control radar. Once in position, Jack and I would get in the water, while the winch man would hoist the fairing over the side and lower away. We would ride it down and make sure it settled flat on the bottom, cast off the lift bridle, affix the coiled float line, and follow our bubbles back to the surface. The water was warm, and very clear. But from the bottom, at 180 feet, we could only barely make out the shadow of the M-boat hovering above. When the *Horizon* arrived with the recorder packages, we would swim them down and pop them into place in the fairings. We hoped to recover them the same way after the lagoon was cleared for re-entry. These records that would tell us how the explosion-wave characteristics varied with distance across the lagoon.

But, no matter what the travel guides say, deep diving is exhausting work. And between dives, we sat shivering in the rain, seeing tantalizing patches of blessed sunshine that never seemed to cross our path. It was strange to be so near the equator, shivering uncontrollably, fingers turning to prunes, and longing for any means of getting dry and warm. The fairing installation took two long days, and even the boat crew heaved a sigh of relief when we pulled up anchor for the last time and headed back to the barn.

That evening, while Jeff and Jack had joined the poker session, I settled in to reread Suzie's correspondence. Jeff had turned out to be a poker fanatic; he knew all the odds and gambits, and seldom quit a loser.

Lacking any worthy tennis opponent, Suzie had discovered a stable down near Pojoaque, 20 miles east of Los Alamos, and reverted to horseback riding. She had grown quite close to Mona, and they shared many evenings together, but the dearth of male acquaintances was beginning to exact a toll. "I guess I'm a one-man woman," she wrote. "When you're not around, I seem to function on one cylinder . . . ." About this time, I must have dozed off, to be awakened rudely by the breakfast siren, Suzie's letters scattered all over the bed. I can recommend scuba diving to anyone afflicted with insomnia!

The *Horizon* crawled through the deep channel early next morning, Thursday, 15 October, and by prearrangement tied up at the H&N dock where we had stockpiled the seamount mooring gear. We were all down to meet her, but before we could even make verbal contact, a bus appeared and shuttled the crew off to be briefed and badged.

The *Hor* had taken quite a pasting from the storm. She had a bridge window boarded up, and the starboard hydrographic winch had been dislodged from its mount; it was chained to the bulkhead to prevent further motion. Both would have to be repaired before going to sea again. But the most obvious attrition was to her cosmetic appearance; what had been white, streaked with rust at the start of the voyage, had now been curiously camouflaged by large areas of navy gray and red rust-primer, where her crew had striven futilely to stem the inroads of salt and wind.

"Where's Henry?" I asked as Bascom spied me coming aboard. He looked beleaguered and exhausted, with a week's growth of whiskers.

"He got off in Hawaii to confer with Roger. The *Baird's* cable still hasn't been shipped. It looks like she'll be stuck there until after the test. Henry should fly in any time now. Lucky bastard; we've had a mean trip."

We went aboard and foraged around the after hold until we found all the goodies we had put aboard. Thanks to Charlie Black's foresight, everything was accessible and with no evidence of damage. We could move it all into our workshop for checkout, so that the *Hor* would be free to start the seismic profiling as soon as she had been patched up.

Back on deck, we saw Walt MacConnell drive up in his jeep with a brisk, young army type, whom he introduced as Captain Max Dunbar, member of his special radiation safety team. "Because of the *Horizon*'s unique station assignment northeast of the atoll during the test," he said, "we'd like to put Captain Dunbar aboard her as radsafe officer during the exercise. He'll have special monitoring equipment, and will be able to report directly to us in Flag Operations in case of any contamination. Since we'll know where the cloud is going, we can vector the *Horizon* to her safest sailing course."

"I'm sure there's plenty of room aboard, Captain," said Jeff. "What will you need from us?"

"Just some dry bench space, and intercom communication to the bridge," replied Dunbar. "If it's OK, I'd like to mount the sensor on the bridge roof, and run a cable down to my equipment."

"Fine," said Jeff, and took him down below to work things out.

Because Walt wanted to see the ship as well, I borrowed his jeep and whipped over to the compound to get the ship's mail. On the way, I stopped at Communications; they had received no response from my latest TWX to Midway. I walked over to Headquarters and caught Ogle between meetings. He said he would look into the problem, and invited Jeff and me to dinner at the Flag Mess. "I'm going back to the ZI for a few days," he said. "If you need help with the *Horizon*, get in touch with Olaf Anderson. Now that the big construction push is over, he's got men sitting on their thumbs, waiting to be evacuated . . . no pun intended."

I got back to the ship just in time to meet the crew, straggling down from the mess hall. Harry Hewlitt, skipper of the *Horizon*, patted his ample midsection. "Not that our food is that bad," he grinned, "but a fresh salad bar and unlimited sirloin steak works wonders after a bumpy sea voyage." I told him about the H&N facilities here, which he allowed would be quite welcome. Except for Heztel, whom we would need for going over the recorders, there was no qualified welder on board.

And so, by mid afternoon, the *Hor* was swarming with workers. Our recorders had been moved into the warehouse lab, and the crew had transferred temporarily to our barracks. Even the weather had eased up, and what had loomed as three or four days of repairs bid fair to be completed in two.

About dusk, Jeff and I walked back to the barracks; work on the ship would continue till midnight. We found that the ship's crew had discovered the floating poker game, and were into it, hands and feet. They had somehow also gained access to the commissary and bought cases of beer, so that a merry mood prevailed, that showed promise of waxing as the evening wore on.

We showered and changed, and ambled down to the Flag Mess, stopping by the compound to check my mail. There, in my basket, were all the missing Midway TWX's, together with a note of apology from COMCGSTAMIDWAY. Communications were established, but with no explanation. When we got to the Mess, I asked Ogle how he did it, and got his usual twinkle: "Sometimes, you have to start at the top." It seemed that the Air Force was conducting an emergency fly-through of fighter aircraft bound for Korea. In the interests of secrecy, they had preempted all Midway communications, except for SAR (Search and Rescue) emergencies. Somehow, Ogle had managed to break the logjam.

Tonight, the Mess was filled to capacity; I recognized most of the task unit commanders of TG-132.1, as well as chief officers and staff of the other task groups. After the dinner bell had rung and we were all seated, Admiral Wilkins announced that tonight's meeting had been called to finalize atoll evacuation schedules. "Bill Ogle and I are off again to Washington tomorrow to try to head off an invasion of VIP observers. We were prepared for ten, but they want to send 120 or so, and we're already hot bunking quite a few crewmen. Hopefully, they will settle for 20 or less.

"Meanwhile, I want to call your attention to the latest revisions of our 15 August Evacuation Plan, which will be posted in the compound tomorrow. Principally because of adverse weather, we are about one week late in most categories. To expedite equipment removal from the outer islands, the navy boat pool will be on 24-hour duty, as of today. We will hold an evacuation drill on D-7; every individual must be accounted for by 1500 hours, but only select personnel will be evacuated during the drill. The muster list will be posted with the evacuation bill. Any questions?"

Having no one to muster but myself, I fell to admiring the menu that graced each place setting. It consisted of a typed paper insert within a cardboard folder, round the border of which a dozen pin-up girls cavorted in scanty costumes. "Which one would you like tonight?" I asked of Ogle, as the steward came by to take our orders.

"I rather fancy Marie Wilson," he chuckled, twirling the last of his martini by the stem. "Actually, though, this menu has an interesting history. The folder dates from GREENHOUSE operation, although the menu is changed daily. Last August, with the big buildup, the army sent over a new chaplain, who took immediate umbrage at inflaming the minds of our country's finest. So he asked General Clarkson if the cuties might be dispensed with—at least on the Sabbath. Clarkson said: 'Sure. Go speak to the cook,'" Ogle gave his order and surrendered his menu to the steward. Then he filled his pipe and lighted it, savoring our attention. "Well, the chaplain went in to see the cook—who is Chinese and only passably fluent in English—and came back quite pleased with his minor contribution to righteousness and decency. Next Sunday, he came to dinner, beaming, and opened his folder. There were all the dancing girls as usual—and, in place of the menu, was a handwritten note: At Chaplain request, there is no menu today."

On Saturday, D-15, the *Horizon* was declared shipshape, and Jeff took her out to run seismic profiles across the atoll rim to determine its subsurface structure. On a line through the shot point on Eleuglab Island, they steamed straight out, towing a hydrophone to detect small explosions being set off by a launch inside the lagoon. Afterwards, they surveyed the seamounts Eddy and Freddy, 30 and 75 miles to the northeast, to insure they were satisfactory for the moored wave recorders. It was too rough to test the taut-wire mooring procedure on the sea mounts, but, by the time they returned Sunday afternoon, Jeff had worked up the seismic data.

"Just like Bikini," he told me at dinner, "the lava substrate is 4,000 feet down, with a coral cap all the way to the surface. No overhangs, no signs of rifts; 'looks as if our 'landslide' conjecture was unfounded. Unless Mike's crater breaks the rim, we have only air blast to contend with."

Monday (D-13), Jeff flew off in a chopper to check his tide-well recorders, while the Bobbsey Twins and I took the *Horizon* back across the lagoon to install Bascom's turtle recorders in their lead fairings. Bounce-diving in pairs, the three of us completed the whole job in one day. Diving in the rain isn't so bad, if you've got a warm place to dry off. It was also comforting to have a ship as large as the *Hor* overhead, so as not to risk being run down by the steady stream of LCU's hauling vehicles and equipment back from the northern islets to base camp.

Jeff returned from Eluklab with his well records Tuesday afternoon, and spread them out on my desk. "It's incredible," he exclaimed, as near to animation as I'd ever seen him. "There is absolutely no difference in the tide phase across the atoll rim. The water must flow through the coral basement like a sponge—even though the reef is more than a mile wide at the shot site!"

"Funny," I said. "It seems so solid on the surface. There must be 100 tons of steel sitting on the Mike slab."

"It is fairly solid . . . on top, although you'll notice that the rain soaks right through. But underneath, it's shot full of big caves and cracks. I'll bet that fish can swim right through it. It's just like I thought it would be . . . like crackerjack."

"So, our little wave experiment might not be so far off," I said. "Henry Engels is due in on Friday. I'll have to be here to show him the ropes. As soon as he gets checked out and you've loaded all the seamount mooring stuff, the *Hor* can take off to install it—and stand by for the test.

"Hell's Bells, this may be our last evening together. Why don't we wander over to the Flag Mess. I'll treat you to the drink of your choice. Yesterday they were featuring strawberry daiquiris."

"I thought the Mess was invitational."

"It is . . . But I'm a member now . . . Perks of being Commander, TU-7.3."

"Oh, Brother. While I'm out there sweating my balls off on the *Horizon*, you're going to be sitting around the Mess drinking daiquiris?"

"Temper, Temper," I laughed, opening the file cabinet and withdrawing a bulky packet of letters. "Don't forget the ship's mail."

Ogle came back on Thursday and called me in. "Among other things we learned in Washington," he began, "Los Alamos now places relatively little credence on Teller's 100-megaton estimate for Mike, but 20 or 30 still isn't out of the question. So, on my recommendation, President Truman has OK'd a general tsunami warning, through regular channels in the event that we think Mike has produced potentially dangerous waves." He paused to let this sink in, and then continued. "All we have to do now is to decide what is meant by 'dangerous', and set up an appropriate verbal code that the *Horizon* can transmit in the clear after they have looked at the tapes from your seamount recorders. Then the task force will alert the Tsunami Warning Service, and have them announce an appropriate 'earthquake'.

"With the AEC's blessing, I stopped by their headquarters in Ewa, Hawaii on the way back, and prepped them on how to respond."

My mouth moved, as if to say "WOW", but nothing came out. I suppose that this was the first time I had come to face with the absolute truth of the whole operation. Until now, it had seemed more like the game of chess in Alice In Wonderland, where real people moved from square to square in purposeful, but aimless, patterns. Suddenly, I was required to make a decision that would have enormous impact on the lives of others . . . thousands of lives . . . no matter what the outcome. I must have stared at Ogle for some time, before I managed: "Henry Engels is coming in tomorrow. Could we get together with you Saturday and work something out?"

"I was going to suggest that," he said, kindly, apparently aware of my quandary. "Perhaps it might be helpful if we took him out to meet Admiral Wilkins, and to see the command and firing stations firsthand before we talk."

Henry Engels arrived at Eniwetok Island at 1430 Friday (D-9). By prearrangement, Ogle and I were there to meet him, carrying an umbrella. As he stepped off the air taxi, clad in lederhosen and knee socks, and carrying a tattered suitcase., the afternoon downpour came down with a rush.

"My word," he exclaimed, "I've never seen such rain. How can anyone work here?"

"Just wait an hour, I laughed, "and the sun will be beating down."

Ogle had explained that because he was a senior scientist and would be spending only one or two nights ashore, Henry would be given the full treatment and be billeted in VIP quarters at the Flag Mess. His badge having been prepared in advance, other formalities were dispensed with, we whisked him to his quarters for a quick shower.

"Dinner's at 5:30." I said as he emerged dripping. "I can come back if you'd like a quick nap, or take you to the Mess for a martini."

"Martini, of course," exclaimed Henry, "How are things going out here? I haven't heard a word since leaving La Jolla three weeks ago."

"Everything's right on track," I said. "You'll have two days to see the sights before the *Horizon* leaves to install the seamount moorings. Then she'll stand by for the test."

Ogle joined us for drinks, but we dined alone, since it was obvious that Henry was nodding. Next morning, after an early breakfast, we jumped into a waiting helicopter and were transported to the carrier *Rendova*, fleet flagship, and headquarters for early re-entry and radiation control. The *Rendova* (CVE-114) was one of those ingenious wartime hermaphrodites resulting from sawing off the superstructure of a heavy cruiser, and replacing it with a 600-ft flight deck. Although she had earlier ferried the fifteen Air sample jets to Kwajalein, she now carried only a small mix of utility aircraft and helicopters.

We were met by the executive officer, CDR Kim Fletcher, who showed us, first, the radiation control and contamination station, where the early survey aircraft would be washed down and personnel monitored. Then we were taken below to the CIC room, from which all fleet operations would be controlled. Here, Henry was introduced to Admiral Wilkins, who apologized that problems with evacuation planning would prevent his joining us for dinner. As we climbed the ladder topside, Henry stifled a yawn and confided to me that he had slept poorly, and would much rather be sipping a martini in the mess than flitting about the fleet.

We next flew to the USS *Estes* (AGC-4), amphibious command ship, Headquarters for JTF-132 (afloat), and scientific and technical nerve center for the exercise. No slouch for size (460 ft., 14,400 tons), the *Estes* was relatively unarmored, and carried a helipad astern. In keeping with her control and communications functions, her superstructure carried a veritable forest of antennas, some fixed, some scanning back and forth, and one continuously rotating.

Below decks, the *Estes* was ideally suited for this type of operation. There was a large briefing room, with convenient office space for each task group commander and his staff. The briefing room also doubled as the Combat Information Center (CIC), having at one end a large panel, upon which charts could be displayed, and magnetic markers deployed to depict tactical situations. For present purposes, the panel bore a chart of the Marshall Islands, upon which a spider web grid of circles and radial lines was centered on the Mike site, on the northern rim of Eniwetok Atoll.

On the next deck above were the Control room, flanked by Communications and Weather. The "Brain" room, as Control was called, contained an array of oscilloscopes and communications hardware by which remote aspects of Mike's behavior could be monitored.

Ogle, sensing Henry's impatience, showed us the Mike firing station, and briefly elaborated the countdown and firing sequence. He explained that I would be standing there beside him, in direct radio communication with Henry aboard the *Horizon*.

"I have just returned from Washington," he said, quietly, reaching for his pipe pouch. "President Truman has approved the revised Ivy Operation Plan, including the recommendation that the United States and other vulnerable Pacific Rim countries receive advance warning in the event of a potentially dangerous tsunami. So, you see, whether or not we activate the Warning System ultimately boils down to your interpretation of the seamount records." He fixed Henry with his intense brown eyes as he packed his pipe.

"Aha," said Henry, thoughtfully. "You know, we did some small-scale experiments that suggest the wave effect is not significant unless the explosion crater breaches into the water . . . I'm afraid I've been under the impression that breaching is rather unlikely . . . Am I wrong?"

"Unlikely? Yes. Certainly? No. It's not a probability we can ignore. In fact, most of our revised operation plan is based on the assumption that Mike might have an abnormally high yield."

"Aha," said Henry. "Perhaps I should review my notes. What type of response would you like?"

"Some sort of number code . . . You know, scale of 1-5 . . . with a recommended action for each number." Ogle glanced at his watch; then winked at me. "If we head back right now, we should have time for two martinis before dinner."

By noon Saturday (D-8), Henry and I had worked out the following codex, wherein, even now—thirty five years later, the corresponding wave properties have been omitted for security reasons:

CODE	WAVES	ACTION
1.	Undetectable	None
2.	Small	None
3.	Moderate	Await Wake Island Report
4.	Large	Issue Conditional Alert
5.	Very Large	Full Tsunami Warning

Ogle reviewed our code with some interest, and suggested we destroy all notes and calculations, as well as the original codex, once the test was over. "At this point, the results are conjectural, and are easily reproduced," he said. "To retain material—even in a classified file—that links the administration with the deliberate risk of producing a tsunami might prove embarrassing."

* * *

Monday 24 October, 1952. The siren blasted at 0530, and Mahatma commenced a protracted litany: "Attention. Attention. Today is D-7. There will be a test rehearsal of approximately 24 hours duration, beginning at 1530 hours today. Every person in the Forward Area will muster at his assigned station, or report to his task unit commander by 1500 hours. Fleet embarkation transport will depart the personnel pier at 15-minute intervals, beginning at 0700 hours. For further information, call extension 400. May God have mercy on our souls!"

Having been duly forewarned, I rolled out of my bunk, shaved and showered, grabbed a hasty breakfast, and jogged down to where the *Horizon* was berthed. Although it had rained heavily during the night, rays of early sunlight were now sneaking between the ragged clouds. Evidently the weather people had picked a good day for the rehearsal; communications were always screwed up by lightning, and the air-sampling program required good visibility and freedom from icing conditions at high altitude.

There was not much activity aboard the *Hor*, although I found Harry Hewitt and Al Hopkins, the cook, having coffee in the galley. Most of the crew had been up until midnight hoisting the seamount gear aboard and securing it for sea. "This is Jeff Knight's show," I told Harry. "I really just came down to say goodbye and wish you luck, in case we don't make connections after the test."

There was a squeal of brakes on the dock, and Walt MacConnell bounded up the gangway, followed by Henry Engels and crisp Captain Dunbar. "Mail Call," thundered MacConnell, tossing a fat packet onto the table. "Where the hell is everybody?"

"Nobody heah but us chickens," growled Jeff, stumbling through the hatchway clad in nothing but skivvies. "Hi, Henry, Walt. I presume you guys had plenty of sleep last night." He sat down, vigorously scratching his tousled mop of black hair, and gratefully accepted the steaming cup Al set before him. Hearing voices, Henry, who had been out on deck, also poked his head through the hatchway. "Harry, isn't the *Horizon* a mess . . . all the rust . . . and different paint colors?"

"Well," said Harry, a little embarrassed, "You know how it is. We keep daubing red primer on the rust spots to keep 'em from spreading. Then, in Honolulu, I bummed five gallons of grey from the navy. Mechanically, though, she's in good shape." He sighed, and pulled a handkerchief from his pocked to wipe his glasses. Then he looked back at Henry and spread his big hands. "If you want to know the truth, white is not my favorite color for a research vessel. What this bucket needs is a complete scrape and paint . . . from truck to keel."

"I know", said Henry, also embarrassed. "The Regents have denied our request for money to paint the ships every year since we got them from the navy. I wish Roger could bring a little more pressure to bear" . . . His voice trailed off, and I felt a stab of empathy for Hewitt. A shipmaster's vessel is his life. To see her gradually degraded, particularly in the eyes of the navy, which now surrounded us, was tantamount to a personal affront.

By way of distraction, I offered to show Henry the seamount mooring gear, while Jeff had breakfast. He was somewhat disconcerted by the great piles of rope, cable, train-car wheels, and buoys lashed down on the *Hor's* broad, open afterdeck, with its giant winch and tall, derrick-like, A-frame at the stern, by which gear could be lowered, piecemeal into the sea. "All this stuff . . . just to measure the water pressure 200 meters below the surface," he murmured. "I'm happy to be a theoretician, who needs only a pencil and paper."

Out on deck, we examined one of the data recorders, upon whose paper scroll a pen would trace in red ink a line representing the oscillations of the sea surface, transmitted from its submerged buoy to the surface raft by its cable tether. "The paper speed is three inches per hour," I explained, "and the wave scale is 0-10 ft. or 0-100 ft., depending on how this switch is thrown. As you may recall, the stations will be about 30 and 75 miles from Ground Zero. I suppose you'll be standing by the more distant station . . . just to give yourselves more leg room. Even though the winds are supposed to be blowing the stuff the other way, the initial expansion of the mushroom cloud may extend out this far."

Henry looked at me, solemnly, his thick glasses giving him the appearance of a barn owl. "What do we do, if we can't outrun the fallout?"

"You've got a rad-safe expert, Captain Dunbar, to monitor the level of radioactivity on board, and an excellent wash-down system. Meanwhile, the skipper will close all outside openings, and take the quickest escape route."

"Let's hope it doesn't come to that," he muttered. "I should hate to commence a four-month expedition on a radioactive ship."

I bade them all farewell, and rode back to lunch at the Flag Mess with Walt MacConnell, where we were joined by Brian Mason, Ogle's tropical weather expert. There was a copy of the evacuation bill lying beside each placemat.

While everyone on the island would be mustered this afternoon, today's rehearsal was intended primarily as an instrumentation and communications test. Although the Air Command at Kwajalein would be going through its first complete cloud-penetration shakedown, only four ships would leave the atoll to rendezvous at their assigned stations. The *Horizon* would be engaged in mooring emplacement 75 miles northeast of Ground Zero, while the firing ship (*Estes*), the fleet flagship (*Rendova*), and the aerial ground-control ship (*O'Bannon*), orbited 30-50 miles to the southeast.

Once on station, at dawn, the ships would go through a mock firing drill, after which the photographic aircraft would commence their intricate flight patterns. An hour later, the cloud-sampling fighters would appear in groups of four, refuel from tankers, penetrate the imaginary mushroom cloud, refuel once more, and return to Kwajalein for sample recovery and decontamination.

Most of this aerial melee would occur at 40,000 feet, directly above us, but far removed from sight and sound, seen only as radar echoes on oscilloscope screens, heard only as radio voices. For all save the *Horizon*, the drill would end tomorrow night; she would remain on station, keeping lonely vigil over her fragile moorings until Mike had flashed his challenge to the world. She would rejoin the fleet for atoll re-entry only after her vital message had been delivered.

MacConnell was the first to finish reading, tossing the document aside and thumping his thick-fingered fist on the table. "Damn nonsense," he snorted. "The air force has turned the cloud-sampling program into a circus. I was in on the early planning. Do you know what the initial mission requirement was?" He fixed us with his glittering eyes, salt-and-pepper chin whiskers bobbing with emotion. "Three pairs of 100-milligram samples at hourly intervals, beginning as soon as practicable after shot time."

He paused to let the steward pick up the orders we had scribbled on our place cards. "Now look at what we have. There will be fifty planes milling around up there within the first three hours after the shot . . . and half of 'em are associated with sampling . . . fourteen jet fighters . . . six aerial tankers . . . two control aircraft . . . three SAR . . . that's twenty-five."

"So, what's your point?" I asked.

"They could do the whole job with three B-47's . . . at much less risk and headache . . . no tankers . . . no controls . . . no SAR . . . plus, three men in each plane to share the workload." He switched his eyes to me. "Am I right, Bob?'

"I'm not sure," I said. "It seems to me they considered 47's last June . . . but they were still talking about fourteen planes . . . they didn't think they could get that many . . . with a war going on."

"Bullshit!" snapped MacConnell. "Glantzberg's an ex-fighter jock. He just wants to show what the 84's can do. What do you think, Brian?"

Brian Mason was a thin, youngish, forty-year-old Aussie, from Adelaide, with round spectacles and an undershot jaw. He was obviously embarrassed by the question. "Well," he said, "it does appear to be a bit of what the British would call the seminal approach . . . You know . . . sending a hundred soldiers to assault a pillbox in the hope that one will be able to pop a grenade through the slit."

"What's seminal about that?" growled MacConnell.

"It's a bit like procreation. You pop in a billion semen, hoping just one will get all the way up to the ovum. What?"

During lunch, we talked about the weather outlook, which was of intimate concern to MacConnell's radsafe activities. Mason explained that we were prematurely well into the wet monsoon season, and that forecasts of more than 24 hours were of little value. In his opinion, the chances of reasonably dry weather on D-day was about 20 per cent. "The Air Force has weather teams sitting on a dozen little islands, tracking balloons every six hours," he said. "They've got ten long-range weather aircraft looking for localized cyclones as far out as 500 miles in all directions. Under normal summer conditions, the forecasts would be a piece of cike. But, with this sniky band of thunderstorms we call the Intertropical Convergence sitting right over us . . . it's a bit dicy. All we can hope is that the bloody snike crawls on a bit, and leaves us a clear spot."

Comfortably sated on fish cakes and San Miguel, a fine Philippine brew, we ambled down to the personnel pier and caught a fleet taxi out to the *Estes*. The postcard weather was still holding, but a wall of black cumulus was massing on the eastern horizon. "Looks like your bloody snike's on the move again," said MacConnell over his shoulder as we ascended the boarding ladder. We signed the muster sheet and were given berthing assignments. I drew the lower in a double cabin; Mason and MacConnell were next door. Knowing that the ship was fully air-conditioned, I showered and changed into clean khakis, and set out to find Ogle. I finally located him standing out on a wing of the bridge, conversing with the *Estes*' skipper, Captain George Kincaid, together with an enormously tall, elderly, bejoweled civilian, dressed in a black business suit. They were obviously standing outside because the older man was too tall to fit under the overhead of the bridge deck.

Ogle beckoned me out, and introduced me to Mr. Ed Pauley: "Dr. Ward is our water wave expert . . . from Scripps." I shook a hand that felt like a plastic baggy full of bread dough, looking up at a mouth that smiled and eyes that didn't. Where had I heard that name?

"Oho," rumbled Pauley. "You must be one of Roger Revelle's boys."

A bolt clicked into place. "Big Ed" Pauley, the oil tycoon . . . Chairman of the University's Board of

Regents . . . One of Roger's few sworn enemies . . . The man who steadfastly vetoed our annual funding requests for repairing the pier . . . painting the ships. My God, if he could only see the old *Hor* now, compared with the spic-and-span navy flotilla.

I suddenly realized that some time had elapsed since Pauley's question. Ogle was looking at me with interested amusement. "Not exactly, Sir," I hastened to say. "I just got my degree under Professor Henry Engels."

"Engels," mused Pauley. "Ah, yes . . . The German chap with the lovely wife. What was her name . . . Martha?"

"Margaretha," I volunteered. Women might remember Henry, but no man ever forgot Margaretha.

Just then, as if in answer to my prayer, a painted apparition slowly emerged from behind the screen of the anchored *Rendova*, turning into the stream on her way out of the lagoon, the full glare of the afternoon sunlight reflected from her bedaubed and rust-streaked flanks. "Look!" I exclaimed, with affected pride. "There goes our ship, *Horizon*, now."

"That . . . is a University of California ship?" croaked Pauley, aghast.

"Yes, Sir," I expanded. "Finest oceanographic ship afloat. Of course, she could do with a little paint . . . but, somehow, our regents can never seem to find the money." Kincaid was biting his tongue to keep from smiling, and Ogle was suddenly busy with his pipe. I put out my hand and shook his dough bag. "It was a pleasure to meet you,

Mr. Pauley. If you ever get down to Scripps, I'd be happy to show you around."

I didn't see Pauley again. Ogle told me he had gone over to the *Rendova* for supper and then flown back to Kwajalein. He and 100 other VIP's watched the test from special observer aircraft. But before the *Horizon* returned from Capricorn expedition, four months later, the Regents had passed a special appropriation for painting all our ships . . . not white, but blue and gold.

General Glantzberg arrived in his chopper at 1645, followed almost immediately by the violent storm front we had seen approaching two hours previously. The deck crew had barely time to get the machine tied down before howling winds and drenching rain blotted out all visibility. According to Mason's "snike" analogy, two consecutive days of good weather was too much to expect. Glantzberg and Ogle huddled briefly with Mason in the Weather room, then went down the ladder and powered over to the *Rendova* in the captain's gig to confer with Admiral Wilkins. They came back an hour later, looking glum.

"The cloud tops are above 20,000 feet," Ogle confided to Walt and me at dinner, "So the fighters can't refuel. We've scrubbed the sampling exercise for this rehearsal, but everything else will go ahead as planned." He raked some breadcrumbs together and pinched them off to his plate. "It's a little unfortunate, you see, because the task group went through a complete aerial rehearsal about ten days ago, communicating with the *Estes*, here, at anchor. As you might anticipate, there were lots of problems.

"Despite all their practicing in Texas and Utah for the past nine months, when they all got together over the ocean, things came unglued. The scale was just too big. The fighters couldn't see the control B29 more than five miles away, and it couldn't locate them electronically with all their magic gimmicks over 20 miles off. Even the ground-control ship couldn't find them when there were storm clouds in the way.

"Part of the problem was that everybody was yelling over the same radio channels, when there were unused neighboring channels. As a result, our communications people, who were supposed to be coordinating everything, were cut out of the picture."

"So, where does that put us?" I asked.

"Well, they've re-assigned radio frequencies to straighten out the communications foul-up, and they've cobbled up a new homing device to vector the fighters . . . but this rehearsal was their only chance to test these fixes. Now, we'll just have to pray that everything works right during the final go-around." He poked a blackened finger into his pipe and relighted it.

"Walt seems to feel that they should have used bombers instead of fighters for cloud sampling," I said, and MacConnell reiterated his lunchtime comments about F84's vis-à-vis B47's.

"You two are not the only ones of that opinion," said Ogle, grimly, "but Glantzberg is not the fall guy. The order to use fighters came from higher up. I doubt that the mechanics of this operation had very much to do with the decision."

As the evening wore on, the downpour waxed and waned. Occasionally a few stars peeped out. I wandered about the Brain room, watching scientists and technicians playing games with their equipment, trying to avoid interfering. Most of it appeared to be diagnostic stuff, monitoring various aspects of Mike's health and well-being, as well as the character of his radiative output after firing. Because of the good-natured banter, I gathered that they were getting the right signals.

Ogle spent most of the time seated behind the firing console. Slightly elevated and centrally located, he could view the entire instrument panorama. With a telephone headset and patch box, he could communicate directly with any task force element. As Test Director, once the fleet was on station, he would be sole command of operations until he elected to relinquish it. The rest of us, advisors and noncombatants, had chairs in a row behind him.

About 2230 hours, we got word that the firing party had left Parry Island. The party was led by Jack Clark, and included Harold Agnew, who had to make last-minute changes to Mike's fueling system, and two EGG specialists in the timing and firing circuitry, Herb Grier and Barney O'Keefe. Also along were two LASL scientists, George

IVY-MIKE

Downes and Abe Schwartz, who were responsible for critical optical experiments, including the notorious gamma ray box that had caused Ogle so many headaches. The party was traveling in a 55-foot motor torpedo boat (AVR), capable of 45 knots in smoother water.

At each station where the firing cable came ashore, the party landed, locked the switches open, and reported to Ogle by radio. There were auxiliary loudspeakers in the control room, so that everyone was privy to their conversation. The party reached Eluklab, the shot islet, at 2335, and began the long arming procedure, each step of which was described and confirmed by radio. By 0030, they had buttoned things up and commenced the tedious return trip. I went out on deck and did some pushups to clear the cobwebs. The rain had stopped, but more was coming. The *Rendova* had gone, and we only awaited the return of the firing party. Mason was still in the weather room, but MacConnell had disappeared. There was nothing more for me to do; I left an 0530 call with the OOD, and slipped away to bed.

Although alone in my cabin, I slept fitfully. At midnight, Mahatma announced D-6, and commenced an hourly countdown that would continue until H-1 hours, after which he would switch to 15-minute intervals. The last quarter hour would be given in minutes; the last quarter minute in seconds. It was impossible to shut off the squawk box, and I was awakened each hour by its crackling—even before our Oracle's gravelly voice intoned the time.

At 0150, I heard the firing party come aboard; at 0300, the anchor chain rattled in the hawse, the engines throbbed, and we headed into the channel. Outside, lulled by the soothing motion of the long Pacific swell and the gentle humming of the ventilator blowers, I dozed.

The wakeup call was redundant; at 0500, the ship's klaxon summoned all hands to general quarters. I waited until the thunder of feet had subsided before venturing out for ablutions, and then made my way up to the Brain room. It was raining heavily outside, and blowing half a gale. Ogle was still sitting in his command chair; judging by the pile of pipe ashes in the tray beside him, he had been there all night. "The control aircraft have encountered icing above 20,000 feet," he announced, wearily. "So, we've scrubbed the entire air exercise. We can't even launch helicopters in this weather. It looks as if we'll have to settle for a general firing and instrument checkout. If that isn't weatherproof, we're in the wrong business."

I helped myself to coffee and a doughnut, and inquired if anything had been heard from the *Horizon*. "She's on station," he said, "but it's apparently too rough to anchor. They're waiting for daylight to assess the situation."

"May I talk to them directly?" I asked.

"Sure," he said, handing me the headset. "They're Blackfoot and we're Cherokee. This is a clear channel. Don't say anything relevant to testing."

I called, and immediately got Jeff Knight. "Bob," he said, sounding a little frustrated, "when we planned this maneuver, we were expecting steady easterly winds, so that we could drop the wire upwind of the seamount and then drift back over the middle of it to lower the moorings. Instead, we've got strong, gusty winds from every point of the compass. I'm afraid we're just going to have to wait until things settle down for a few hours."

"Understand," I responded. "Why don't you give me another status report about 0800. This is Cherokee, out." I handed the headset back to Ogle. "They probably won't get the moorings in until the wind lets up. They'll send us a fictitious wave report about 0800."

"Fine," he answered, pressing his palms over his eyes. "If things continue in this vein, we'll probably be back in the lagoon for lunch . . . But I think it might be a good idea to get you a separate radio channel to Blackfoot, just in case we both need to talk at the same time."

By 0600 the control room was filling up, and Ogle began running through a long checklist of task unit readiness reports. Jack Clark and Herb Grier had reappeared, and were monitoring Mike's vital signs, including the liquid levels in his deuterium, hydrogen, and nitrogen chambers. Despite the fact that this was only a practice exercise, last evening's levity had given way to serious concern; as if this were not a drill, but the actual test of the world's first thermonuclear device . . . perhaps a thousand times more powerful than the bomb dropped on Hiroshima, and, seemingly, a thousand times less certain of success.

At 0645, Mahatma began the H-1 hour countdown. Again we heard the rumble of feet, as all crew members not essential to operating the ship were mustered on deck, handed dark goggles, and assembled to face away from the blast direction. For the past two hours, the *Estes* had been heading directly away from the shot site, partly to protect the bridge windows, and partly to optimize the directivity of her many radio antennas.

At 0729, Ogle lifted the protective cover from the firing switch, and awaited announcement of the 15-minute warning. At the tone, he pressed the button that initiated the firing sequencer. Mike was now on automatic, and all of us not directly concerned with the firing mechanics filed out onto the bridge deck and donned our goggles. It was broad daylight now. Though the clouds were lowering, the rain had let up and the wind considerably abated. But the relentless voice of Mahatma followed us outside . . . counting, now in minutes . . . finally in seconds. Then, the klaxon . . . and the announcement: "Now hear this. The firing drill is over. All hands will report to normal duty stations."

At 0800, back inside the control room, we got the wave report from the *Horizon*. Henry Engels sounded a little breathless: "Cherokee, we are Blackfeet. We have Code 10 waves. Do you comprehend?"

"Blackfoot, this is Cherokee," I responded. "Understand Code 10. Todos es perdidos . . . Cherokee out." Ogle was shaking his head . . . but I don't think he was really angry.

PART V

THE TEST

    I spent the last four days before final evacuation back on Parry Island. Most of the facilities were still operating, and with the withdrawal of support units from the outer islets, Parry had become a hive of activity. As vehicles and equipment arrived by ship, they were marshaled in prearranged storage areas, drained of combustibles, and covered with heavy canvas. Larger buildings were secured by stakes and cables to better enable them to resist the gust-like wind pressure expected from the distant blast.

    As the task force "tsunami expert", I suddenly became very popular, and was bombarded with questions: How high should the sand embankments be to protect fuel tanks? What locations would offer best natural protection for stored equipment? In what depth of water should moorings be placed for craft too small to be evacuated to sea?

    Throughout these preparations, the weather continued foul, with bursts of heavy rain, separated by an hour or two of hazy sunshine. Despite light bulbs burning in our clothes lockers to combat fungus, nothing ever dried out. I wondered, vaguely, how the natives of this region could prosper under such conditions. I could picture them, sitting in their thatched huts, choking in the smoke from damp coconut shell fires, and peering out at the sodden landscape. My boyhood concept of tropical nirvana was sadly at odds with this image.

And where were the local natives now? With the buildup of the Pacific Proving Grounds, several years before, the residents of Eniwetok and Bikini had been "temporarily resettled" among other islands to the south and east. Of course, there would be reparation for all this inconvenience. When we were through turning these islands into radioactive deserts, we would plant new trees, build them new tin houses, give them Coca Cola machines to rot their teeth, and hamburgers to plug up their heart arteries. But, in the meantime, they would have to move in with Aunt Nellie and Uncle Jim for a few generations.

While the outer island message traffic had been coming through with encouraging regularity, mail seemed to arrive in batches, as if someone were saving it up until there was a plane headed our way. A big packet appeared on Monday, 26 October (D-5), together with a notice that all further deliveries would be suspended until after the test. As usual, most of it was for the *Horizon*, but there were three letters for me.

I opened Ray Smith's letter first; it was bursting with exuberance and gratitude. Johnston Island was a skin diver's paradise. The local hobby group had somehow crafted a glass-bottom boat, in which he was taking diving aspirants cruising over an endless labyrinth of shallow reefs. He had speared the world-record Moray Eel, which had been frozen and shipped to a specialist at USC. Enclosed was a snapshot of Ray and his new centerfold girl friend standing on either side of the record eel, which was hanging from a fish-scale. On the back he had scrawled: "The Eel is the one with the gills."

Ted Folsom wrote merely to apologize for having missed two message days (I hadn't missed them). One was caused by a flat tire on his bike; the other to some malfunction of Li'l Mollie, later diagnosed and corrected. The weather at Wake had turned fine, and he had found a German-speaking island employee, who was giving him grammar lessons. He had made peace with Deadly Dudley; they played chess every evening.

Suzie's was also short: "Dearest Bumpkin," (New nickname? I used to be a Prince). "I've got a bad case of the Jeebies. There is absolutely nothing for me to do here until Dr. A. gets back. So I've decided to take leave until this whole thing blows over. I'm just going to drive around the Southwest. Maybe go down to Guaymas. Somewhere I can go swimming and lie in the sun. Mona will be here, answering the phone, and I'll keep her posted on my whereabouts, just for emergencies. All my LOVE, S."

Wednesday (D-3) marked the embarkation of most Army personnel aboard the transport, *Gen. E.T. Collins*, and most of the Holmes & Narver people on another, the *D.C. Shanks*. Except for a handful, most of the northern camps were now closed; most technical and scientific personnel would observe the test from the seaplane tender, *Curtiss*, which had brought Mike out to Forward Area. Under the blessing of prevailing low cloud cover, Admiral Wilkins had successfully shunted the 150-odd VIP "observers" to Kwajalein. Although accommodated under rather primitive circumstances, they would witness the test from the safety and comfort of pressurized aircraft, circling Ground Zero above 20,000 feet, and 100 miles away.

Wednesday also marked the closing of the Flag Mess. We few diehards, numbering perhaps twenty, and including Walt MacConnell and Jack Clark, were accorded free martinis during an impromptu happy hour. Brian Mason was not there; he was just beginning his three-hourly forecasts aboard the *Estes*, that would continue right through the test, until the airborne radioactivity had disappeared from the entire island complex. Talk was subdued. It was the calm before the storm. Mike's final fueling, commenced on D-5, was now completed; I could picture him standing there, sweating, fuming, and impatient. The last fueling truck would remain, to top him off as needed. It would be sacrificed for lack of any means of removing it.

"My, oh my," sighed Jack, taking a first sip, and nibbling at his spitted olive. "Nothing like a cold martini after a hard day's night." Although slender by nature and bronzed by an outdoor existence, he looked gray with fatigue, and a two-day stubble of white beard competed with his sparse, brown crew cut.

"Tell me, Jack," I asked. "How come none of the big-name scientists who worked on Mike are out here to watch the show? . . . You know, the people I met at your party last June."

Jack finished his first drink and signaled the steward. "Well, those theoretickers live in a different world. Once the ink's dry . . . that's the end of it. Besides, Mike was Teller's baby. Now, he's gone off to his own lab at Livermore, and everybody else is working on the next generation devices. You see, they've gotta beat Teller's record."

"Tut, tut . . . Jealousy among scientists?" chuckled MacConnell.

"Naw. Not jealousy . . . Just friendly competition. And besides, most of the really big names have gone back to their ivory towers. They've proved the point, and are happy to let the young fellers show their muscles."

There was a burst of rain on the roof, and we all involuntarily lifted our eyes. "Of course, if the weather doesn't let up a little," Jack continued, "they might all have to come back and design us a waterproof device."

"Jack, if you aren't a theoreticker, what are you?" I asked. "Ogle says you have a physics PhD."

"Oh, there are all kinds of physikers. I guess you'd call me a practiker. Norris Bradbury and I went to Stanford together, when they were turning out mostly practikers . . .

only he ended up pushing papers, and I ended up pushing buttons."

But Jack was just being modest. Nobody was in a hurry to go anywhere, and with the inducement of a few more martinis I learned a little of his history. After college, he had worked at the Army's Aberdeen proving grounds, studying "interior ballistics . . . how fast a bullet moves down a rifle barrel." He became an expert on explosives, then, during the war, an officer in charge of explosives testing. After the war, Bradbury had invited him to LASL to do similar work, but related to atomic weapons. Ultimately, he gravitated into field testing . . . in Nevada. Ivy was his first Pacific test. "I just had to make sure the fellers were doing everything right."

Thursday (D-2). With the shore facilities closing down and the weather continuing bad, most everyone without specific duties ashore moved back aboard ship. Actually, we were rooted out; a work crew appeared with a big truck to strip all the beds and bedding for temporary storage. They secured the shutters open . . . "to let the blast blow through", and shut off the plumbing. Being advised, in the worst eventuality, to plan for permanent departure, we took all our possessions. MacConnell had six bottles of Black Label he was unable to cope with single-handed; we divided them between us to "equalize the burden." My own excess burden was a string bag of diving paraphernalia.

Struggling up the boarding ladder of the *Estes* with all this hardware occasioned some interested amusement among the crew. At the gangway, we set everything down, proffered our badges to the security guard, and were mustered aboard by a yeoman with a clipboard. "Dr. Ward, Sir, your berth will be 11B, A-Deck. Dr. MacConnell will be in 11A. If you gentlemen will leave your gear right here, we'll have it brought up. Would you care to join the Bomb Pool?"

"Bomb Pool?" I echoed.

"Yessir . . . Five dollars to join . . . Nearest guess to the bomb size, announced at 1200 on D+1, takes the pot. There's a pool aboard every ship. The boat-pool bos'un's in five of 'em."

"I'll just join the *Estes*' pool," I said. "Where do I sign up?" I was going through all sorts of mental gymnastics, wondering how the world's most secret number could be bandied about among the 12,000-odd Ivy personnel.

"Right here, Sir. Just take this gizmo and punch out a number."

Aha! The secret was out. It was an ordinary punchboard. There was no magical connection between the Mike yield and the winning number, which the ship's executive officer would punch from an identical punchboard at noon on D+1 day. I paid up and took my punch. The number was 001050. I tucked it into my pocket. "Are you in, Mac?" I tendered him the punchboard.

"No thanks," he laughed. "I only bet on liquor and women."

"Excuse me, Gentlemen." It was the OOD, who had been talking to another officer during our conversation with the yeoman. "Sorry I didn't see you come aboard. There will be a meeting of all task unit commanders at 1300 in the JTF Briefing Room, 'midships, B-Deck. Also, you'll find a mess bill on your bunks. Owing to very crowded conditions on board, we're having double mess hours. We'd appreciate your being as prompt as possible." The OOD was a young, nervous Lt. JG, with a cap that appeared much too large for his slender features.

"Thanks, Lieutenant," I said, with a straight face. "I'm a pretty fast eater . . . but you may have some trouble with Dr. MacConnell, here. He tends to fletcherize."

Our cabin had a porthole, and a small desk, and a wash basin. "Pret-ty nifty." observed MacConnell, peeling off his rain slicker and tossing it on the lower berth. "OK if I sleep downstairs?"

"Be my guest," I said. "After tonight, neither of us will be getting much sack time until it's OK to move back ashore. How long did Ellingwood say it would be before atoll would be habitable . . . 24 hours?"

"Bullshit!" snorted MacConnell. "He said that the significant local fallout would be over in 24 hours, but the ground radiation levels would only be down by a factor of a thousand. That means a place reading 100R at one hour might be down to 100mR . . . OK to visit, but not to tarry. More likely, it'll be a couple of weeks before one can wander at will among the tulips."

"But, if there's no fallout at Parry Island, then we can return after the fallout stops, right?"

"Right! . . . And that's the purpose of our early chopper radsafe survey . . . To map out the initial levels all around the atoll . . . and appraise the fallout situation. This will be a balance between wind transport of the mushroom cloud away from the atoll, and local rainfall, which brings down the finer stuff. By the way, didn't Ogle say you were going along on that trip . . . a wave damage survey or something?" He fumbled in his pack and produced a can of peanuts. "Care for a snack before lunch?" I shook my head, and he began popping them by the handful.

"Yeah," I said, without much enthusiasm. "I guess I'm slated for that survey."

"Worried about radiation?" he said, putting a hand on my arm. "Forget it. You'll be with the experts. We'll take it very slow, and stay out of the squalls."

I felt a sudden burst of affection for this forthright, indignant little man, with his knobby knees, his bristly chin, his rimless spectacles. "How'd you ever get into this racket?" I asked.

"Oh . . . I don't know . . ." He paused in his chomping. "Combination of failed physicist . . . failed medico . . . failed marriage, I suppose. And somewhere, a desire to be useful. Haven't you noticed? There's quite a bunch of us hiding out at the Lab . . . specialists in obscure and occult arts . . . There's the mess call. How about some chow . . . we've got a briefing at 1300?"

Before the briefing, I ran up to Communications to see how the *Horizon* was making out with the seamount moorings. I got Jeff on the horn; he sounded a little dispirited. "Both moorings are in. But you were right about Carlucci and his sea sickness," he observed, dryly. "He's spent most of the time in his bunk, and seems unable to cope with even the simplest tasks. In fact, we've had the same problem with Captain Dunbar. But I've learned to operate his gear, and can probably fill-in if push comes to shove." I signed off, wishing, but unable, to add some note of cheer.

By 1300, the briefing room was filled with some two dozen now-familiar faces, including Major Frank Davis. He looked a bit haggard, and explained that he had been spending most of his time shuttling between Honolulu and Kwajalein, catering to the needs of VIP "observers."

The briefing was chaired by Stan Buriss, whom I had seen little of during my Eniwetok sojourn. He summarized matters succinctly: "We're here to discuss alternatives to the current Operation Plan, if the weather continues to exceed our scheduled maxima for public safety and data recovery.

"In that regard, we originally thought we had some flexibility. Ideally, we'd like to have east-northeast winds of 10-20 knots below 10,000 feet, with 20 per cent cloud cover, and clear above 5,000 feet. Under these conditions, most of the fallout would occur over the open sea, and the atoll could be cleared for re-entry within a few hours.

"However, as you all know, we've had a normal year's rainfall in October alone. We've had 80-90 percent clouds, and variable winds to 40 knots as high as 25,000 feet. If these conditions continue into D-day, our first fallback will be a 24-hour postponement. This could be announced as late as H-1 hour, when our entire operation is deployed at sea, or in the air between Kwajalein and Eniwetok.

"The Mike fueling, and most essential diagnostics, can survive a 24-hour hold without serious dysfunctions or data loss, and it's a long enough interval for the Air Force to recall the planes and start over. In fact, we could have a 6-hour hold without any change in plans. But, any delay longer than 6 hours means that the aerial tankers and photo planes have to go home, and we would automatically reschedule for the following morning. Then we would have another 6-hour window." Buriss stopped for a drink of water, and shuffled his notes before continuing.

"If we are forced into a second weather hold, it would have to be for a minimum of three days. All ships will hold stations, except the *Curtiss*, the *Estes*, and the *Rendova*, which will re-enter the lagoon to refuel Mike and recheck all instrument channels. Air Ops at Kwaj will also need that much time to fall back and regroup.

"Meanwhile, we would have to secure approval for a new firing schedule from AEC Headquarters in Washington. Considering that our next window would fall on a Presidential Election Day, it is possible—even probable—that permission will be denied. In that case, we would most-likely have to cancel the operation, and go automatically into re-entry and roll-up modes."

Buriss laid down his notes and mopped his forehead with a handkerchief. "Needless to say, we're all hoping for a weather break. Dr. Mason tells me that the outlook for tomorrow, D-1, is favorable. All we need is 36 hours of passable weather to wind up this exercise as scheduled. Any questions?"

The was a flurry of hands, but I slipped out. The outer islands had no deadlines, short of a message to discontinue recording and go home. The *Horizon* could be sent necessary delay messages. My chief concern was how long the seamount moorings could survive. That, again, would depend upon the weather.

"It's what he didn't say that bothers me the most," Ogle confided to me at dinner that evening. "Most of the congressmen and other VIP's who've been sleeping in leaky tents down at Kwajalein for the past week or two have expressed some disenchantment with this enterprise. About a third of them have already gone home. The cutoff on Election Day is not just weather . . . it's money . . . the three million a week it takes to keep 12,000 warm bodies sitting around out here in the rain. Congressmen just don't understand why we couldn't have shot this thing back in early October, when the weather was fine . . ." He paused, as if searching for the right words. "The ironic thing is that we could have shot it two or three weeks ago, except for these same congressmen, who insisted on a fixed firing commitment so that they could come out here to watch it."

Then, changing the subject abruptly, he asked me what I planned to do after Ivy was over. "I don't really know," I said. "Maybe hang around Hawaii for a week or so . . . visit the other islands . . . Why?"

"I've got a small job I'd like you to finish up for me in Honolulu. It'll only take a couple of days. But it'll save me a week if I don't have to stop over on my way back."

"Sure," I said. "I'll be happy to help out. What do you need?"

"I haven't quite figured out the details yet. How about checking with me just before you leave the Forward Area. OK?"

I wondered what he could want. Probably a preliminary report of results. I'd have to write a detailed report as soon as I got back to La Jolla. And what about Suzie, flaked out in Guaymas or Mazatlan, wasting all the vacation we might have spent together. If I'd had an ounce of brains, I'd have invited her to come out to Hawaii. Now, I couldn't even reach her.

In a black mood, I went up to my cabin and found Walt MacConnell, propped up in his bunk, reading a paperback and sipping a tumbler of Black Label. "High-ho," he sang out. "Care for a little libation? You look like you need some liquid cheer. Last night of liberty, etcetera."

Pouring about three fingers into my water glass, I resisted the sacrilegious impulse to dilute it, and took a healthy swig. "Easy, there," croaked MacConnell. "That stuff runs $2.10 a fifth at the commissary—and the commissary's closed until further notice."

I coughed as the fiery jolt hit bottom and anchored itself. I sat down in our only chair, wrong-way, facing him, and raised the glass again. "Your health, Sir. There's nothing wrong with me that two days of benign weather and a week in bed with my beloved wouldn't cure." I took another belt, but smaller.

"Ah, sweet simplicity of youth," said MacConnell, placidly. "Perhaps I should grant your wish—at least, the first part." He put his book on the desk and rose to a sitting posture, folding his legs together, Yoga-fashion. Then he took a deep breath, closed his eyes, and pressed his clenched fists against his stomach. He held this posture for some time, looking as if he were trying to suppress hiccups. Then he relaxed and returned to his former supine position. "That should do it," he said. "Why don't you take a look outside?"

Deciding I could use some air in any case, I stumbled out into the passageway and followed it forwards to the companionway issuing onto the main deck; then continued out on deck as far as the anchor windlass. From here, three-quarters of the night sky was visible. Mac was right; the dark, serried ranks of rain cloud were blowing off to the west; the eastern sky was perfectly clear. And a quarter-way around the globe in that direction, Suzie slumbered in some unknown bed, tucked up in a fetal position. I hoped she was dreaming of Prince Robert of Ward.

I must have slept very soundly. I didn't hear the klaxon at all, and only caught the end of Mahatma's message: ". . .

today is D-1. All personnel will muster at duty stations for atoll evacuation by 1500 today. This is not a drill".

"It's on!" I cried, sitting up abruptly, and whacking my skull on the overhead. MacConnell was already shaving. "Of course!" he observed, carefully circumscribing his short mustache and the tuft of whiskers on his chin. "Exactly as I willed it. I trust you're suitably impressed by my psycho-kinetic powers."

"I am indeed." I said, tenderly palpating the lump already rising on my occiput. "Why didn't you bring them into play earlier in the month? You could have saved this operation incalculable anguish."

"That would have overtaxed my limited ability." He wiped away the lather and slapped on a little skin bracer. "I saved everything for the big push. How about some breakfast?"

By 0700, the Brain Room was buzzing with activity and an atmosphere of guarded optimism prevailed. The latest weather report suggested that Mason's snike had indeed crawled on, opening a kink in the convergence pattern that: "should persist for at least 24 hours."

As a result, every task force facility was testing communications, and all 27 channels to the *Estes*' radio room were swamped. It was 1030 before I managed to send off coded messages alerting my four island operators to an impending "typhoon" condition, so that they would be standing by their instruments on D-day, waiting to report any unusual wave activity. I also spoke to Jeff and Henry aboard the *Horizon*, using the new 2-megacycle transceiver Ogle had provided. They were comfortably anchored to seamount Freddy, with the wave raft only a quarter of a mile away.

There was a final meeting of the task force command staff in the briefing room, but I wasn't invited. They broke up at 1130 and dispersed to their respective duty stations. Generals Clarkson and Glantzberg remained aboard the *Estes* with Stan Buriss; Admiral Wilkins to his flagship, *Rendova*, and Colonel Burritt to the *Collins*. Glantzberg was in an ebullient mood. The Air Force had already completed a completely-successful mini-Mike operation this morning, including twice refueling two F84G's on mock penetration flights from Kwajalein. "A piece of cake," he beamed, slapping a closed fist into his opposite palm. "All we need is another four hours of clear skies tomorrow."

After lunch, with everything humming like clockwork, I made a quick tour of the ship, more for exercise than anything else. Down many ladders, I reached the engine room, with its oil-fired boilers and massive turbines. I peeped into the shaft alleys where propeller shafts as thick as tree trunks turned the 16-foot screws at 180 revolutions per minute, or thereabouts. Then up through the laundry, the galley, the mess halls, the sleeping quarters of this 500-room floating hotel, climbing past officers' cabins, meeting rooms, communications, to the bridge; finally ending up on top of everything, except the massive tripod structure supporting the 30-foot radar, like a tennis net spinning about its mid-point.

IVY-MIKE 319

From this high vantage point, I watched the transport *Shanks* head north to Teiteripucci to join the *Curtiss* in removing last-minute workers and security guards, saw the *Oak Hill*, a sea-going dry-dock, scoop up and stockpile 24 LCM's, saw two fleet tugs towing strings of barges to Kwajalein. The surface of the placid lagoon was spider-webbed with the wakes of small personnel boats scurrying to evacuate the last people ashore; scurrying to meet the 1500 muster deadline.

* * *

The problems started with the muster. When heads were counted at 1500, six civilian technicians were missing, who should have boarded the *Curtiss* at Teiteripucci, while the *Collins*, anchored off Parry Island, had an extra man aboard. The civilians had last been seen walking down the small boat dock, but somehow never reported aboard their ship. Nobody was seriously alarmed—men don't just drop out of sight. Every vessel ordered a recount. Seven hours later, all six appeared aboard the *Collins*; they had not even realized they were on the wrong ship.

What complicated the recount was that five people were simultaneously missing from the *Collins*; in fact, they had been gone since the morning of D-2. Dr. Fred Foster, a radio chemist from the Navy's Radiation Defense Laboratory, San Francisco, a technical assistant, and three seamen from the small boat pool, had requisitioned an LCM and set out to circumnavigate the atoll for the purpose of setting out and activating fallout collectors on every islet. Dr. Foster was a late arrival at Eniwetok, and this experiment was not included in the revised operation plan. Its details were, in fact, known only to a small group from the Armed Forces Special Weapons Project (AFSWP), who were sponsoring a group of "effects" experiments on a "not-to-interfere" basis.

Dr. Foster's party had made it halfway round by Thursday evening (D-2), and spent the night at Teiteripucci. They had departed early Friday morning to do the eastern half of the atoll, and should have come back by noon. The LCM had a radio transmitter, and the weather was good. Nobody had missed them until the muster.

When this bit of news filtered topside, a chopper was launched from the *Rendova*. Flying the route counterclockwise, it found the LCM within a half-hour, beached on lonely Biken Island, in the remotest part of the atoll. The chopper crew helped them set a stern anchor to hold the LCM until after the test, and delivered the party to the *Rendova* about 1930. "The damn fools lost their alternator on the way out," Ogle told us later. "They didn't notice their batteries were weak until they tried to start the diesel this morning. Then, they elected to continue the trip, keeping the diesel running while they were ashore, until they ran out of fuel. Then, of course, they couldn't use the radio to yell for help."

In the midst of the muster flap, the Headquarters Command got word that one of its far-flung net of

P2V patrol planes had detected three unidentified ships approaching the Control Zone around Eniwetok, measuring about 1,000 miles on a side. The plane had contacted two of the ships, and diverted them so as to avoid the CZ. But the third had not responded, and was continuing on a course that would bring her within 200 miles downwind of the shot point at the time of detonation. Low on fuel, the plane was now en route to her base on Kwajalein.

This straightforward exigency was responded to by dispatching a second P2V from Kwaj. to intercept the interloper, the round-trip distance being about 2,000 miles because Kwajalein was at exactly the opposite corner of the Control Zone. But, at 1630, we heard a May Day from the second interceptor. She was 150 miles northwest of Eniwetok, with one engine out and the other running ragged. She had not made contact with the unknown ship, and was attempting to reach the closed-down runway at Eniwetok; short of that, she would ditch at sea.

"Oh, my God," groaned MacConnell, standing beside me in the Brain Room. "If that plane goes down, we've had it! There's no way we could rescue the survivors at night, and very little chance of finding them tomorrow."

Responding to the May Day, the *Rendova* ordered the patrolling destroyer, *Carpenter* to divert to the flight path of the ailing aircraft, and sent an emergency crash crew over to the Eniwetok strip to turn on the landing lights and stand-by if needed. Additionally, the Coast Guard dispatched an amphibious SA16 aircraft from Kwajalein to rendezvous with the P2V and escort her back. A third P2V, returning from patrol, was diverted in a last attempt to intercept the oncoming ship.

"We now have four independent reasons for postponing Mike," said Ogle at dinner, more depressed than I had ever seen him. "It will take something of a miracle to resolve them all before the time comes to push that button. I'm not a religious man, but I sometimes get the feeling that somebody up there is trying to tell me something."

But the fun was far from over. The next news was good; the Foster party had been found. The muster was now complete, and ships could commence evacuating the lagoon. In the fading twilight, we watched a long file of smaller vessels, led by the giant *Oak Hill*, thread their way through the narrow ship channel between Parry and Japtan and disappear from view.

Meanwhile, there was a continuous stream of voice traffic between the stricken P2V and the Coast Guard SA16, which was approaching Eniwetok from the opposite direction. The P2V was down to 90 knots on one rough engine, and flying at "zero" elevation with half-flaps, to provide a little extra lift. The *Carpenter* was racing at flank speed from the north. At 2015, we picked up both aircraft on the *Estes*' radar. At 2020, the Eniwetok runway lights flashed on, and we heard the control tower come on the air, talking the wounded bird in to a squeaky landing. She was followed almost immediately by the SA16, which took her crew aboard and headed back to Kwaj, while the rescue crew secured the P2V against blast damage and scurried back aboard the *Rendova*. "Three down and one to go," breathed Ogle, as the *Rendova* heaved up her massive anchor and signaled her departure.

But the words were hardly out of his mouth when the next blows fell. Brian Mason appeared with the latest weather. The light easterly breeze that had been freshening all afternoon had backed into the northeast, and a squall line was coming down. It had already bypassed Eluklab, and was expected within the hour. This was the worst of all possible directions for surface winds; it could carry the fallout directly over the entire atoll, and to the fleet beyond. Had Mason's snike wriggled backwards, or was this just some vagary of the Convergence? The winds aloft were southerly, swinging to east at high altitudes, the usual sign of stability for these latitudes.

Ogle huddled with Clarkson, Mason, and Glantzberg. It was decided to wait until the 0300 forecast, when all the fleet was at sea, before deciding whether to postpone the test. With clear air aloft, Glantzberg was guardedly optimistic about the Air Force mission. But Clarkson had larger concerns: "I'm worried about our last P2V, out there in messy weather, trying to head off that stupid ship," he rumbled. "Shouldn't we send the *Carpenter* over there instead?"

"Not enough time, I'm afraid, General," answered Ogle. "We worked out that problem before the *Rendova* left. It would take the *Carpenter* five hours to reach the ship, and six more to get back on station; but we shoot in nine hours, assuming no further calamities. That leaves the ship relatively close, and right in the fallout path. As things stand now, the plane should reach her by 0100, much farther out, and with almost seven hours to divert to a safer position."

They were interrupted by Jack Clark's voice on the speaker: "Kiowa calling Cherokee." It was 2230. Evidently the firing party had reached Runit on its outbound leg.

"Go ahead, Kiowa," said Ogle.

We're at station seven, Bill . . . er, Cherokee. We've got a little problem with the firing cable . . . the resistance has dropped below ten megohms on eight out of 48 conductors. It looks as if some moisture may have penetrated a splice we put in last week. Herb Grier says it's no big sweat unless they go below one meg. Maybe we should get permission to fire from here, just in case things get worse by the time we come back again to close the switches."

"Roger that, Kiowa. We'll put it in the hopper and advise you when you call in from station six. You might inventory that bunker to see if you need any supplies; we've still got time to send a boat over."

Ogle put his headset down and turned back to Clarkson. "Looks like I spoke too soon," he grunted, tapping the dottle from his pipe and refilling it. "Now we're back to three down and three to go." He got up and stretched his arms over his head to relieve the tension. A number of the technical people, hearing the announcement, had left their stations and clustered around us.

"Firing from Runit, is that practical?" asked Clarkson, adjusting his rimless glasses, a worried frown appearing on his forehead. "I mean, we'd have no way to evacuate them in case of any emergency."

"Oh, I don't think there's any particular hazard... Only a little inconvenience. Runit has always been our fallback station. Remember, we were going to fire from there until the Big Bang flap. Then, when it got around to evacuating the atoll, we decided to shoot from the *Estes*. Actually, the bunker could withstand the blast pressure from a 100-megaton shot. All the vents can be closed. It has auxiliary power. It seems to me all they really need is food, water, and a few comic books to pass the time until we can get them out." Ogle lighted his stove and looked around at the group of anxious faces. "Any of you guys see any unforeseeable problems? Walt, Bob?"

"No, not really," said MacConnell. "We've already agreed not to fire unless the weather cooperates. They shouldn't have much fallout to contend with."

All eyes switched to me. "Waves?" I said. "Hell, I don't know. Our experiments suggest three or four big ones... probably less than a minute duration. With the bunker vents closed, even if the run up inundated the whole area, it should drain off fairly rapidly. At worst, the surges might knock the dike down and pile sand against the doors; make them difficult to open. They might drown the auxiliary power unit. But . . . ten miles away, and a quarter-mile inland, it seems a bit unlikely."

Ogle turned back to Clarkson and Buriss. "Well, you guys, I guess the ball is in your court. Technically, there are some advantages to hardwire firing from land. No radio problems . . . No sloping decks. I'm a great believer in solid-earth operations."

"Let's go for it," said Buriss. "The sooner we decide, the longer we'll have to make the switch."

"I agree," said Clarkson. "Let's go for it."

"Fine," said Ogle. "I'll alert the *Rendova*, and ask them to set up a chopper to bring the heroes back after the shot."

Advised of the change, the firing party wended its way up the island chain locking the switches open. Meanwhile, a tender was dispatched to Runit with food, blankets, and flashlights . . . and a chess set, at Abe Schwartz's request. At 2335, Clark called us from Eluklab: "Got a couple of problems. First, it's raining a storm up here . . . Thunder, lightning, and shots of hail as big as pea gravel. Also, the wind is from the north, which I suppose your weather types all know about."

The second problem was more serious. They had found a frozen blow-off valve on the liquid nitrogen feed line. The pressure in Mike's cylindrical cooling jacket was rising slowly as the liquid evaporated. Moreover, the liquid level was falling because the feed pump could not supply more nitrogen from the reservoir against the rising pressure.

"We've thawed it out twice by pouring sea water on it," explained Jack, "but the pump just runs till the level gets back to normal; then it shuts off and the valve freezes up. Agnew has timed it. He figures that it'll take about four hours for the pressure to rise to where it might endanger the system. So, in view of the present weather hold, we're proposing to just stick around here until the situation clarifies. If the weather breaks, we'll arm the device, bleed the pressure off manually, and head for Runit about 0500. That'll give about us two hours to get back here and disarm it if we have a misfire. If we have a weather hold, we'll shut everything down, and take the valve to Parry to rework it. OK?"

"What do you think, Stan?" asked Ogle. "You're a boat type. The only risk I see is if they have trouble with that AVR." In nautical matters he was clearly out of his depth.

"That torpedo boat has four 2500-hp Packard engines," said Buriss, who had once been a PT exec. "At least one of 'em ought to work. In a pinch, both of us know how to shut the system down. We could get there by chopper from the *Estes* in half an hour." Again, General Clarkson nodded assent.

"OK, Kiowa," responded Ogle. "Your proposed action is approved here. We will provide an updated weather advisory at 0300. This is Cherokee, out."

At midnight, the siren wailed, and Mahatma announced: "Attention. Attention. Today is D-Day. Standby to synchronize clocks. At the tone, it will be 0000, exactly." We could all hear the WWVH signal. Precise timing was vital to many experiments. As Ogle had earlier explained, "If you've got a camera that shoots a million frames a second, and you're one second off, you've wasted 20 miles of film."

I had by now discovered Mahatma's true identity. He was a jolly, little Italian sound engineer named Frank Strabola, who habitually wore nothing but swimming trunks, tennies, and a shark tooth necklace that he had traded for a radio tube from a Marshallese native. He taped all his broadcasts in advance. "I'm gun shy," he told me. "If I tried to do a live countdown, I'd blow it, for sure." Frank had worked for EGG for eight years, mostly at the Nevada Test Site. In addition to broadcasting, he was in charge of EGG's hardwire timing group, who furnished precise timing signals to anyone who needed them. Like Hetzel, he was a master at his peculiar craft.

At 0130, we heard that the P2V had located the errant vessel 300 miles northwest of Eniwetok, completely blacked out except for her running lights. When she failed to answer on the radio distress channels, they had buzzed her twice with their landing lights on. This brought a belated radio response; the ship was diverted, and would be out of danger by dawn. "She is the British merchantman *Hartismere*," said the pilot. "I guess everybody on board was asleep."

He had hardly finished when Mason burst out of the weather room. The vortex that was driving the squall line had moved on to the west. "The wind has shifted to south," he said, excitedly. "So far as we can see, there are no other disturbances headed this way for at least 12 hours."

Ogle had just returned from the coffee urn with a brimming cup. His fifteenth? "Well, I'll be damned," he said, carefully setting the cup down. "A clean strikeout, with the bases loaded. Gentlemen, we've still got a ball game!" Glantzberg was dancing a jig, and Clarkson's stony visage cracked into a broad smile. Ogle reached for his headset. "Let's get back to the arming party and tell them it's clear sailing."

But before he could press his Mike button, Jack Clark was on the air, calling us: "Cherokee, Agnew has whipped the valve problem, and the storm seems to have blown by. We'd like permission to arm this monster, so we can get back to the coffee and sandwiches you were going to send over to Station 7. Over."

"Roger that," said Ogle. "We now have affirmative weather clearance, so we are in Condition Green. Proceed with arming as rapidly as possible. We cannot depart Area 1 (the lagoon), until your AVR is secured and we take its crew on board. Over."

I didn't hang around to hear the arming details a second time. As a result of too much coffee and the whirlwind succession of events, I was suffering from what my sainted Aunt Winifred used to call "nervous prostitution." I slipped down to my cabin. MacConnell was already in the sack, snoring like a trooper. I lay down, unable to sleep. I could shut the body off, but not the brain. Condition Green. The long wait was over . . . All those months of sweat and travail, now culminating in the measured voice of Mahatma, counting off the hours.

Someone was shaking my arm gently. "Doctor Ward, they want you in the Control Room, Sir." I fought my way up through layers of sleep, into awareness. From the slow heaving motions, I knew we were at sea. My watch read 0510. MacConnell was still snoring. I splashed some water on my face, and headed topside. Out on deck, it was pitch dark, and the air had that purple velvet warmth known only to the tropics. The sky was mostly clear, and a billion stars loomed down, glowing softly, not the hard, brilliant points of the California desert. There was a gentle breeze, but which direction? I tried to orient myself by the stars, but could find none of the familiar constellations in that panoply. Was that Orion, almost overhead, but upside down?

In that soft moment, it was hard to rationalize our purpose here, waiting, in the middle of nowhere, to make our own star . . . a harbinger of eternal peace, or the war to end all wars?

The Control Room was nearly empty; in one corner there was a chess game in process, with a few kibitzers. Ogle sat slumped in his swivel chair, headset on the desk, dead pipe, cold coffee. I touched his arm. He lifted an eyelid, then sat back, yawning, stretching his arms over his head. "Where is everybody," I asked. "Is this the calm before the storm?"

"Probably in the briefing room," he grunted. "The air circus has already started. They've got to get 26 aircraft aloft and into position by shot time."

0530. First call for early breakfast. I asked Ogle to join me but he demurred. "They're bringing up trays for us setting hens," he said. "See you back here at 0700, OK?" I went below and had a Cattleman's Special: Fresh papaya, steak, eggs over easy, fried potatoes, and four cups of coffee. Who knew when the next meal might be forthcoming?

0600. Up to the briefing room. Plenty of action here, mostly brass, but few technical people. Despite the exhaust fans, the room was blue with smoke. I helped myself to coffee and sat down next to Frank Davis. "Good to see you, Bob," he grinned, punching me on the arm. "I hear they've been keeping you busy."

"It goes with the job," I smiled. "Not exactly what I foresaw when I signed up . . . Sort of fascinating, though, to see an operation of this kind all coming together . . . The moment of truth, so to say."

"The moment of truth," he echoed, "and if we're lucky, by this time tomorrow it'll be history, and most of us will be looking ahead to our next assignment."

"Where will yours be, any idea?"

"I've put in for Washington, the Pentagon . . . got a plug from the Old Man . . . But, in the peacetime army, who knows? I could end up teaching tank tactics at Fort Benning." We both laughed, and I don't think there was the slightest doubt in either of our minds where young Major Davis was headed.

The large magnetic panel, or "situation board", at the end of the room displayed a patch of ocean 1,000 miles wide (east-west) by 600 miles high (north-south). At this scale (100 miles per foot), the islands of the Marshall group appeared as black circles a few inches across. Eniwetok was in the center, Bikini near the right margin, and Kwajalein in the lower-right corner.

A cluster of tiny magnetic ships clung to the southeast sector of Eniwetok. Only the *Estes*, the *Rendova*, and the *Curtiss* were labeled. Three isolated markers showed the current positions of the *Horizon*, 75 miles to the northeast, the aircraft control ship, *O'Bannon*, halfway between Eniwetok and Kwajalein, and the errant merchantman, *Hartismere*, 300 miles north of Eniwetok, and headed eastward.

As Frank and I talked, Colonel Jack Parsons, Glantzberg's aide, had outlined a dozen ellipses in colored chalk, showing the orbiting patterns of aircraft already aloft. There were three photo planes, at 10, 15, and 20,000 feet, respectively, equally-spaced around the shot point, and 40 miles distant; three VIP observers, at 15,000 feet, ditto; two controller aircraft, 50 miles southeast, at 25 and 35,000 feet; two aerial tankers beneath the controllers; and two Coast Guard SA16's at low altitudes, for search and rescue.

Parsons stood back, as if to admire his handiwork; but it was only to perceive from better vantage how to fit five more tracks into the scramble already present. Three B50 bombers, specially instrumented to measure fireball radiation, altitude 35,000 feet, distance 50 miles; two B47 jet bombers, to penetrate to 10 miles and run away, testing blast effects on their structural integrity. And far out to the north and east, weather planes scouted for rain squalls. The movements of this planetary multitude were being directed by the lower control aircraft, a B29 bomber converted into a flying control tower, and monitored from below by the *O'Bannon*, equipped with its huge ground-control radar. All of the voice traffic relevant to keeping the planes in position was piped into loudspeakers here in the CIC, and also into the Brain Room, where General Glantzberg could order changes as he saw fit. Despite my years of private and commercial flying, I was hard put to understand their cryptic military jargon, particularly since most aircraft were identified only by alpha-numeric codes: Echo-1, Peter-2, etc.

Still to appear, of course, were the twelve jet sampler aircraft, led by two jet "sniffers", which would appear in groups of four, at hourly intervals, beginning one hour after detonation. However, even as Parsons finished his chalk work, we heard the sniffers, Scouts 1 and 2, announce that they were airborne, and climbing to rendezvous with their respective tankers at 0645. "Take it easy, Frank," I said. "Time to attend to my knitting."

As I left the CIC, the klaxon sounded, and Mahatma announced H-1 hour. I suddenly realized I was shaking inwardly and my mouth was dry. We were now fully committed, and nothing less than a major equipment failure would alter the inexorable march of time to detonation. One hour to wait—that was the problem, the waiting, with nothing to keep my mind occupied. Here we were, on the brink of a cataclysmic experiment, fraught with enormous uncertainty, and with very little margin for error. Mike had been designed for 2-megatons yield, upper limit of 5. Then, Teller had said it might go 100. But our back-of-the-envelope calculations suggested that 20-megatons might rupture the atoll rim, generating a major tsunami. And the *Horizon* had three men out in a little boat, waiting for the waves to arrive. If the rim ruptured, how high might these waves be? 100 feet? 1,000 feet? Our calculations were at least as uncertain as the best yield estimate. I debated whether to call the *Hor* and suggest they keep the men aboard until the waves passed. They could tow the skiff. If the waves were really big, they wouldn't need the record to warn us. If not, they would lose little time getting back into the skiff and powering over to the instrument raft. Then I decided against any last-minute changes.

In the Brain Room, the flyers' conversations were muted. Ogle was talking to Jack Clark at station Seven. Since all timing signals originated aboard the *Estes*, Ogle was still running the countdown, even though Jack would actually push the button that actuated the 15-minute sequence timer. After detonation, control would revert to Ogle. Locked in their airtight bunker, the firing party would know only that the lights were green at the time of detonation. Radio contact would be lost until Mike's radiation field stopped jamming the airwaves—probably 10 or 15 minutes later.

As during rehearsal, the Brain room was filled with technical people, each attending his particular instruments, most of which were connected by individual radio circuits to transmitters scattered along the atoll rim. Their connections, too, would cease on detonation; their sole function was to monitor instrument readiness up to the last second, or to initiate some late-stage sequence of events. Every panel was aglow with colored lights; green lines traced delicate patterns across banks of oscilloscope screens; relays chattered; quiet voices muttered prayers, imprecations. Unlike the rehearsal, the row of kibitzer seats was nearly empty. Anybody with nothing else to do was down in the CIC, watching the air show.

I switched on my radio, put on the headset, and called the *Horizon*. The radio room was next to the bridge, and Harry Hewlitt answered. I explained my concern about the small boat operation, and asked his opinion. He said: "Wait one," and left me on hold for a few minutes. Then he came back on. "We've been drifting for about an hour, planning to run slowly back toward the raft at H-hour to pick up the boys," he said. "I've been watching them with binoculars, though, and I just took another look . . . There are only two people in the boat. Somebody's actually sitting on that raft!"

"Good God," I groaned. "They weren't supposed to board the raft until the waves have passed."

"I know. But, under the circumstances, neither Dr. Engels nor I think we have time to reorganize this procedure . . . we're just too far away."

"Understand," I said. "This is Cherokee, standing by."

The wall clock crawled toward 0645; the stretch of time now seemed immense. Then Mahatma: ". . . the time is now H-30 minutes." Outside, the thunder of feet; the off-duty watch assembling, a half-hour later than rehearsal, to give the stewards and galley crew leeway to complete their chores. Ogle, slipping one earphone forward and turning to Buriss: "Everything's green at Runit." Then, to me: "How about the *Horizon?*"

I decided against sharing my alarm. "All ready, and standing by."

"Fine. Let's check the air show." He flipped a panel switch, called: "Control-1, Control-2, this is Cherokee. Status, please?" Switching to his channel, I could monitor the conversation. Buriss, sitting beside Ogle, had his own headset. MacConnell, beyond Buriss, was chattering over his own radio.

"This is Control-1. All units in position. Clear above 8,000. Visibility unlimited. Temperature fourteen. Over."

"Control-2. Scouts refueled and ready. Red Flight on standby at Mother-1." The sniffers were poised; the first four jet samplers were awaiting takeoff from Kwajalein. The sampling operation was being controlled by the huge B-36 bomber, orbiting above Control-1 at 35,000 feet.

"OK," said Ogle, flipping another switch, "let's hear from the *O'Bannon*. "Control-3, come in, please."

"This is Control-3. We have 20 goblins (radar images), and two more coming. Clouds 70 per cent. Temperature 84 degrees. Dew point 78. Over."

"Hell," exulted Ogle, reaching for his pipe pouch. "This is more like it. The bases are loaded, and we've got a Big Hitter coming to the plate! Who'd like to get me some more coffee?" Davis, behind us with Glantzberg, grabbed his cup. Switching back to Runit, Ogle eyed the wall clock, crawling toward 0700. He announced, tersely: "Station-7, standby for sequence time tone."

Then, Mahatma's booming voice: "Attention. Attention. At the tone, it will be H-15 minutes . . . Ten . . . Niner . . . Eight . . ." the seconds ran down. Then, the tone, heard throughout the fleet, in the air, and in the sealed bunker on Runit, where the sequence timer had taken over. Barring human intervention, the die was cast! Not quite true . . . a malfunction of any of several vital diagnostic instruments could interrupt the timer until the last millisecond. But, all that we mortals could do now was wait.

Dark goggles in hand, I followed Clarkson and Glantzberg out onto the abbreviated deck adjacent to the briefing room, and aft to where it ended, overlooking the helicopter platform on the stern. The main deck below us was crowded by the off-duty watch, sitting in orderly rows, backs to the northwest and the invisible atoll from which Mike's fireball would erupt. The *Estes* was steaming slowly eastward, spearheading an echelon that included the *Rendova*, the *Curtiss*, and the destroyers *Fletcher* and *Radford*.

The sky had all the earmarks of a perfect tropic day; clear above, but flanked by avenues of cumulus. The puffy clouds, were cut off flat underneath by the thermal inversion, where the temperature dropped below the dew point. In the east, the rising sun, lighting both the clouds from beneath and the sky above them, suffused our limited world in pink opalescence crowned with gold. The western horizon, yet untouched, lay dark and somber.

Again, Mahatma's measure cadence, counting the minutes, then the seconds. What were the last thoughts of condemned men? Turning away from the blast and adjusting my goggles, I could see nothing, not even the white bulkhead before me. "five . . . four . . . three . . . two . . . one . . ." Then, the tone.

Instantly, everything was visible. The bulkhead. The railing beside me. The after kingpost, with its array of antennas. The white hats of sailors on the deck below. Everything was bathed in white, shadowless light. I could feel the heat on my back, as when the summer sun emerges from behind obscuring clouds. A ragged cheer rose from the deck, but otherwise there was no sound . . . the shockwave would take 150 seconds to reach us. It worked, I thought. It really worked. For no reason at all, I felt like laughing. "Sonafabitch!" exclaimed General Glantzberg.

The light dimmed. The warmth faded. The loudspeakers barked: "Attention, all hands. You may now remove goggles and face the blast." We turned, and could now see the fireball, a semicircle of red light, like the sun just rising . . . filling a quarter of the sky. Detaching itself from the horizon, it rose rapidly, becoming enshrouded in lenticular cloud wreaths of its own manufacture. Still rising, it slowly faded, blending with the prevailing cumulus.

Finally, the shock wave, which had been traveling outward all this time at the speed of a rifle bullet; a sharp report; a gust of warm dry wind; a protracted, thunderous rumble. The ship shook, and then recovered. Almost simultaneously, burgeoning above the nearby clouds like a genie, the towering head of the distant mushroom rose into the clear sky. Glantzberg raised his arm and sighted at its top. "About 50,000 feet already, I make it," he said. "'Going straight up at 600 miles an hour! 'Guess I better run down to the CIC and catch the action." I glanced at my watch. It was only H+3 minutes . . . the first tsunami waves would reach seamount Freddie in another twenty.

The Brain Room was in a state of restrained jubilation. Instrument banks, no longer needed, were dark, or flashing aimlessly. Everyone was on his feet, cheering, laughing, gesticulating, shedding nine months of accumulated tension. "Twenty," I heard someone shout, ". . . at least twenty. Maybe thirty." Could he mean megatons?

At the control console, heedless of the melee, sat Ogle, Buriss, and MacConnell, all wearing headsets. Seeing me, Ogle beckoned, pointing to his headphone. Then, catching Frank Davis's attention, he swept his hand in a circle and pointed to the door. Davis instantly sprang forward and commenced clearing idle celebrants from the room. I sat down, adjusted my headset, and switched to the *Horizon*'s channel. "Blackfoot, this is Cherokee. Come in, please."

"Cherokee, this is Blackfeet," Henry Engels came back, instantly. "Bob, Bascom is still on the raft. We are drifting about 200 meters away. It is beginning to rain here; we can't see very much. Do you have any source information?"

"Blackfoot, Cherokee. The experiment was apparently successful . . . I have an unverified estimate of moderate to large signals. Over."

"Roger, Cherokee. We have nothing yet to report, except that the sea appears unusually calm. Over."

Ogle was frowning; he had apparently been monitoring our overlong conversation. So I said: "Roger, Blackfoot. Standing by for your report. This is Cherokee, out."

It would take them at least ten minutes to analyze the recorder signals, so I switched my left earphone over to Ogle's channel. He was listening to Jack Clark, calling from Runit. There was a great deal of static:

"OK here . . . dust from shock . . . bunker swayed . . . earthquake . . . water, lots of water . . . basin drain spouted to ceiling . . . electrical conduits, too . . . half an inch on floor, including everything we ate yesterday . . . stinks pretty bad . . . when will wave hazard . . . over? . . . want to open door . . . check activity."

Ogle glanced at me. It was H+10 minutes. I had estimated 13 minutes for waves to reach Runit . . . duration five minutes? I held up ten fingers. He relayed this to Clark, and signed off, pulling an earphone aside. "What could put all that water in the bunker?" he asked.

"Too soon for water waves," I said. "Maybe the overpressure pulse behind the shock front. That might force lagoon water back up through all the waste plumbing, or through the coral basement into the electrical conduits."

"Then why didn't it happen on GREENHOUSE? That was only six miles away."

I hunched my shoulders. "Smaller shot . . . lower pressure . . . shorter duration?"

"Live and learn," he grunted, twisting his channel selector. "Let's see what's happening upstairs. Control-2, this is Cherokee. Status, please."

"Cherokee, Control-2. We've really got a house-of-fire up here. We've climbed to 40,000, and moved away to about 60 miles from GZ. At H+10 minutes, we estimated cloud top 110,000, width 40 miles, bottom 60,000, stem width 15 miles, very ragged, and dirty brown. There's lots of low-level cloud cover, with rainsqualls obscuring the lower stem. Scouts now en route to explore and report back by 0800. Red Flight now airborne from Mother-1 . . ." There was more, but my right earphone had come alive: "Cherokee, this is Blackfeet.

"We have Code 3 . . . Perhaps Code-4. It's very mysterious . . . a sort of step in the record. We suggest you assume Code 4, until you receive island reports. Captain Dunbar says we're getting some radioactivity on deck. Over."

I acknowledged, and turned to report to Ogle, but MacConnell was there, requesting departure of the first radsafe helicopter from *Rendova*. "Is that the survey you wanted me to go on?" I asked. "The *Horizon* reports a possible wave emergency."

"No, we'll go later, when the situation clarifies. This is just a preliminary sniff at "Wetok and Parry, to see if it's safe to send in work crews to get the facilities operating. So far, our spies on Runit haven't reported any activity. Go ahead, Walt. If the base is clear, let 'em fly north until they pick up the first traces. If that cloud is really 40 miles in diameter, it may extend over most of the atoll." He turned back to me: "OK, what's the wave picture?"

I reiterated Henry's message, including his reservations. Ogle sat forward, eyes shut, massaging his temples with his fingertips, thinking. "Why don't you send Colonel Jacobs a TWX," he said, "recommending a conditional alert, but not to be activated until we confirm. That way, it won't come as a shock to the Warning Service if the island reports look ominous. We can always cancel if things improve . . . . and tell the *Horizon* to get the Hell out of there . . . flank speed. Head north until we advise you otherwise."

About 0800, we received some disturbing news from Runit. Fifteen minutes previously, they had cracked the door and found no water outside. They then tested the air with a Geiger counter and read nothing higher than the residual 1-2 mR left from GREENHOUSE Operation the previous year. Outside, they had placed the counter on the concrete doorstep, and looked around for information of use to us back at the command post. They found some singed grass, and saw that the blast wave had knocked the doors off two instrument trailers. The water waves had not advanced closer than 100 yards from the dugout, but already (H+35 min) the edge of the mushroom cloud was overhead, and its red, blotchy stem appeared no more than five miles away. Low clouds were advancing, and it was starting to rain.

As they returned to the bunker, they heard the counter clicking busily; the needle read 25 mR, and even as they watched, climbed to 50, then to 100. Although this level was only equivalent to about one chest X-ray per hour, it was going up fast. By the time Jack had gotten everyone inside, it was reading 1 R outside, and 25 mR inside the control room!

"That was ten minutes ago," said Jack. "Now, with the airtight door shut, we're reading 10R near the door, and 150 mR in the control room. Abe Schwartz thinks it's coming through the roof. There's ten feet of sand up there, but the rain could be carrying radioactive fallout from the crater down through the sand.

"Anyway, we've moved into a back room where it's currently only 10 mR. As long as the generator runs, we've got lights and the radio, although it's too hot to man the radio continuously. We'll send somebody in to check with you every 15 minutes or so. This is Station-7, back to you."

"Roger, Seven," said Ogle, "we've got a chopper sniffing up your way right now. It's big enough to carry you all if the situation permits. If not, you'll just have to sit tight until things cool off, or we can think up a better plan. What can you do if it gets any hotter?"

"We can go downstairs... But that's where all the sewage has collected. There's about four inches of water on the floor."

"Well, here's hoping you don't have to sleep down there tonight. Rotsa Ruck. This is Cherokee out." Despite the joke, his face was grim. He turned immediately to MacConnell and Buriss and summarized the problem. "What's the story on your sniffer flight, Walt?"

"Eniwetok is clear. They're on their way to Parry... Should report any minute."

"Good. If Parry is clear, have them make a stab at Runit, but don't let them exceed 1R total exposure. As I read it, the fallout levels should peak out within an hour or two. By that time, we should have the airfield and wash-down facility reactivated. I'd hate to bring a hot machine aboard the *Rendova*, unless Runit becomes an emergency."

0815. H+1 hour. The radiation level was holding at Runit. Control-2 reported that Echos 1 and 2 had returned. Mike had topped out at 120,000 feet well into the stratosphere. The cloud was now 60 miles in diameter; the stem 20. Red Flight 1 and 2 had finished refueling, and would penetrate the stem at 45,000 feet in half an hour. Red 3 and 4 to follow as soon as the leaders had emerged. "Just in and out, until you get the feel of it," were their instructions. It was estimated that they would require about an hour of total time inside the smoky column for effective sampling.

Back at Kwajalein, crews were waiting in flack suits, with giant tongs to open the wing-tip canisters and transfer the gauze particle collectors, intensely radioactive, to lead cylinders, cylinders to boxes, boxes to jet transports, for the long flight back to Los Alamos. Other crews waited to wash down the jet fighters with fire hoses; to assist the pilots to emerge, to disrobe, to shower; scrubbing their hair, eyes, noses, fingernails, every crevice, until the Geiger counters stopped screaming, stopped clicking. Then, the debriefing; every action, thought, impression, response to be dictated in case the in-flight recorders were not working.

By 0830, the Walt's radsafe sniffer had encountered no radioactivity over Parry or Japtan islands, and was proceeding north toward Runit. "It's very strange," reported the pilot. "We've been under the main mushroom ever since we reached the atoll. But it's very high, and we haven't seen any activity. The stem is just ahead . . . It's surrounded by little rain squalls . . . I can see lightning flashes . . . almost continuous . . . The main column has almost reached Runit, but seems to be moving eastward . . . out to sea." His voice broke, and then came in again.

"Holy Cow! We just passed through some rain . . . We're plastered with little mud drops . . . We're getting 30R outside . . . Apache (*Rendova*), This is Peter-1 . . . Daddy is coming home . . . ETA . . . fifteen minutes."

"Damn, damn!" said Ogle, switching to the distress frequency. "Apache, this is Cherokee. Implement Plan Able, immediately. I want those birds in the air before Peter-1 arrives. Send Peter-2 to pick me up. Please acknowledge." Then he turned to Frank Davis. "Get Mason in here. I want his 0900 wind report, pronto.

"Walt, Bob. You guys will have to hold the fort. I've got to get out to Boken to salvage some films, or our main diagnostics may be destroyed. The Able crews will reactivate facilities at Eniwetok and Parry. Your job, Walt, is to keep track of things at Runit, and to keep the fleet out of the fallout path. Bob, you've got to standby for your outer island messages and issue appropriate responses. Stan Buriss, of course, will be in charge until I get back . . . probably two hours. With luck, the atoll might be clear for re-entry by tomorrow morning."

Mason came in with the wind charts. As anticipated, the main cloud was moving east at about 30 knots with the high-altitude flow, while the upper stem drifted southwest with the trades. Unexpectedly, however, the lower stem, containing most of the heavy particulate fallout, was taking a sluggish westerly path between the *Horizon*, to the north, and the remainder of the fleet, to the south. Runit had been right in its path!

"What do you think, Brian? I asked. Should we have the *Horizon* continue north or head northwest?

"Difficult to say," he mused. "The lower stem might be caught in an eddy, in which case it could swing around to the north. I'd suggest having the *Horizon* continue north."

"I concur," said Ogle. "Runit is probably out of danger now. All they have to do is sit tight until we can go in and pick them up. The important thing is to keep the *Horizon* from being clobbered . . . Gotta run, here comes my taxi." He was out the door and down the ladder before any of us could say a word.

"There's going to be big trouble aboard that chopper," laughed Frank Davis, bending down to pick up something from under Ogle's chair. "He forgot his pipe pouch."

0915. Save for Walt, Buriss, and myself, the Brain Room was again empty; people had slipped off to bed or were down in the CIC watching the air circus, which was just now getting into full swing. Having explained the situation to the *Horizon* and given her sailing instructions, I had nothing specific to do but wait for the island reports. The waves should have passed Wake by now, but Folsom had four miles to pedal, and then to encrypt his message. Guam would be next, and then Midway. I had decided to wait for all three reports and then to confer with Henry Engels before deciding how to respond. That would still give the Tsunami Warning Service two hours to alert local authorities.

Walt had been in touch with the Runit group. They had moved into the flooded basement, where the radiation level had not exceeded 5 mR. There was no furniture, except for two desks. It was 90 degrees, and damp. Their generator had died, but they had flashlights and a battery-powered radio . . . Its signal was very weak. Jack had said, "Have you every tried sleeping on a desk with two other guys?"

Fighting an overwhelming desire to sleep, I switched to the air-control frequency. Red Leader, the first jet sampler aircraft, was just about to penetrate the cloud stem. From the pilot's steady monologue, I gathered that he was calling out his cockpit gauge readings, so that they could be taped by Control-2, as well as by his on-board voice recorder.

"I am straight and level at 42,000 feet, speed 400 knots, visibility unlimited; outside temperature 10, inside 50, radiation zero, dosage zero; fuel 3/4, all other needles normal. Heading for small cloud segment projecting from main stem; Red-2 is on my right wing; entering cloud . . . now."

There was a long silence . . . perhaps half a minute. Then, "Wow! WOW! Whoa there, Nellie . . . This crate's buckin' like a Brahmin steer. I'm not flyin' . . . jes' hangin on! I'm in a dim, red tunnel; visibility zero; outside temp. 110; dose rate 12 R per hour! Total dose 2.6R already! Gyro is floppin' . . ." Then his transmission was overwhelmed with bursts of static; his words fragmented; impossible to decipher; vanishing altogether. Finally, we heard: "Red-2 . . . is Red-1 . . . hanging left ninety . . . now . . ."

There was nothing more for several minutes, until they apparently burst into the clear. "Red-1, this is Red-2. I have you at 10 o'clock, high, closing."

"Roger that. Control-2, this Red Leader. We are at 40,000, outbound. Fuel one-half. Request vector to Control-1. Do your read? Over."

"Red Leader, Control-2. Descend to 20,000 on radial 165. Contact Control-1 on channel 6. Acknowledge . . . Nice work, fellas."

Out of the corner of my eye, I saw General Glantzberg seat himself beside Stan Buriss, and adjust his headset. Red Leader was cautioning Red-3 and Red-4, who were approaching the main cloud stem: "Cut it very thin," he said. "It's a blast furnace in there. The needles don't seem to read right, and your controls will feel very mushy . . . And watch that dose rate needle; it spins like a stop watch."

At this point, Glantzberg broke in and identified himself. "Red Flight, you can forget about spending an hour inside the cloud. At the levels we're getting, five or ten minutes should be plenty. Remember, you must exit before your total dose exceeds 20R! Good luck, this is Top Bird out."

At 0928, Red-3 and Red-4 penetrated the stem, flying under roughly the same conditions as their predecessors. As a communications experiment, Red-3 had been counting as they entered the cloud, and got only to "eight" before he was cut off by a burst of radio noise. Five minutes dragged by . . . then ten more, while Control-2 continued to call at one-minute intervals. Glantzberg had risen from his chair, fists clenched, jaw set.

Suddenly, we heard from the *O'Bannon*: "Control-2, this is Control-3. We have a transponder echo from grid secter George-6 . . . Very weak. Might be one of your bandits."

"George-6?" exclaimed Glantzberg, banging his huge fist on the desk . . . "How in hell did he get way over there? He must have flown clear through the damn column. I'll bet he's hotter than a roasted potato."

"Red-3, this is Control-2. We see your transponder. If you read me, try your VHF . . . channel 8."

"Roger, Control-2. This is Red-3. I've been in the clear, flying around in circles for five minutes with no contact . . . Apparently all my radios were out . . . plus, I have no gyro or magnetic compass. I am now at 33,000, fuel one-third. Total dosage 14.6 R. I have lost Red-4. Do you copy?"

"Red-3, Control-2. We read you loud and clear. You are on the northwest side of the cloud stem. Fly towards the sun and reset your gyro compass to 097 degrees. Mother-2 (Eniwetok) is now open. Vector 063, 70 miles. Report Red-4 if you make contact. Control-2, standing by on channel 8."

"Roger that. I've got almost an hour's fuel. Guess I'll spend some of it hunting for my buddy."

"Jesus!" exclaimed Glantzberg to Buriss, shoving one headphone back. "We may have lost Red-4; the radiation field seems to have kayoed his electronics. Is that possible, Stan?"

"I suppose it is possible . . . We just haven't had any experience with these conditions. It's not something you can duplicate in a laboratory experiment. I'll alert Mother-2 and ask them to have choppers standing by. What about White and Blue Flights, General?"

"White is refueling now. With your permission, we'll hold them until Red Flight is . . . clear."

Control-2 and Red-3 continued calling every few minutes until 1005, when Red-4 suddenly responded. He had apparently tumbled out of control within the churning cloud stem, temporarily losing consciousness, and had finally been ejected at an altitude of 23,000 feet—20,000 feet lower than his point of entry. His transponder was still non-functional, but he had picked up the Eniwetok beacon on his direction-finder, and was now headed toward it. Control-2 had deduced that he was about 10 miles farther from Eniwetok than Red-3, 10,000 feet lower, and had about the same fuel reserve—very little.

Everyone's overwhelming jubilation at finding Red-4 now gave way to tense anxiety as the two pilots fought to conserve their dwindling fuel supplies. Some factors were in their favor. Ogle's survey chopper reported that the Mike cloud stem was now drifting northwest, entirely clear of the lagoon. Radioactivity seemed to be confined to islands north of Runit, and the southern half of the atoll appeared uncontaminated. Two helicopters were airborne from Eniwetok strip and heading west toward the approaching jets. Control-1 had also directed one of the Coast Guard SA-16's to highball it for the lagoon, in case either of the planes had to ditch. Working against them was the poor glide angle of the F84G without power, which Glantzberg likened to that of a "streamlined brick."

While most of us were glued to the drama unfolding aloft, Stan Buriss had been busily directing Plan Able, the reactivation of shore facilities and the mapping of radiation levels around the atoll. The object was to get task force headquarters re-established ashore as soon as possible, so that the scientific people could organize their data recovery programs. Firing Mike successfully was only half the job; it still remained to find out what had happened. Meanwhile, speculation was rampant among the scientists aboard, with the consensus hovering between 10 and 20 megatons . . . It was H+3 hours, and still no word from Wake. Had we generated a dangerous tsunami or not?

Suddenly MacConnell was calling me, while pointing to his headphones; I had slipped mine forward temporarily to relieve the pressure on my ears. I put them back and received an earful of incoherent ravings: "Oh my God, my God . . . all going to die . . . fallout . . . hundred Roentgens on deck . . ." Then, a clatter, and silence. It was the *Horizon*'s frequency, but I couldn't place the voice.

A minute or so later, Jeff Knight came on, his usually placid voice somewhat anxious. "It's Captain Dunbar. He seems to have gone off his nut . . . raving about deadly fallout. I've asked the crew to restrain him, and Bascom has gone to check his equipment. I've closed up the ship and started the wash-down. We're now about 100 miles north-northwest of you, with calm seas, and a little rain for the past half-hour. The cloud is still over us. This is Blackfoot, over."

"Blackfoot, Cherokee," said MacConnell, "Stand by while we investigate." Then, to Buriss, who had been monitoring our dialogue: "The *Horizon*'s getting fallout. Maybe the stem has caught up with her. I'd like to send one of the cloud trackers over to see where it's coming from, OK?"

"Of course," said Buriss, "just ask Control-1 to . . ." He held up a finger. "Hah . . . Red-3's just landed at Eniwetok . . . flamed out at 50 feet. Can't call it any closer then that. Red-4 is 10 miles out and gliding . . . he can't make it, so he's going to bail out over the lagoon at 3,000 feet. The choppers are out there waiting . . ."

I switched my left ear to the tower frequency. General Glantzberg was sweating through his clean drill shirt. He had a hand over his eyes. One of the chopper pilots was reporting: "Mother-2, this is Rufus-3. I am at 3,000, in the glide path . . . I think I have him. Yes, I have visual contact. He's too low to bail out . . . he's trying to stretch it. Rufus-4, do you copy?"

"Rufus-4 . . . Roger that. I am at 500, range two miles. He's just ahead, pancake landing, wheels up . . .

bouncing ... nose dive. He's down ... sinking. I don't think he released his enclosure. I am right above him. I see a seat cushion ... nothing else. Mother-2, do you read?"

Glantzberg: Suddenly assuming command of the situation, bellowing instructions, setting up a search. The SA-16, just arriving, had taken a short cut through the remnant cloud stem and gotten clobbered ... total dosage: 19.6R! There was nothing for her to do but land for emergency wash-down. What a mess, I reflected. An hour ago, a perfect exercise ... now, everything was coming unglued. I switched to Control-1 and heard MacConnell giving instructions for the cloud tracker. Christ, I had forgotten all about the *Horizon.* My right headphone crackled. It was Jeff, good old Jeff, with his calm, lucid explanation: "Cherokee, Cherokee. This is Blackfoot. We are OK. Repeat, OK. We are reading 100 milliRoentgens on deck, not 100 Roentgens. Dunbar had his equipment switch on the wrong scale. We have the wash-down system going, and are heading south. Will return to recover records. Should rendezvous with you tonight. Do you read?"

"Roger, Blackfoot. Understand 100 mR on deck. This is Cherokee out." In my left ear, Control-1 was vectoring White-3 and White-4 to their respective refueling tankers. Evidently, the second cloud-sampling attempt had been successful. Blue Flight was now en route to penetration.

Then, Walt was at my elbow, handing me a cup of coffee: "Ogle is on his way back from circling the atoll.

He says the crater is intact. He'd like to know what you've heard from your island stations."

I looked at my watch. 1045. Three and one-half hours since detonation; more than enough time for all stations to have responded. "I haven't heard anything, Walt," I said. "Do we have direct voice communication with Wake Island?"

"I don't think so. Everything outside the CZ goes by teletype. We have a weather station there . . . right in the terminal building. Why?"

"I'd like to send a cable query to my operator, highest priority we can muster."

Walt scribbled the cable address, and priority, 1B; I walked over to Communications and filed my short message. The cables officer glanced at it and whistled. "Don't get many this hot," he said. Then, "Dr. Ward? I think we have some coded traffic for you . . . came in this morning . . . Haven't got around to decrypting it yet . . . too much higher priority stuff from Washington." He leafed through a stack of messages and extracted four sheets; one each from Wake, Guam, Midway, and Johnston Island. I couldn't believe my eyes! All the work we had gone to, and the bottleneck was right here on the command ship.

"Can you decode these right now?" I asked. "They're of critical importance to the test."

"Sorry, Sir," he replied. "I've got to handle all traffic according to priority."

"OK, then, don't send my cable to Wake. Just wait right here." I steamed into the Brain Room and over to where General Clarkson was standing behind Stan Buriss and General Glantzberg, and briefly summarized the problem. Clarkson steamed into Communications and ten minutes later I had my four messages.

"I don't understand it," I said to Henry Engels over the radio. "You got Code-4 waves at Freddie, and I seem to have Code-4 responses at four islands. But we have confirmed that the reef crater is intact. The waves should reach Hawaii in two hours. What do we say to the TWS (Tsunami Warning System)?"

"Well, Bob. You're the specialist. What would you say?" The ball was back in my court. Wasn't I the world's tsunami expert?

"Why don't we announce a magnitude 6.5 earthquake? They'll send out a conditional alert. Then, if waves develop, they'll be prepared, but if nothing happens, nobody will be disappointed."

"Let's do that," said Henry Engels.

I sent off the priority earthquake message to Sutter Street, together with routine dispatches to my four island operators, complimenting their efforts and advising them that they should discontinue observations and return to the ZI at their own convenience. Then I hung around the Brain Room, listening to the air show winding down. There were no further sampling problems, and the last pilot of Blue Flight had returned to Kwajalein by 1110.

About 1130, Ogle came back on board, having first been thoroughly decontaminated at Mother-2. He was smoking a cigarette, which he immediately stuffed into the sand box when he saw his beloved pipe pouch on the instrument console. Then he settled into his chair, puffing up a storm, hands behind his head, and proceeded to fill us in about events ashore.

"We started out clockwise around the atoll, mainly to avoid the airborne stuff, which appeared to be going off to the west. If you think of the shot point as 12 o'clock, and Parry Island as 5 o'clock, we actually got clear around to about 9 o'clock before we could pick up any ground radiation, and to 10 o'clock before we saw any significant blast effects; you know, trees knocked down, wooden buildings blown away, tents burned up. "At Bogallua, which would be about 11 o'clock and six miles from GZ (Ground Zero), it was still too hot to land, and there were signs of extensive flooding, but the instrument bunker seems intact. From there, on in to GZ, everything has been washed over by waves, and most concrete structures are damaged.

"Eluklab Island has entirely disappeared; just a great big hole in the reef, full of milky water. Must be a mile across. We flew around it twice. It came within 100 yards of breaching into the ocean, but the rim is perfectly intact. So much for tidal waves, eh?"

"We're still not sure." I told him about the outer island records and my message to Mike Jacobs. "We should hear something by this afternoon if anything unusual occurs in Hawaii."

"Fine, you did the right thing," he grunted, and then continued with his account. "Coming back the other way, it was much the same, except the radiation levels were higher. Even at Runit, it was still reading 100R on the ground. It seems clear that we've got to stage a special snatch operation this afternoon to get those guys out of the bunker. I tried to reach them with my walky talky, but no response. Any ideas, Walt?"

MacConnell put his finger tips together and looked at the overhead for a moment. "Two choppers . . . Two crew in flak suits, carrying sheets . . . Bang on the door, cover them up and run for it . . . Abandon the sheets before entering the choppers. Shouldn't take more than five minutes. If we wait until 1700, the ground dose rate should be down to about 30R per hour. That's about 2.5R per fugitive."

"OK, set it up," said Ogle. "Let's use equipment that's already contaminated. We've got to save some clean choppers for data recovery." He looked at his watch and yawned prodigiously. "How about some lunch, you guys? I haven't had a square meal since Thursday."

The speakers crackled: "Attention all hands. The winner of the *Estes* Bomb Pool is number 1050. The prize of $833 can be claimed at the Purser's office." I fished in my pocket for the wrinkled slip . . . sure enough, I had won!

Like many of the technical people, I slept most of the afternoon, and awakened for supper to mixed tidings.

The bad news was that despite four hours of searching the sampler pilot was never sighted after his plane sank, and was now presumed to have been trapped inside it. "He was so damn close to the runway," said Ogle. "If only he had bailed out as announced, we could have wound up this exercise with a clean slate. He must have thought he had a chance to belly-in if he didn't make it. Glantzberg tells me quite a few fighters have survived water ditchings."

The good news was that no serious wave effects had been detected in Hawaii, and that the firing party had been snatched from the Runit bunker like Ex-lax, and were now recovering from their ordeal in the newly re-opened Flag Mess on Parry Island. Walt MacConnell had participated in the rescue, and was now at Eniwetok directing all radsafe operations. The southern half of the atoll had been declared habitable, and nearly all facilities were back in operation.

Despite the air accident, which had drawn General Glantzberg back to Kwajalein, an air of exultation pervaded the dinner mess. For most, the scientific rewards of protracted effort were yet to come in the data still entombed in concrete bunkers. But for me the battle was all but over. Despite two stiff belts of Black Label, incautiously abandoned by MacConnell in our cabin, I could not match the general exuberance

Ogle, particularly ebullient, sensed my mood. "Why so glum, young Robert? You Scripps people have done a bang-up job."

"Anticlimax, I guess. We've been on this runaway freight so long, it's hard to believe we've really stopped. After this ride, oceanography's going to seem pretty tame."

"Well, if it get's too boring, you might think of coming to LASL. With all the projects we've got coming up, we could probably use a tsunami expert . . . and don't forget to let me know before you take off."

"I won't . . . and thanks for the offer."

PART VI

THE AFTERMATH

At 0930 hours, on Sunday, 2 November, 1952, the *Rendova* re-entered Eniwetok lagoon. The rest of our impressive fleet followed, single-file, with the weather-stained *Horizon* bringing up the rear. The *Hor* was asked to anchor to leeward at some distance, because of her "contaminated" condition. No one would be allowed ashore until ship and personnel had received radsafe clearance. Normally, this would have been the responsibility of Captain Dunbar, but he was still under sedation in the *Hor's* "infirmary".

About 1100, Walt MacConnell led a survey group aboard her, where they found the general radiation level on deck to be below 1 mR, probably owing to many hours of assiduous scrubbing and hosing. Jeff later owned that they had deep-sixed a large pile of net-bound glass floats and miles of nylon rope that had stubbornly resisted decontamination. Even so, their film badges were taken ashore to be processed, to make sure that nobody had accumulated a total dosage in excess of 3.9R, the AEC standard allowance for Operation Ivy.

The radsafe party returned to Eniwetok about noon, stopping by the *Estes* only long enough to drop off Jeff and Henry Engels. In the stern of the survey boat, I glimpsed a dejected Captain Dunbar, elbows on his knees, face buried in his hands. As Ogle had remarked about himself: "Some men are just not cut out for a life at sea." Jeff looked wan and tired, a consequence of overexertion and little sleep, but Henry was his own smiling self. He had a three-day stubble, and was carrying a small ditty bag.

"Bob," he said, "I wonder if I could shave and shower in your cabin. We seem to have used up all the fresh water on the *Hor*. The evaporators are still not working right. Harry Hewlitt is wondering if you could arrange to have someone look at them again."

"Of course," I said. "It's No. 11 on the next deck. Why don't I go see about getting the *Hor* in work, and we'll meet for lunch in the wardroom?"

Fortunately, H&N could furnish two mechanics immediately to work on the *Hor's* evaporators, a rather critical problem because it would be almost three more months before she would see a port equipped for such repairs before returning to San Diego. For the crew, it meant two or three days of shore liberty after a hard week at sea; for me, it meant having to use an LCM to dive for the turtle records, once the northern lagoon had flushed itself clean. How long this would take depended mainly on the winds, which were still holding in a favorable direction. I left word for the Twins to ready the diving gear for possible use in the morning, and went down to lunch.

I found Henry and Jeff sitting with Ogle and Captain Kincaid.

There was a moment of silence while I sat down, and then Henry Engels asked Ogle if there was as yet a reliable estimate of blast energy.

"Ten, plus or minus one, megatons, is the best number we have so far," said Ogle. "That's from fireball size. We should be able to improve that estimate as soon as we get the bunker data. You might also be interested in some crater dimensions we've gotten from photo over-flights at H+3 hours: diameter, 6,300 feet; distance from reef edge, 340 feet!"

"Good grief," said Jeff, softly. "If Mike had gone to 14 megatons, it could have breached the reef and created a real tsunami."

Ogle raised his eyebrows, and relit his pipe. "I'd say we pretty much lucked out all round . . . except, of course for the sampler pilot. And he'd have made it if he'd just happened to eject from the cloud a thousand feet higher up. Sometimes it's a mighty thin line between success and failure."

There was a squeal of bosun's pipes over the speaker system and Kincaid rose to his feet. "The Admiral's coming aboard," he said. He called this morning to ask a favor of you Scripps people. I guess he's come over to put it to you in person. If you gentlemen will be kind enough to wait a moment, I'll bring him up."

Admiral Wilkins shook hands all round and stirred sugar into the coffee the steward had rushed to bring him. "General Glantzberg has asked me to continue the search for the lost sampler aircraft, which is now presumed to still contain the unfortunate pilot's remains. Although we feel his point of entry into the lagoon is known within a mile, neither yesterday's air search, nor a sonar search by the *Fletcher* this morning has located the plane on the lagoon floor."

Wilkins smiled quizzically and fixed me with his penetrating gaze. "Bob, I've been wondering if the resources of the Navy might be more successfully augmented using the your . . . what do you call that equipment?"

"Aqualungs, Sir. We can tow a diver at 60 feet, and he should be able to see the bottom at about 150 feet. But, the water near the South Pass, where the plane went down, should be clearer . . . and the plane will undoubtedly reflect sunlight. We could determine the optimum towing depth by lowering a fish flasher to the bottom, and then swimming down until we can see it. How big an area would we have to cover?"

"We've buoyed off an area about a mile square, centered on the best radar fix we could get from the Eniwetok tower. I'd suggest you try towing right down the middle, lined up with the runway. Then, if you don't find it, work out to the sides."

"Fine, Sir," I said. "We'll try to get our best operating depth worked out this afternoon, and hit it first thing tomorrow."

But, in the end, it all came to naught. The rainy weather had returned with a vengeance; the flasher was useless, and we had to tow at 80 feet to see even the larger bottom shadows. That limited Bascom and the twins to 30 minutes per dive and three dives apiece, so as to avoid recompression and the risk of getting the "bends". Even so, when our compressor finally blew a head gasket late Monday afternoon, we had managed to survey a strip a mile long and about 200 yards wide, without finding anything. Despite the fact that two helicopters, the tower radar, and at least six people on the runway itself had seen the plane go down, they still had not been able to pinpoint its location to that degree of precision. So far as I know, it still sits on the bottom of Eniwetok lagoon, essentially intact, with its grisly cargo

When our dive boat dropped me off at the *Estes,* I found myself on an empty ship; all the scientific and command functions had been transferred back ashore during the day. Somehow, despite the rain and my fatigue, I felt the need for familiar companionship, so I packed my duffel, signed out with the OOD, and caught a water taxi back to Parry Island.

Inside our barracks, the poker game was in full swing, but Jeff was in his sack, snoring up a storm. I showered, got into dry clothes, and poured two belts of my dwindling whiskey supply into separate glasses, before I woke him up.

He opened one eye, then the other. "Wow," he said, reaching for his glasses, which were tucked into the springs of the bunk above. Then he struggled to a sitting position. "Slept twelve hours last night . . . can't seem to catch up." He took a sip of the drink I offered him and shuddered all over. "Good stuff. What is it?"

"Johnny Walker, Black Label . . . courtesy of Walton MacConnell. How's the *Horizon*? Where's Henry?"

"The *Hor* should be ready by morning . . . those Holmes & Narver guys are real workers. Henry is over at the flag mess, catching up on his politics. Going to be a big blast there tomorrow night; we're all invited, including the Twins—because of the diving today."

"Where are the Twins, now?"

"Working on the compressor . . . so you can dive for the turtle recorders tomorrow."

We let that ride for a while, sipping our scotch while the rain drummed on the metal roof. Finally, I said: "Jeffo, how did you really feel, sitting out there, waiting for the waves?"

"I was scared shitless. But, as you pointed out, I figured if it got really big, we wouldn't need the record—Bascom could just bail out and swim for the skiff . . . How was it on the *Estes*?"

"Sort of exciting . . . Lots of things happening . . . very fast." I told him about the firing party in the Runit bunker, the sampling operation, the hang-up with the outer island reports. "I can hardly believe it's over. How goes it with your wedding plans? When are you heading back?"

"First plane out," he laughed. "I just sent Mona a coded message. We'll be married in La Jolla, and have about three weeks together before I have to fly out to Fiji to meet the *Horizon* for the rest of Capricorn expedition. I don't know where we'll honeymoon; Mona's handling all the details. How about you . . . will you be available as Best Man?

"I really don't know," I said, slowly. "Ogle wants me to take care of some things in Honolulu . . . I don't know where in hell Suzie is. Everything's kind of up in the air."

"Well, the mail comes in tomorrow. Maybe you'll know more then. How about some chow? I'm famished."

It really poured all night, varying only in intensity. I woke up several times and lay there, thinking how fantastically lucky we had been to have two consecutive clear days, exactly when we needed them; thinking about Suzie in Guaymas, baking in the desert sun . . . Suzie, driving her little red beetle through Sonora . . . Suzie, in the shower with me . . .

In the morning, it was still raining, but intermittently. The *Horizon* was not ready; we would have to use the LCM again to dive for the turtle records. There was nothing to do but bundle up, grit our teeth and go for it. Mercifully, the rain stopped about noon and the sun peeped out from between towering banks of cumulus. But, of the five instruments we had emplaced so tediously, we could find only the three most distant from Ground Zero. The marker buoys for the other two had evidently been destroyed by the blast.

After of couple of hours of futile groping on the bottom, we gave up, and headed back across the lagoon.

Pounding along against the choppy seas in the wind and the rain, I looked across at the Twins, the solid dependable Twins, huddled together opposite me on the steel-grate flooring of the LCM. "A penny for your thoughts," I yelled to Charlie Black against the thunder of the diesels.

"Cost you a lot more than that," he yelled back, his white teeth glistening through his soggy black beard. "Jack and I've just been figuring how much we'll be making when we come back here on our own and go diving for Killer Clams . . . they're all over the bottom out here!"

We tied up behind the *Horizon* at the H&N dock shortly before dusk; Jeff and Henry were there to greet us. As the Twins were heaving the diving gear up onto the dock, Jeff handed me a postcard, with a mischievous look. It was a view of the beautiful crescent beach at Bahia San Carlos, near Guaymas; but it had been posted October 28, from Santa Fe, N.M.! There was nothing on the reverse but the outline of a heart, with the letter "S" inscribed within it.

Suddenly, all my emptiness evaporated. I stood there, grinning foolishly, with the rain dripping off my chin, soaking the postcard, only gradually becoming aware of Henry's insistent inquiry: "Bob, the records, have you looked at them yet?"

"Not yet, Henry. We could only find three of the turtles . . . I was afraid to open them in the rain. Let's get them up into the *Hor's* dry lab."

With the aid of Hetzel and the Twins, we muscled the heavy steel cases aboard the ship and into the instrument room on the main deck, where Hetzel unscrewed the six bolts around each housing and pried the halves apart. One of them had leaked, but the other two were perfect. On each smoked aluminum disk, the thin bright line traced by the stylus rose abruptly with the shock wave arrival, then decayed over several minutes to a smaller, negative value, finally rising smoothly to its original level, about which it oscillated slowly.

"My God," exclaimed Henry, peering myopically at the shiny trace. "There are no waves . . . The bomb simply pressed the lagoon surface down, and then sucked it up. These late oscillations are the whole lagoon, sloshing like a bathtub . . . how fantastic!"

"No wonder the toilets flooded the Runit bunker," I said, and related the travails of the firing party. They all laughed mightily at what now seemed an obvious oversight. Then Jeff said: "We now have three different kinds of wave records from this test: in the lagoon, at seamount Freddie, and at the island stations, none of which we completely understand. It seems to me that about all we have learned is that it's safe to detonate a multi-megaton device on a coral reef big enough to contain the crater." Prophetic words? I was to spend the next ten years pondering the same problem.

The farewell party was in full swing before we members of the Scripps contingent walked into the Flag Mess. On such short notice, the mess staff had done a masterful job of creating a festival atmosphere. Nets and fish floats hung above the bar, colored ribbons spiraled everywhere, and clusters of balloons hugged the gabled metal ceiling. An enormous photograph of General Clarkson graced an impromptu stage, where a small military orchestra played loudly, if not tunefully, amid an arboretum of potted palms. There was liquor aplenty, and a bibulous atmosphere prevailed.

Before the level of insobriety exceeded that of recollection, we had a few short speeches. General Clarkson thanked us on behalf of the JTF staff for outstanding cooperation in a successful operation; Stan Buriss told us that there would be no official public announcement of Ivy, and that all aspects of the test would remain secret until released by order of the President; and Walt MacConnell announced that the last remnants of the Mike cloud had been detected by tracking planes at high altitude over Guam, 1050 miles to the west, maximum intensity less than one-quarter mR. All radiation exclusion zones were now lifted, and air and sea traffic routes cleared for normal service.

Lastly, Bill Ogle, who more than any other had borne the brunt of responsibility for the scientific success of Operation Ivy, rose to air his views. Bronzed by the sun, and with glossy black hair now tending to shag after six weeks away from civilization, he more than ever resembled my uncle's Apache chief.

"We have just completed the largest of all human experiments," he began. "There will probably be larger experiments, but not much larger; we are simply running out of places to conduct them. As most of you know from the recent defection of Klaus Fuchs, the results of our labors have not been lost upon our Soviet friends, and we can confidently expect some competition rather shortly.

"I am not a politician, so I won't try to second-guess the long-term implications of such competition. But, I expect we will continue in the testing business for some time to come. I have made some good friends in the course of this operation, and look forward to seeing many of you the next time around." My recollection of the remainder of that evening is rather dim, probably owing to the high concentration of alcohol fumes in the air.

The *Spencer F. Baird,* sister ship of the *Horizon*, arrived at Kwajalein lagoon on Sunday, after being held outside the radex zone for two days while the Mike cloud dissipated. The *Hor's* evaporators had been repaired, and she would leave in the morning to join the *Baird* on Leg III of Capricorn expedition. Henry flew over to Kwajalein to bring Roger up to date on the Mike test results.

The Flag Mess was closed down, and Eniwetok seemed deserted as H&N set about cleaning up the island, just as Olaf Anderson had said. Ogle had somehow arranged transportation for Jeff and me aboard a MATS flight to Hickam field, Honolulu, departing Eniwetok tomorrow, Tuesday November 4th, at 0600 hours.

Jeff and I made the plane—but just barely. Pitch dark outside and raining steadily. Fortunately, my duffle was still packed. No time for breakfast . . . just catch the van to the Compound, the grasshopper to 'Wetok, turn in our film and ID badges to a sullen security type, and scramble aboard the three-tailed Lockheed Constellation, as the gray dawn portended another soggy day in Paradise. Canvas bucket seats; rubber Mae-Wests, with a tin whistle to blow to attract sharks. Most of the passengers were civilians, but nobody I recognized.

Aloft, in the bright sunlight above the cloud layers, we got juice, cinnamon rolls, and gallons of black coffee from a battery of thermos jugs forward. It was very pleasant to feel cool and dry for a change.

About five hours later, and one day earlier, we began our descent to Midway Islands, so named because there are three small islands compressed into the southern sector of a lovely lagoon. It was early afternoon of Monday, November 3rd, and despite the bright sun, there was a chill in the air, for Midway is on the northern edge of the tropics. We had an hour on the ground for refueling, the engineer told us; time enough for a drink at Midway's new officers' club.

The O-club was right on the beach in a little sandy cove, barely six feet above the lagoon level, and surrounded by Scabiosa and palms. The gravel walk that lead to the BOQ was lined with murex and helmet shells. It had only opened two days previously, and we found the mess officer, Lt JG. F. N. Parks, checking off bottle stores, while sailors in dungarees were just unwrapping and setting out the last of the rattan patio furniture. We complimented him on the layout and asked him to join us for a beer.

"A lovely spot," I said, "but rather close to the water. Looks as if a good blow might raise the lagoon level and flood you out."

"Too far north for typhoons; too far south for northers," said Parks. "The Old Man's a Coast Guard airman. He's checked the met situation pretty thoroughly. Only thing he's worried about is tsunamis. But there's only been one this century. He figures the odds are pretty good."

"Well," said Jeff, "you're looking at the world's tsunami expert. What do you think, Bob?"

"Shouldn't be much effect on a small island," I said. "I agree; the odds are with you." Midway had had bigger waves from Mike than Wake, but not nearly so large as those from Guam, a much bigger island. I was still quite anxious to check the Honolulu tide gauge to see if anything had shown up in Hawaii.

"You guys part of that Scripps tsunami study?" asked Parks. "We just had a Dr. Meyer here for a month. Little guy with a beard?"

"That's Meyer all right. Did he give you any trouble?"

"Oh, no. Never said a word to anybody. He was always out in his pith helmet and a long-sleeved shirt, hunting for Gooney birds. Didn't find many, though. I think it's the wrong season."

"Gooney birds?" I echoed.

"Laysan albatross," supplied Jeff. "They nest here and on other islands of this archipelago in spring, and spend the rest of the year at sea. They have a two-meter wing-span, and can soar forever on the updrafts over wave crests. Pretty awkward on land, though, it takes the fledglings about four months to learn to fly. They tumble ass-over-teakettle on takeoff."

"Is that all, Professor?" I asked; Lt. Parks was now goggle-eyed at his burst of erudition.

"Well, I'd say they used good sense coming here to breed . . . Midway's a very lovely island."

"Pretty nice duty out here," agreed Parks, sipping his beer. "Hard to believe this is still part of the good old USA. Tomorrow is Election Day. Who's going to take it, Acheson or Eisenhower?"

"Acheson hasn't a chance against a military hero, I'm afraid," said Jeff. Lots of people are sore at Truman for sacking MacArthur after he had driven the Chinese clear out of Korea. Nobody likes to lose a war for political reasons."

"Drink up, Jeffo," I said, attempting to head off another discourse. "I see the fuel truck pulling away from our aircraft." We thanked the MO, and strolled back to the terminal.

The sun and the beer must have had a soporific effect; I fell sound asleep the instant my seatbelt was fastened, only awakening when the captain announced our final descent into Hickam Field, Hawaii. It was pitch dark again, eight pm Honolulu time; according to my watch it was still three pm in Eniwetok.

After landing, we taxied interminably, finally stopping in the middle of nowhere, and completing the trip to

Hickam terminal by bus. While waiting for our bags, Jeff went over to the travel desk to see about a commercial flight to San Diego—by spending eighty bucks, he could save four or five days over military air. Meanwhile, per Ogle's instructions, I phoned Sutter Street. The duty NCO told me I was expected; they would send a driver over to take me to a hotel. I was to check back with Colonel Jacobs in the morning. Very strange, I thought. Why not the BOQ?

The driver arrived just as we had retrieved our bags. Jeff had found a midnight PAA flight to the coast, so the driver agreed to drop him off at Honolulu International, which, in those days, lay on the opposite side of the airfield. We were putting our bags in the car, when the terminal public address system suddenly broadcast an emergency announcement:

"Attention all military and civilian personnel. There has been a large earthquake in the Western Pacific. It has now been confirmed that this earthquake has generated a major tsunami—or, tidal wave. The tsunami is expected to reach Hawaii at approximately 2300 hours, local time; that is, eleven o'clock, Hawaiian Standard Time. All military personnel will report to local command authority. Civilian personnel are warned to evacuate the terminal area and to seek refuge on higher ground. This terminal will close immediately to all traffic, and will remain closed until the tsunami warning has been terminated."

The message was repeated, as bedlam arose inside the terminal. People were running everywhere in seemingly aimless confusion. "My God," said Jeff, "let's get out of here before they lock the gates." As we drove away, our driver switched on his radio, which was carrying the same message on most stations, but with more details. The earthquake, Richter magnitude 8.3, had occurred at 5:15 pm, Hawaiian time, and large tsunami waves had already been observed in Japan and at Attu, in the Aleutian Islands. All commercial ships had been advised to clear Honolulu harbor, and the Navy had ordered emergency evacuation of ships from Pearl Harbor. Police and civil defense units were mobilizing to alert citizens in all low-lying areas of Hawaii . . .

As we pulled into the Honolulu terminal departure area, there was a new announcement. Tsunamis waves had inundated the Midway Islands runway, and totally demolished the new $25,000 Officer's club, completed only last week.

"So much for science," I said, a little sheepishly, "Looks like we got out of Midway just in time. Lt. Parks and his CO are probably frothing at the mouth . . . What would you like to do, Jeffo, take your chances at the airport or stay over with me tonight?"

He hesitated, and then said: "The airport, I guess. That way, I can catch the first available flight."

"OK, I'll call you mañana, as soon as I know my schedule."

Half an hour later, in the heart of Waikiki, the driver turned off Kalakaua Avenue into a curving driveway, graced with beautifully landscaped tropical shrubbery, and stopped beneath an arched portico. A red carpet extended from curbside to the great glass doorway, above which was incised in stone: Royal Hawaiian Hotel. A red-coated doorman with gold epaulettes opened the car door and beckoned me out.

"I . . . I can't stay here," I stammered. "There must be some mistake." Only pride and embarrassment kept me from blurting out that the University's per diem rate outside California was $8.00 per day, whereas rooms at the Royal started at $20.00.

"I was instructed to bring you here, Sir," said the Driver, who was Hawaiian. "I think you find everything taken care of. Mahalo, and have nice stay in Hawaii."

Mystified, I allowed my bags to be piled upon a dolly, tipped the doorman a quarter, and followed the porter down the long, carpeted hallway to the registration desk, acutely conscious of my travel-worn appearance in such elegant surroundings . . . shorts, flip-flops, wrinkled aloha shirt, 24-hour stubble. A group of well-groomed ladies standing at the desk, parted, recoiling in shock, as if a mongrel had wandered into a championship dog show.

The Chinese-Hawaiian reservation clerk raised his hand, palm out, as if to arrest my progress. "Sorry, Sir . . . we have no rooms . . . none at all!"

I gave my name. Had not a reservation been made? At that point, I would gladly have gone next door to the Moana . . . or back to the Niumalu. I just wanted a shower, a drink, and twelve hours sleep, in that order.

"So sorry, Dr. Ward ... No room ... ah ... One moment, prease." He plucked an envelope from his reservation file, opened it, read the card. They say the Chinese do not perspire, but beads of sweat sprang out above his eyebrows. With masterful restraint, he pulled himself erect. "So sorry, Dr. Ward ... Yes, we have very nice room." He pulled a key from its slot and pounded the desk bell. "Would you prease sign the register?" More mystified than ever, I followed the bell boy to the elevators. The ladies had not budged.

Number 301, the Princess Kaiulani room, was enormous. It had a smoky green carpet, pale ceiling, and red velvet walls with gold moldings. A large four-poster double bed with an embroidered coverlet was almost lost in the vast expanse, which also contained a rosewood table with four padded velvet chairs, a book case, a writing desk in its own alcove, a large rosewood clothes cabinet, and a high dresser with an oval mirror. The windows were shrouded by velvet curtains, parted to show pleated gauze drapery, and a cut-glass vase on the table held a spray of white orchids. Perfect Victorian elegance in a tropic setting!

A little uncertain of protocol, the bell boy stood my duffle bag carefully in an empty corner, and placed my net diving bag and briefcase inside the cabinet. Then he stood there, waiting, as if to see what I might do next. I reached in my pocket ... no change. In my wallet, the smallest bill was ten dollars. I hesitated a moment, and then thrust it in his hand. "Laundry," I said. "Can you have my laundry done by tomorrow morning?" I untied the top of the duffle back, and shook it from the bottom, so that its entire contents of rumpled, soiled clothing cascaded onto the carpet.

The bell boy looked at the pile of clothes, then at the bill in his hand . . . a good day's wages "Yessir," he said. "I fixum, wikiwiki."

The bathroom was also large, containing a marble pedestal lavatory, and a huge, porcelain tub, standing on lion's feet. Its concession to modernity was a free-standing chromium shower loop and curtain. A long, hot, shave-as-you-go shower did wonders to brace the sagging spirit, and I regretted not having asked the bell boy to bring me a tall rum drink in the bargain. I whipped a bath towel about my waist and dialed room service. However, before they answered, there was a knock at the door.

"Come in," I said, and the door swung open, revealing four waiters in red trousers and starched white jackets. Two of them were wheeling a large serving cart, loaded with covered chafing dishes; one carried a tripod-mounted silver ice bucket containing a magnum of champagne; the last, a tray supporting a carafe of iced martinis and two frosted glasses.

"Wrong room," I ventured. "I didn't order this stuff."

"Dr. Robert Ward, room 301?" asked the headwaiter, as the others proceeded to arrange two place settings at the table, lighting two tall candles, rotating the champagne and wrapping it in a napkin. I nodded, too stunned to move. "Compliments of the management," he said.

"Mahalo, and have a pleasant stay in Hawaii." They went out, closing the door softly.

I stood there, looking at the two place settings, the two martini glasses, the two candles; a germ of suspicion burgeoning in my mind. "SUZY!" I cried. "Where the hell are you?"

Then, the familiar little giggle. She came through the curtains from the balcony, in a tailored muumuu, barefoot, wearing a gardenia lei and carrying another. She slipped it over my head, and suddenly we were welded together, she standing on my insteps so her mouth could reach mine, our hearts pounding as though they must surely burst.

After an eternity, I picked her up and carried her to the bed. "FF or EF?" I asked, kissing her neck as I unzipped her dress.

"I give up," she whispered, nibbling my ear. "What does it mean?"

"EF means Eat First."

She rolled out of my embrace, slipped off her clothes, and turned out the room lights. Then she went to the table, poured two martinis, and brought them back to the bed. "I think we ought to eat first, Darling," she coaxed, pulling me to my feet. "You're going to need all the strength you have tonight."

We sat there, quite naked in the candle light, gazing into each other's eyes, drinking, eating . . . saying all the wonderful, nonsensical things that lovers say, and slowly sinking into that wonderful euphoria generated by martinis followed by champagne. Then, over the murmur of surf through the balcony doors, I heard the faint sound of sirens . . . coming nearer.

"The tsunami!" I cried. It's supposed to arrive at eleven." We rushed out on the balcony, which overlooked the pool terrace. Beyond the slightly-elevated terrace lay twenty yards of sand, and the broad reef, over which the famous Waikiki surf rose and tumbled, glinting white lines in the waning moonlight. The terrace was crowded with onlookers, who were boisterously resisting the attempts of hotel staff to herd them back inside. The sirens were louder now, and I could hear loud-hailers urging people to evacuate the streets and to ascend to the second floors of waterfront buildings.

"Will there be big waves, Darling?" asked Suzy, tremulously, insinuating herself into my embrace.

"I don't know, Sweetheart. In 1946, tsunami waves ran a quarter-mile inland on the other side of Oahu. But it isn't a single big wave . . . it's like the tide, except it rises and falls every half hour, instead of every twelve hours."

Then, as surely and inevitably as the moon was setting, we saw the surf line advance . . . each little surge on the beach rising higher than that which came before, until the water overran the lower terrace of the hotel next door, and trickled into the common walkway to Kalakaua Avenue. Small wavelets were now breaking against the Royal terrace, and the crowd below had vanished.

Fifteen minutes later the water retreated, as smoothly as it had advanced, and then the whole process was again repeated, but this time cresting lower. "It's over," I said. Suzie was shivering, so we went back inside and tumbled into bed.

"It's absolutely crazy," I said, crooking her in my arm and pulling her to me. "I've been studying tsunamis for five years . . . and now I've actually seen one!"

"Mmmm," whispered Suzy, sliding her leg over mine and nibbling my ear. My ardor was rising . . . but my head was whirling; the trauma of last night's party, too little sleep, the long flight . . . then Suzy, the liquor, the tsunami . . . Suddenly, an utterly incongruous thought burst upon my brain. With Herculean effort, I struggled upward to my elbows.

"Darling," I said, "do you realize that, if this tsunami had occurred three days ago . . . when we shot the bomb . . . , nobody would ever have believed it was a coincidence?"

"Darling," she murmured, tracing two letters on my chest with her index finger, "do you realize what we might be doing right now if that tsunami had occurred three days ago?"

"E.F.," I said, purposely misreading her message. "Darling, I really don't think I could eat anything more right now."

"Bastard," she cried struggling to break loose. But I rolled to my knees above her, pinioning her tiny wrists.

"Now, it's your turn to say Uncle."

"Uncle," she moaned, thrusting upward . . . "Oh, Dearest . . . Uncle . . . Robert."

And that is what she has called me ever since: "Uncle Robert."

Made in United States
North Haven, CT
26 May 2023